BLOOD
SISTERS

Also by the same author

BLOOD SISTERS

CAN A PLEDGE MADE FOR LIFE ENDURE BEYOND DEATH?

JULIE SHAW

Certain details in this story, including names, places and dates, have been changed to protect the family's privacy.

HarperElement
An imprint of HarperCollins*Publishers*
1 London Bridge Street
London SE1 9GF

www.harpercollins.co.uk

First published by HarperElement 2017

1 3 5 7 9 10 8 6 4 2

© Julie Shaw and Lynne Barrett-Lee 2017

Julie Shaw and Lynne Barrett-Lee assert the moral
right to be identified as the authors of this work

A catalogue record of this book is
available from the British Library

ISBN 978-0-00-814279-7

Printed and bound in Great Britain by
Clays Ltd, St Ives plc

MIX
Paper from
responsible sources
FSC™ C007454

FSC™ is a non-profit international organisation established to promote
the responsible management of the world's forests. Products carrying the
FSC label are independently certified to assure consumers that they come
from forests that are managed to meet the social, economic and
ecological needs of present or future generations,
and other controlled sources.

Find out more about HarperCollins and the environment at
www.harpercollins.co.uk/green

As well as dedicating this book to my wonderful family, my parents, husband, kids and grandkids, and of course my huge extended family of Hudsons and Jaggers, I want to make special mention this time to the best friends of my younger days. Sharon Thornton and Bridget Hone were my true blood sisters, and yes, we did the whole cut and touching blood thing! Memories of our escapades certainly played a part when writing this book.

Prologue

Clayton Village Hall Youth Club, Bradford, 1983

It's late on a summer Friday, the sky just turning peachy, and two twelve-year-old girls who've been best friends since nursery are hiding behind the stage curtains in the village hall.

They're making a solemn oath. It's the most important kind of oath. Which is why they've taken the trouble (which has been both a risk and a challenge) of 'borrowing' the craft knife from the art drawer in the hall kitchen, which they are now using, in turn, to slit the skin on their right thumbs.

The blood forms beads, dark and glossy behind the drapes, as they squeeze, and in perfect synchrony, despite neither of them consciously timing it, they touch their thumbs together, allowing the blood to mix.

'I solemnly swear,' whispers Vicky Robinson, who is the taller of the two, 'that no boyfriend will split us up, or anyone else come between us. I swear we will be sisters for the rest of our lives ... Your turn,' she then finishes, smiling at her friend.

'I solemnly swear,' agrees Lucy Briggs, her voice equally low, 'that no boyfriend will split us up, or anyone else come between us. I swear we'll be sisters for the rest of our lives ...'

'Blood sisters *forever*!' they both whisper, in unison.

Then they put the knife back in the drawer, roll up the waistbands of their skirts, and, giggling as they both re-apply a sheen of lip gloss, feel their way round the edge of the musty stage curtains and go back to join the boys in the smoking shed.

Life was good in the summer of 1983.

Part One

Two are better than one, because they have a good reward for their toil. For if they fall, one will lift up his fellow. But woe to him who is alone when he falls and has not another to lift him up! Again, if two lie together, they keep warm, but how can one keep warm alone? And though a man might prevail against one who is alone, two will withstand him – a threefold cord is not quickly broken.

Ecclesiastes 4:9–12

Chapter I

Clayton, Bradford, July 1987

The world always seemed to melt away when Vicky was doing her make-up. Particularly her eyeliner, which, being a posh liquid one, required total concentration: lips slightly parted, brows raised, good light and a steady, steady hand. Even Rick Astley, who had up to now held at least half her concentration, seemed to oblige by taking a breath so she could get the line exactly right.

'Victoriaaaaa! *Door!*'

Vicky swore under her breath as she lowered the eyeliner brush. Her bloody mother. And, judging by the way she was bellowing her name, this wasn't the first time she'd yelled it up the stairs either.

She slipped the brush back into the tube and reached for a cotton-wool ball. One day, perhaps *one* day, her mam would stop yelling, get up off her fat backside and actually answer the front door herself. But she doubted that would be happening anytime soon.

'Mam, it'll be Luce!' Vicky yelled down through the open bedroom door. 'Let her in, can't you? Please? I'm not dressed yet!'

Though she ought to get her skates on, she realised. She'd been getting ready for over an hour now, and she still wasn't done. Though, in her defence, she decided, as she spat on the cotton wool and carefully wiped the outer edge of her left eye, this was their first night out as working girls – no more school, *ever* – and she was determined to look old enough to get into every pub and club in town. She just hoped Lucy had done a decent enough job of stuffing her bra with socks. She hadn't yet been blessed with Vicky's natural assets, and they were always so bloody strict down at the Caverns.

'I'm not your bleeding slave!' Vicky's mum yelled back up the stairs, predictably. And she had a point, Vicky conceded, as she redid the final flick of eyeliner. Most of the time, these days, it felt like the other way round. But she also felt the tell-tale breeze that meant the front door was open, so she got up from her dressing table and danced across to her bed, humming along with Rick, in her bra and knickers.

'Whoah,' came a deep voice, moments later. 'Now *that's* what I call a welcome.'

Vicky whirled around, astonished, then grabbed the bath towel from the back of the dressing-table chair. 'Oh my God – Paddy!' she exclaimed, colouring. 'What the hell are you doing here? I thought you were off out with the lads!'

Paddy's gaze travelled appreciatively over her as he shut the bedroom door. Bold as you like, as per usual. What on earth had her mam been *thinking*, letting him come up?

'Well, I'm not now, am I?' he said, grinning as she tried to wrap the towel around herself. She thought he might try and yank it off her, but instead he nodded towards the tape player. 'And you can get that shit off, for starters,' he added, pulling something from one of his jeans pockets and flinging it on the bed. It was a worn-looking cassette tape. One Vicky recognised immediately, because she'd sat there, bored to tears, while he'd made it. 'Put that on for us, will you, babe?' he asked. 'Please?'

That was the thing with Paddy. He walked into a room and had this disarming way of owning it. That and filling her stomach with butterflies. It had been almost a year that they'd been seeing each other now and the way he made her feel never seemed to change. Her mam always went on about how all that fluttering hearts stuff soon wore off and then you saw the sort of man you were *really* dealing with, but her mam was just bitter, because of her dad up and leaving. Still bitter, despite it being years ago now; they'd seen nothing of him since and though Vicky had heard he was with a younger woman in Leeds now, she never dared mention it, because any mention of him got her mother in such a state that she'd go on a crying and eating binge that could last for days.

No, her mam *really* didn't get it. Paddy wasn't a bit like her father. He was different. He worshipped the ground Vicky walked on. *Literally.* Only last week he'd flung himself down on the pavement outside the Oddfellows Arms to prove it – just like that, after she'd torn him off a strip, with everyone watching. She'd called him an idiot

– it had been raining, and he'd got his new jacket soaked – but, secretly, she'd loved how he didn't care who knew it. Loved that he didn't do that whole offhand thing so many of the lads her own age thought was cool. No, the butter-flies were still there, and she loved that.

She breathed in the scent of his aftershave as he ambled across to kiss her. 'And you know, you don't need to get dressed on my account,' he whispered, tugging playfully on the towel.

Wriggling away from him, she reached for the black dress she'd hung out to wear, and quickly slipped it over her head, letting the towel flump to the floor just a calculated couple of seconds before she'd properly smoothed the dress down her thighs.

'I bloody do,' she said, picking the tape up and going over to the cassette player, pressing the button to eject her beloved Rick Astley and replace it with his Northern Soul compilation. She thought she could probably recite the tracks at will. Paddy was a die-hard fan, and used to go to the all-nighters at the Mecca on Manningham Lane all the time before they started seeing each other. Though Wigan Mecca, where it all started, before he was old enough to be a part of it, was like *the* Mecca as far as Paddy was concerned.

'No, you really don't,' Paddy said. 'Trust me, Vic. You were just fine as you were.'

'Pad, babe, I am dressed because I am going *out*. With Luce,' she added, picking the towel up. 'Remember?'

'No, I don't,' Paddy said, as the tape began playing. 'Moonlight, Music and You', one of his favourites. Granny music, she'd called it once. Which had gone down like a lead balloon.

'Babe, don't be dense,' Vicky said. 'I told you about it ages back. *And* I mentioned it Monday. It was our last day today, remember? I am no longer a schoolgirl. And we are going out to celebrate the fact. *Remember?*'

Paddy turned up the tape player. Vicky resisted the urge to turn it down again. Next thing she'd have her mam screaming up the stairs at her. Which she really didn't want, since the one thing she *did* want was to cadge a fiver off her.

Paddy pulled a face Vicky knew well. 'So what about me, then?' he asked her, sticking his lower lip out.

'What about you?'

'What am I supposed to do while you're gallivanting round Bradford with that gormless friend of yours? It's me you should be celebrating with, not her.'

'Don't call her that,' Vicky said. 'And how am I supposed to know what you're supposed to be doing? You were *supposed* to be going out with the lads and I'm going out with Luce and Gurdy. We can celebrate together tomorrow night' – she blew a kiss at him. 'As per the *plan.*'

Paddy rolled his eyes. 'Gurdy? That Paki twat? Jesus,' he countered, 'why the fuck do you want to hang around with him tonight?' Despite his harsh words, he was still grinning as he inched nearer to her, moving in and whispering things in her ear that would have her mother's toes curl if she could hear them.

She wriggled away from him again, despite feeling the familiar tug of animal attraction, and began transferring what she needed into her clutch bag. 'Paddy, I'm going out. O.U.T. No arguments. Luce will be here any minute. And there's no point in you trying to sweet talk me, because it won't make any difference ...'

Though, even as she said the words, it already was. He was nuzzling at her neck now and, infuriatingly, she was enjoying it. 'I wasn't planning on sweet *talking*,' he said, purring the song lyrics into her ear, and pinioning her within the circle of his ridiculously strong arms.

'Paddy, stop it,' she said firmly. 'I'm going *out*.'

He let her go then, and flung himself down on her bed with a heavy sigh.

'What?' she said.

'Nothing,' he answered. 'Leave me then. Go on. Leave me all on my lonesome so you can go and chat up all the other lads in town.' His gaze travelled up and down her again. 'And they'll be all over you, dressed in that. Actually—' He sat up again, grabbed her wrist and pulled her onto his lap. 'I reckon I ought to come with you. Keep you safe from wandering hands ...'

'Pad, I'm *sixteen*,' Vicky pointed out, already imagining Lucy's face at the thought of having Paddy chaperoning them. Lucy was as fond of Paddy as Paddy was of Lucy, i.e. not at all. And, increasingly, it was becoming tedious to have to deal with. Not least because Vicky loved Paddy, and her loyalties felt increasingly divided, and Luce never quite seemed to get that. Never quite seemed to get that, actually, Vicky didn't *mind* that Paddy could wind her round his little finger. Because it worked both ways. He'd do anything for her. He'd give his life for her. She *knew* that. Luce didn't quite get that bit either, Vicky reckoned.

Still, tonight was different. They'd made a plan and she was determined to stick to it. 'Seriously,' she added, climbing off Paddy's lap again, 'I can look after myself.'

'That's not what I'm worried about,' Paddy said. 'It's all the lads that'll be trying it on with you, that's what *I'm* worrying about.'

'Okay,' said Vicky, seizing on a way to turn things to her advantage. 'How about me and Luce go out, like we'd planned, and then we meet up with you later on? We've much more chance of getting into places if you're there, after all. Go on, that'll work, won't it? You go and find someone else to play with for a bit, and then we'll meet up at Jokers. How about that?'

Paddy reached out and slid a hand up the back of her thigh. 'But I want to play with *you* …'

Nothing for it. She'd have to be firmer. 'I'm telling you,' she said briskly, batting his hand away. 'Cut it *out!*'

'God!' he said, sighing theatrically for a second time, as he grabbed the packet of cigarettes and lighter Vicky was just about to put in her bag.

'Oi!' she said as he lit one. 'Smoke your own! That's all I've got.'

Ignoring her, he drew on it deeply and blew the smoke out in rings. Then stood up and walked through the cloud he'd created, first turning up the volume and then picking up her dressing-table mirror and setting it carefully down on the bedroom floor.

He'd done it countless times. He loved to dance, and particularly in Vicky's bedroom because of the lino on the floor. All the better to practise his moves. She stood and watched him, as she always did, even though it wasn't really her music. Loved to watch how he lost himself so totally in the music, his eyes on the mirror as his feet slid and flicked across the floor. He was so good. So impossibly, mesmerisingly good. And then, predictably, almost, he reached out a hand to her, parked his fag in the ashtray and swept her up with him.

It was crazy. There was no room to swing a cat, let alone her. But she went along with it anyway. Giggling as he twirled her, losing herself too, just like she always did when he let her come to the Mecca on Manningham Lane with him, happy to be led by him – he was such a brilliant exhibitionist – basking in the oohs and ahs and loving all the comments about how amazingly they danced as a couple.

And then, as the track ended, he reeled her in towards him, cupped a hand round her buttock and began kissing her again.

'Pad, babe,' she started. 'Look, you know I can't resist you, but I'm on a promise and I *have* to go out, okay? I—'

There was a cough. 'Not on my account, you don't.'

It was Lucy's voice, from the doorway, the light spilling across their feet as she pushed it open wider.

They both span around. 'Luce, you're here—' Vicky started, conscious of Paddy deliberately taking his time lowering the hand that had been kneading her left breast.

'With brilliant timing, as per usual,' he finished dryly.

'So it seems,' Lucy said, her eyes darting between them. 'So if I'm interrupting …'

'Course you're not,' Vicky said, snatching her bag up and shoving her fags into it. 'I'm just about ready. Just got to grab my jacket and see if I can scrounge a couple of quid off Mam. God, just think,' she said, conscious that she was beginning to prattle, 'this time next week we'll both have pay packets. Can you imagine?'

She was aware of Paddy behind her, crushing his – *her* – fag out. Then bending over the cassette player and getting his tape out. She reached across Lucy to switch the bedroom light off.

'I won't,' Lucy said, and her voice was flat and hard. 'I'm on a monthly salary, aren't I? It's going to seem like an age.'

'What d'you expect?' Paddy said, as he slipped the tape into his back pocket. 'That's what you get for working in an office, isn't it?' He managed to make it sound, Vicky thought, like it was some sort of offence. 'Anyway,' he then added brightly, 'where to first, then?'

Vicky felt her friend's eyes on her before she turned to meet them. Accusing. Questioning. Boring into her back, as she led the procession back downstairs. She met them at the bottom of the stairs and frowned apologetically. But she could see Lucy was not in the mood for an apology.

Her eyes narrowed and she looked behind Vicky, to Paddy. 'What, *you're* coming?' she said to him.

'Course I am,' he told her. 'Got to keep an eye on my girl, haven't I? Why?' His voice was challenging. 'You got a problem with that?'

Lucy ignored him. 'Seriously?' she said to Vicky, looking exasperated. '*Seriously?*'

'Is it such a big deal?' Vicky responded, feeling her hackles rise, despite herself. 'It's not like Gurdy won't be out with us, not to mention half of bloody Lidget Green, for that matter.'

Lucy's expression hardened. '*Yes*, actually, Vic. Yes it *is*. Because it means I get to play gooseberry while he bloody paws you. Great girls' night out that's going to be. Cheers, mate.'

Vicky could see Paddy's satisfied grin forming out of the corner of her eye, and for a moment it crossed her mind to tell him that, actually, Lucy was right. That he needed to go somewhere else and amuse himself for a bit – Christ, he knew every-fucking-body, didn't he? But something stopped her, or at least made her hesitate, and she wasn't quite sure what it was. Or maybe she did know. It was frustration. Couldn't Lucy just roll with it for once? Why did she have to make everything to do with Paddy so bloody difficult? Because Lucy knew as well as she did that when they got to the Boy and Barrel or the Crown or wherever they were going first, he'd be off on the dance floor, or off with some of his cronies, within minutes of them so much as stepping into the place. So why couldn't Lucy just let it *go*?

'Look, let's just go, shall we?' she said. 'Let me just go talk nicely with Mam, yeah? Won't be a second. Where's Gurdy going to be anyway? He'll be wondering where we've got to …'

Not waiting for an answer, she headed off into the back room, where her mam was, as ever, full-length on the sofa, fag in hand, tea at her elbow, telly blaring.

'I'm off, Mam,' she said. 'And I was wondering …'

Her mam ferreted in her cardigan pocket before she'd even got the rest out. 'And that's only a sub,' she said, pushing a five-pound note into Vicky's palm. 'Not a gift. And now you're earning, I'll be expecting keep off you too.'

Vicky slipped the money into her bag and headed back into the hall. Paddy was standing on the doorstep, the open door allowing a balmy summer night's breeze in. It had a sweet, exotic scent to it, heralding the start of what she was determined was going to be a brilliant night. Lucy would get over herself. She usually did.

Paddy had his back to her, but turned around when he heard her and smiled.

'Where's Lucy?' Vicky asked, looking past him into the street and not seeing her.

'Stomped off, as she does,' he said mildly. His hair had the same inky gloss as next door's black cat. He ran a hand over it now, smoothing it down, feigning innocence.

'Christ, Paddy! What did you say to her?'

'*Me?*' he looked astonished. 'That one could start a fight with a fucking plant pot. Stomped off in a huff because I even fucking *exist*. Seriously, babes,' he said, hooking the letter-box knocker to close the door behind them. 'You don't get it, do you? She doesn't *like* me. And there's fuck all we can do about that, is there? Seriously,' he began again.

'Pad, I feel *awful*. Where'd she go?'

'I have no idea. She obviously didn't feel like enlighten-ing me.'

Vicky felt dreadful now. Dreadful and, all too belatedly, so bloody *wrong*. 'Well, which direction did she go, then?'

'This way,' he said, as they fell into step. 'She'll be prop-ping up the bar by the time we get there, you wait and see. But you know, babe, you've left school now and you've got to face facts. She's got some high falutin' job now, not to mention seeing a fucking copper's son.'

'So what? What difference does that make?'

Paddy slipped his arm around her shoulder and squeezed it. 'Babe, you really need to ask me that? It makes *all* the difference. Sometimes,' he squeezed her shoulder again, 'you've just got to let friendships go. Hey!' he added, as she raised a hand to belt him, albeit lightly. 'I'm just saying. That's all, babes. Just saying.'

Chapter 2

It was going to be such a lovely night. That was the thing that really pissed Lucy off, as she stomped disconsolately round the corner into Terrington Crescent. It was just getting dark now, the sky coral at the horizon, and the air was warm and fragrant. Almost tropical in fact. One of those nights when everyone spilled out onto the streets, and you could half-believe you were in somewhere like Spain. A rare night, in fact. And it had all gone to pot. What the hell was she supposed to do now?

She shouldn't have stormed off, and she cursed herself for it. Because that was exactly what he wanted her to do. So he'd called her a prick-tease. Putting it out when there was nothing on sale, and taking a none-too-subtle look up and down her. So what? She'd been called a lot worse in her time. And what the hell did he know about it, anyway? And the satisfaction of telling him to go and stick it where the sun didn't shine, for all that she'd felt it, had been all too fleeting. And now what? All dressed up and nowhere to bloody go. Not unless she bit the bullet and went to Caverns anyway. Let Vicky persuade her to ignore her horrible boyfriend and get on with their evening as planned.

But would she? There was no sound from behind, so it didn't look like her friend was rushing to catch up with her, did it? But then who knew? Paddy could have told her anything, couldn't he?

So, home then? She dismissed the idea as soon as she thought it. All she'd get would be a tedious interrogation from her mother and that told-you-so look from her dad. And she definitely couldn't stomach going to the phone box and ringing Jimmy. She might cry if he felt sorry for her. Which he obviously would, because he'd known how excited she'd been about her night out with Vicky. Unlike Paddy bloody Allen, who was a shit and a lech of the first order, *her* boyfriend was kind and considerate and decent. And, besides, it would only add fuel to the fire if she told Jimmy. And there was quite enough heat between the two lads already. Oil and water, best never mixed.

No, she was done up for an evening out, and she was having an evening out. She'd have a walk down to Lidget Green and see if she could find Gurdy, and if not, she might get lucky and bump into some mates who might fancy a few drinks in the Second West or the Oddfellows. Half the school would be out celebrating tonight, after all. And she didn't need town anyway. Not if *they* were going to be there. She stuck her chin in the air, fluffed her hair up a bit, and teetered off in determined mood down Bradford Road.

Gurdy had obviously seen Lucy before she saw him. Because the first thing that alerted her to his probable whereabouts was an ear-splitting and familiar wolf whistle, coming from the bench outside the cricket field at Lidget Green. It had taken him a while to get the hang of it, but since he'd mastered the art, Gurdy now wolf whistled at any opportunity, much to the disgust of his prissy mother.

It hadn't taken very long to track him down, and Lucy was glad she'd chosen to walk there. Had she braved the bus into town on her own she'd have missed him. And now she had an evening in prospect again, her relief was huge. Her spirits lifting finally, she even found herself smiling as his familiar scrawny figure resolved itself from in front of the backdrop of trees and he waved an arm wildly in greeting. Such an odd choice of friend – lots of people seemed to think that – a scrappy Pakistani, and a boy, as well, of course. But she and Vic's friendship with Gurdy went back a long way; back to the day when they'd come across him being beaten up by a trio of scuzzy third-formers from Scholemoor, and, in a fit of righteous fury that neither fully understood, they had bravely waded in and seen the astonished bullies off.

They'd not known at that point that he was actually a year older than they were; he'd been a second year then, same as Lucy's Jimmy. Just a very, very small one. And the sort of kid who had absolutely nothing going for him. Insubstantial, Indian (so not even a 'Paki', as it turned out), funny accent, class clown and, a greater crime than all of them – and half the reason for the bullying – invariably dressed for school as if off to see the Queen – something the girls decided, once they'd finally met Mr and Mrs Banerjee, was actually on their wish list for both of their

19

sons. They even had a picture of the royal family on their mantelpiece.

And Gurdy's dreams were only slightly less ambitious. Now seventeen, he'd worked in his dad's grocery shop on White Abbey Road since he'd left school, but his ambition was to eventually own his own curry shop, no less.

So, yes, an odd friendship, but also a dear one.

'Wow, Luce!' he said, pinging away a cigarette as she neared him. 'You going on the game later, or what?'

He'd scored an unwitting bullseye. It was now a doubly sore point. Not just because of Paddy, but because her dad had said pretty much the same thing earlier – the heels, the ra-ra skirt and off-the-shoulder crop-top designed not for traipsing about Bradford before it was even properly dark, but for the far less disapproving light of a nightclub. It certainly wasn't the right kind of clothing for sitting on a bench by the bloody cricket pavilion. 'Shut up, Gurdip,' she said, aiming a friendly punch at his shoulder, before sitting down. 'Anyway, what you doing here? I thought we were supposed to be meeting up at the pub?'

'Meeting a mate for a bit,' Gurdy told her and she didn't ask him to elaborate. 'Meeting a mate' could mean stuff she didn't want to know about. 'Anyway, what are you doing here, for that matter?'

Lucy pulled her cigarettes from her handbag and handed one to Gurdy. 'Don't ask.'

He sat down again. 'Come on, what's up, duck?' he asked as she held out her lighter. 'What gives, divs?'

'Bloody Paddy Allen! That's what's up,' she said once

she'd lit her own cigarette. 'Honest to God, Gurdy, if I were a bloke, I'd kill him. I *hate* that horrible bastard. Hate him.'

She turned to him then, recognising his silence for what it was. 'Sorry,' she said. 'I know you're okay with him and that but, oh, he gets me so *mad!*'

Gurdy got on with most people. It was kind of a thing with him. Not so much religious, or because that was how his mam and dad had brought him up, but because the years of bullying had taken their toll. Gurdy was a bit of a people pleaser and if there was one thing Lucy wished she could better drum into him it was that you didn't have to try and make everyone like you.

But his friendship with Paddy, irritatingly, seemed genuine. Yes, he was better friends with her Jimmy – they'd been in the same class at school, and at one point it looked like Gurdy might do a plumbing apprenticeship with him too – but he spent increasing amounts of time with Paddy, helping him out in his garage (which wasn't actually Paddy's garage) and doing God knew what else. She could see nothing good coming from it, but Gurdy actively wanted to work all hours, so he could add to his curry-house-buying stash.

But he was always happy to listen to her rants. 'Go on,' he said, nudging her. 'What's he done now, then?'

'Well, as you well know,' Lucy started, 'me and Vicky were meant to be going out tonight, weren't we? And before you say anything, he had no business turning up in the first place. This was planned weeks ago – months ago. And it's supposed to be a girls' night, you get me?' She nudged him back. 'Present company excepted, of course. But it's like he thinks he bloody owns her! Like she's his property or something. Like Emmeline Pankhurst never bloody existed!'

'Emme-what?'

'Never mind. You won't have heard of her. Not off your mam, at any rate. And, of course, Vicky—'

'—sides with Paddy because that's what she always does, and you go off on one and have a row with him and off you trot.'

'God, I know! I *know* I shouldn't rise to it, but what else am I supposed to do? Just trot along behind, playing goose-berry while he gropes her? It's the principle. My Jimmy doesn't give me any of that sort of nonsense, does he? I tell you, Gurdy, I swear it's like he really does think he owns her. Doesn't want her going out on her own having fun in case another bloke so much as looks at her. And she might just look back. You know what I mean? Where's the trust in that? And, of course, she can't even see it.' Lucy crushed her fag out beneath the sole of her shoe. 'Sorry for ranting on. Anyway, I couldn't go home, could I? I'm out now and I'm flipping staying out. So I'm glad I found you. You up for some fun?'

'Bad news, kiddo, I'm skint. My dad's being a prick – said he's putting my wages away this week so I can buy some bloody auntie that I don't hardly know a wedding present.'

'That's alright,' Lucy said, patting her glossy black hand-bag. 'I thought I was hitting the town, nightclubs and all, didn't I? So I've got a whole fifteen quid on me. I think that's enough to get us both pissed, don't you? Pernods on me, mate,' she added grimly.

Gurdy had mixed feelings about being out with Lucy when she was in this sort of mood. Though he hesitated to use the word 'classy', because that wouldn't be the right one – particularly given tonight's tiny, frilly skirt – Lucy was definitely the more posh of his two friends. Where Vicky was starting a hairdressing apprenticeship, Lucy was going up in the world – she was starting next week as a telephonist at a swanky firm of solicitors in central Bradford. But the combination of her annoyance and the fact that she was determined to get smashed made it odds-on that she'd soon leave her posh telephone voice well behind her. He wondered aloud if she should call Jimmy, and let him know her plans had changed now. 'Don't you think,' he suggested, 'he might want to come down and join us, after all?'

'No way!' Lucy said, as he held the door of the Second West open for her. 'You think he needs any more reasons to hate that cocky bastard? Nah, we're fine on our own, and the night is still young. And who knows who'll be in later?'

Hopefully not Vicky and Paddy, Gurdy thought. Still, Luce was buying and, as she said, the night was still young. Then he noticed something that made him grin. 'Oh, my God, Luce – have you been stuffing your bra again?' He pointed at her chest, unable to stop himself laughing as she frantically stuffed the toe of a grey-looking sock back down her top.

'Piss off, Gurdy,' she whispered as they entered the busy pub. 'Here, take this,' she added, handing him a tenner from her handbag. 'You get the drinks in while I go to the bogs and take them out. I only put them in there because we were supposed to be going to Caverns later, weren't we? The bouncers there don't care how old you look so long as you have tits.'

Gurdy took the money and joined the crush at the bar, while Lucy went to the toilets to sort her chest out. It always amazed Gurdy that Western women went to such extraordinary lengths to make themselves look attractive to men. He'd watch the girls doing their make-up and look on in wonder as they transformed their faces sometimes almost out of recognition. His brother, Vikram, who was only a year older than him (but often seemed a world away when it came to such matters) had gone to great effort to try and educate him in these various practices, which he could never imagine his mother having indulged in ever.

'Women are wily, Gurdip,' Vikram had explained to him a couple of years back. 'They wear these things called Wonderbras,' he'd explained. 'I swear they make their tits look massive, man! But then when you cop a feel, it's all padding,' he'd added, disgusted. 'All a terrible con – there's nothing there! I swear, man, don't be taken in. If they can't show you their tits up front, in the flesh, chances are they are as flat as chapatis!'

Gurdy had no desire to see anyone's chest, large or not. Padded or otherwise. In fact, just the thought of it made him wince. Relationships, especially that kind, confused him greatly. His parents, though always polite, barely spoke to each other, and his brother seemed to use girls like toys – endlessly bragging on about how he would shag them and leave them while he waited for the right – as in unsullied – woman to come along. It was a world away from Gurdy's friendship with his two warrior girlfriends, whose intervention when he was being spat on and hit and humiliated all those years back still ranked in his mind as one of the wonders of the world – he'd never known girls could, or would, ever do such a thing.

But now, with them both seemingly coupled up with their boyfriends, everything was getting more and more complicated. Lucy and Jimmy seemed solid enough, but to Gurdy they seemed far too young to be so committed. It was all messed up, really, in his untutored opinion – as, increasingly, he listened to one or the other of them ranting, expecting him – like he knew anything! – to make all the right noises, so they believed he was as invested in their fucked-up relationships as they were, when in truth everything about them was completely alien.

Lucy returned from the toilets and Gurdy inspected her breasts – if only analytically – to observe the extent of the difference.

'One day,' she said obscurely, as she followed his gaze and then joined him in the queue, 'or maybe never. What the heck? Jimmy loves me as I am. So, doubles, you reckon? Might as well crack on, mightn't we?'

And crack on they had. And even more so when a couple of her other mates had showed, and Gurdy, who they'd seemed to adopt as some kind of mascot, had long since lost count of the drinks that were bought for him.

But, unlike Lucy, he could hold his drink – as Vikram told him, that was just basic science – so he was perfectly capable of helping Jimmy, who he'd nipped out and rung just before last orders, in manhandling her home. Well, to Jimmy's home, it being a good deal nearer, and a good deal further from the doubtless tyrannical machinations of her mother. 'Her dad'll be fine with it,' Jimmy assured him. 'He knows what she can get like when she's off on one, and it's only the last day of school once, isn't it? So what happened anyway? Why you here? And where'd Vicky get to, anyway?'

Gurdy gave him a substantially edited version. After what Lucy had said earlier it seemed the diplomatic thing to do. Jimmy's feelings about Paddy were as entrenched and unequivocal as Paddy's were about Jimmy. Not so much chalk and cheese as North and South.

'Well, I'm glad she found you,' Jimmy told him. 'Thanks for looking out for her. To be honest, mate, I'd rather her be pissed as a fart with you than be sober anywhere around that fucking dick.'

The package delivered, all legs and groans and giggles, Gurdy said goodnight, tucked his hands in his pockets and set off back to Listerhills, looking up at the stars as he walked. In a perfect world, all four of his mates would be friends, but he knew that would never happen; that he was destined to remain piggy in the middle. Some things, he decided, as he weaved his way home, were like oil and water and couldn't be mixed. But others – and he was pleased with his bit of philosophy – were like a stick of dynamite and a lit match. Safe separately, yes, but if they ever got too close …

There could only be one outcome – boom.

Chapter 3

Gurdy rubbed his hands together briskly in an effort to warm up. How could it be this chilly in the bloody summer? Or what passed for a summer in Bradford, at any rate – the 'two fine days and a thunderstorm' one of his teachers had once told him when he asked why the sun never came out.

It was the following Monday – never a day with much to recommend it, and with shoulders hunched against the chilly morning wind, he peered miserably out through the filthy window of the garage to check if he could see Paddy arriving. No sign as yet, though, and Gurdy wished he'd spent an extra half hour in bed.

It was a long walk out to the garage, because it was on an industrial estate. A long disused industrial estate, inhabited mostly by rampant weeds now, and suitably isolated and away from prying eyes. It was a big place, too, as in a former life it had apparently been a scrapyard, with a large garage, several outhouses and a big outside area for breaking up cars. There was also a paint and spray shop and next to that a building with a pit, which also served as storage for tyres and car parts.

Gurdy decided to pass the time while he waited for Paddy by admiring all the new tools his friend had recently acquired. Gurdy knew better than to ask, but he knew the tools would have been nicked from some other poor mechanic's garage. He picked up a large, shiny cutting tool and ran his finger down the edge; they were clearly worth a few bob as well.

Paddy's garage – or, more accurately, Paddy's boss Rasta Mo's garage – was always filled with stolen gear. From tyres and wheels to car parts, and all kinds of tools. And often there'd be whole cars in as well, waiting to be chopped, or cut and shut, to then sell on to some unsuspecting punter in a town miles away. Local branch of Kwik Fit it wasn't.

Because Rasta Mo wasn't just in the car 'repair' business. He was also one of the biggest drug dealers in Bradford, which took up most of his time and, as Paddy was a decent mechanic, Mo let him have full run of the place. And he was certainly that – all the time Gurdy had known him, he spent all his free time with his nose under the bonnet of a car; fixing cars, he'd always said, was in his blood.

Though he wasn't just employed as a mechanic. In return for the privilege of more or less being Mo's number two here, he also had to dirty his hands with the drugs. And that was where Gurdy came in. He didn't remember when or how he had been roped in to all that stuff for Paddy, but he knew the money was good for doing very little, and though it wasn't quite the sort of thing he wanted to be doing, nobody said no to Paddy.

'Now then, me little Paki mate!'

Gurdy jumped. How did Paddy *do* that? Manage to creep up on people like that? And why this pleasure in scaring the pants off people all the time? 'Fucking hell, Paddy!' he said, as he was slapped roundly on the back for good measure. 'I almost shit myself! Anyway, where you been, man?' he said, while pressing a hand against his chest to still its thumping. 'I've been here ages. I thought you said eleven o'clock?'

Paddy winked. 'Vicky wouldn't let me get out of bed,' he said, grinning. 'You know what the birds are like for a taste of the old Padster!'

Gurdy didn't know, and didn't want to. He felt his cheeks begin to burn. He didn't like it when Paddy started going on about his exploits in the kip, especially when he was on about his friend.

'So?' he asked, keen to move on to other topics. 'What's on the agenda for today then?'

Paddy burst into song, which was another of the things he often did. 'I've got a braaaain, pickled in cocaaaaaine,' he crooned, and in an accent that was a pretty fair rendition of the Dillinger reggae hit, even if the words were, as ever, completely wrong. He then pulled a paper package from the inside of his parka and slammed it on the wooden workbench with a grin. 'And this, my little Paki mate,' he said, stroking the package lovingly, 'is the best coke that Bradford will have seen or tasted for a long time. So good, in fact, that it's *too* good for most of them, so if you look in that end cupboard, you'll find a big tub of baby talc. I need you to get to work mixing it up for me, okay? And then the usual weighing and bagging before you take it out on the road, mate.' He slapped Gurdy on the back again, though this time he was braced for it. Paddy winked a second time. 'Big bucks for us this time, my friend.'

Gurdy did as he was asked and took the talcum powder from the cupboard, but couldn't help his nerves beginning to jangle. He always felt like this – exposed. Mo could stroll in at any time, couldn't he? 'Does Mo know?' he asked. 'I mean, you know – he's probably already cut it himself, hasn't he?' Gurdy licked his dry lips. 'He'll do his nut if we're doing it again.'

Paddy put down the tool he was inspecting and without warning – not even so much as a change in his demeanour – shoved Gurdy against the brick wall. It wasn't a violent act, exactly – almost casual, if anything. And his expression wasn't hostile, just ever so slightly irritated. It wore the kind of look a weary teacher might give a dozy pupil, who needs telling the same thing over and over. As ever, at such times, Gurdy cursed himself. Why didn't he just keep his trap shut?

'What have I told you about all the fucking questions, eh? Eh, mate?' Paddy asked him, almost conversationally. As if the flat of his hand wasn't pressing hard into Gurdy's sternum, pinning him to the wall. 'Do I go poking my nose into your dad's business?' Gurdy swallowed and shook his head. 'Exactly. No, I don't,' Paddy said, removing his hand and wagging a chastising finger. 'So if you know what's good for you, you'll just keep your trap shut and get on with it, okay?'

Gurdy nodded, rubbing his chest as he took the talc to the bench. He hated it when Paddy got rough with him, even if it was half in jest. Even if he knew, and he did know, that Paddy would never hurt him. That it was all front. Vicky had told him that countless times. Told him Paddy thought a lot of him. He just didn't say so, because that wasn't his style.

But Gurdy hated that he still had so much to learn; mostly because he never quite knew what was going to set Paddy off. Which, as he was quickly learning, could be the slightest thing. For now, anyway. One day, not too long away, he knew he'd earn Paddy's respect.

'Alright, mate,' he said, more comfortable now there was a bit of distance between them. 'There's no need to start on me, is there?' The talc still in hand, he started looking around for a knife to split the package open with. 'I just *wondered*, that's all. Last thing I want is Mo chasing us with a fucking cleaver, innit?'

Paddy smiled. 'Chasing *you*, you mean,' he corrected, grinning as he placed his hands on the bench behind him and hoisted himself up onto it. 'Give us a smoke, will you?'

That was another thing. Paddy was always cadging his fags. He fished in his jeans pocket for his ten Benson & Hedges and a book of matches. 'Here you go, mate,' he said, almost certain Paddy would have a pack of twenty of his own inside his parka.

Paddy lit a cigarette, then blew out the match. 'So,' he said conversationally, 'how's things, then?'

He clearly had nowhere to be and no inclination to help. Perhaps he'd start work on his Capri when he was done smoking. 'Doing my fucking head in,' Gurdy admitted. 'Expecting me to work for them all the fucking time – morning, noon and bloody night. Like I don't have a right to my own life.'

Paddy chuckled. 'You know what you wanna do? You wanna tell them to fuck right off, mate. Fuck. The. Fuck. Off. Just like that.'

Gurdy chuckled too, imagining Paddy saying that to his mother. She'd freak. Or probably faint. But at the same time, he knew, there'd be this little bit of her that would be slightly in thrall to him. He had that kind of charm. She'd probably drag him into the kitchen and feed him.

'Just like that,' Gurdy repeated. 'Yeah, I'll do it tonight, mate.'

'Well, it's your bed, mate. So you've got to lie on it, haven't you? They've got different values, haven't they? They'd have you out planting rice, or whatever it is they grow out there. Till you're fucking forty! No, you got to put them straight. Point out that you make more dosh working a day for me than slaving away all bloody week serving cheapskate customers in their little shit hole.'

Yeah, he was really going to do that. *Just so you know, Mam, I'm a joey for Paddy Allen.* Like it was the easiest thing in the world. But it seemed to be for some – those who didn't have *his* parents – and for Paddy, especially so. He got away with murder with his mum and dad. Always had done apparently. They owned a bakery, with a shop at the front, and they worked all hours too – the difference was, though, that they never asked Paddy to help out. Far as Gurdy could see, he never lifted a finger.

He was always loaded as well. Or, at least, he seemed to be. And with money that didn't come from the drugs or the garage. Even as a kid, he always seemed to have pockets full of money. Not that Gurdy was stupid. Lucy had told him once that they gave it him to keep him out of their hair; plied him with cash to get shut of him, essentially.

So, on balance, which was better? He wasn't sure. He peeled off the tape and carefully opened up the package of cocaine, smoothing out the paper that had surrounded it. 'I wish I could tell 'em, Pad, I do. But my dad's an arsehole. A proper arsehole,' he added, warming to his theme. 'Why me all the time? Why do I have to work in the fucking shop all the time? When our Vikram does fuck-all?'

'Because your Vikram's not a soft touch like you are, mate,' Paddy told him. 'Your Vikram's got his mam round his little finger.' He chuckled again. 'And his finger in …' he laughed out loud. 'God, you are such a pussy, Gurd! Well, don't you worry, mate,' he said, dropping the cigarette on the floor and sliding off the bench to grind it out. 'You keep saving all the money you're making from me, and you'll soon be able to tell him to fuck off as well.'

That was the main thing. That was the thing Gurdy hung on to. That, for all that the drug dealing caused him anxiety, he already had quite a stash thanks to Paddy – and for relatively little work. All he had to do was turn up outside Arthur's Bar on Lumb Lane any Friday or Saturday night and, within an hour, all his tiny wraps of coke would be gone. It always amazed him how much people were willing to pay for it. Especially the prostitutes and their pimps.

Perhaps they needed it to get through their particular line of work. At any rate, they were the backbone of his trade, and, as they ran pretty lucrative businesses themselves, they were a willing and rich market too.

Win-win. And Gurdy always got a fair share of the proceeds. That was one good thing about Paddy – he paid bloody well, and that was down to the fact that he had no need to be greedy. Money always came to him, and he was always very generous. No, one day, he'd get there. He'd have his own curry restaurant. Be free of his parents' shackles once and for all.

'Oh, and I nearly forgot,' he said, noticing that Paddy looked as if he might be leaving. 'It's our Vikram's eighteenth next weekend and he asked me to invite you and Vicky. Mucky Willy's,' he added. 'Next Saturday at eight.' He pointed down to the gear he was now carefully mixing, and grinned. 'I'll have this lot gone by then, too. Should be a good night.'

'Should be,' Paddy agreed. 'Well, if that fucking Lucy and her knobhead boyfriend aren't there. But I'm guessing they will be.'

Gurdy nodded apologetically, while mentally rolling his eyes. All of them. Always singing the same bloody song. 'Course they will, Pad. You know how things are.'

Paddy crossed the garage and clapped Gurdy on the back a second time. 'Don't wet your pants, my little friend. We'll be there. Be a laugh.' He cracked his knuckles. 'You know how much I enjoy seeing that pair of cunts squirm.'

'Pad, I don't want no trouble. My mam and dad …'

'Can fuck right off, remember? I'll even tell 'em for you, if you like, since I'll be seeing them. Cos you'd really like that, wouldn't you? *Joke!*' he boomed then, as he headed back out the door. Gurdy could hear him laughing all the way down the street.

Chapter 4

The salon Vicky worked at was called The Cutting Edge, and was on Market Street, in the town centre. Despite the trendy name, it was considered a bit of an old-fashioned hairdressers, and catered mainly for an older clientele. Nevertheless, its position in the town, and the relatively cheap cuts and perms they offered, meant that there was always a stream of regulars to keep them busy. Vicky loved it when after six weeks of slog as a Saturday girl, she'd been offered a permanent job there. The days had mostly flown by – they certainly got their money's worth out of her and her feet knew all about it – but today she was clock-watching as the hands crawled to home time, because Paddy was coming to pick her up.

She knew it was childish but she so wanted to show him off. Not least to Leanne, the more senior apprentice she worked under, because, as Lucy once put it when she started seeing Jimmy, she felt a powerful need to put her marker down; she'd clocked the way Leanne had looked him up and down last time he'd come to collect her.

Leanne grinned at her now, glancing across as she washed her last client's hair. Vicky sometimes felt as if she could almost read her thoughts.

'Honestly, Vic, it doesn't make the time go faster the more you look at the clock, you know. He'll get here when he gets here.'

Vicky pursed her lips. 'Silly mare,' she muttered, as she wiped round the adjacent sink for the second time. 'That's not why I'm clock-watching. I just want today to be finished because I'm going to a party, that's all.'

And, despite Leanne being right about Paddy – which was infuriating – she was as keen to get to the party as anything else. It had been over a week since she'd had any sort of communication with Lucy and, since their last chat, when Vicky had phoned to apologise and Lucy had been so chippy, it was constantly preying on her mind.

She wondered if this was the way it was going to be between them now. That without the glue of school – the easy companionship, the shared endeavour, the physical proximity to one another – their friendship was destined to wither. They were both working full-time now, several miles away from one another, and Vicky still smarted at how Lucy had so casually alluded to the new workmates she had been going out with that night.

But key to all of it (and Vicky still cursed herself for letting Paddy dictate terms that night, even as part of her felt Lucy had been over-reacting) was the increasing enmity between their respective boyfriends. Yes, it was true that she had her own issues – she knew she should stand up for herself more, rather than be dictated to by a best friend and a boyfriend with such strong personalities – but none of that would be an issue without the boys.

She checked the colourant trolley to see if it needed restocking. She simply couldn't see what Lucy saw in Jimmy. Yes, he was okay looking, but he was about as much fun as a wet weekend in Blackpool, and, being a copper's son, was often hard to relax around. Like Paddy often said, you really could almost see him sniffing the air, looking for signs of wrongdoing to tell his dad about. His dad who wasn't just any old copper – who was a detective inspector with the vice squad.

That Paddy hated Jimmy was a longstanding and under-standable fact, particularly now, when he was getting in so much deeper with the terrifying Mo. About which she gnawed on a kernel of constant worry, and could only hope that the garage, under Paddy's capable stewardship, did well enough that he could leave off the drug dealing. Lucy's voice kept coming back to her, increasingly coolly and crit-ically. *He's a bloody criminal, Vic. That's what I don't like about him. But if that's the sort of lad you want ...*

That was the problem. She did.

Her client's hair washed, Leanne had taken her back to be blow-dried, and both were now looking at Vicky through the wall mirror. Leanne bent down slightly to chat into her client's ear. 'We know different, don't we, Mrs Gallagher? We clocked the way she fluttered those eyelashes of hers last time he was in.'

It was banter, that was all. Everyday hairdressing gossip. Nothing meant by it particularly. Just a bit of teasing. But already she was finding it irritating. And, as she went to make a last cup of coffee of the day for them all, it was with a riposte on her mind, if not actually on her tongue, that last time Paddy had been in, if she wasn't mistaken, it had been Leanne who'd been fluttering her bloody eyelashes.

It shouldn't matter – she knew that, because Paddy so obviously adored her – but Leanne was pretty, too. And, if Vicky's hunch was correct, she wouldn't let the small matter of Paddy being taken bother her, not if she really had set her sights on him.

'Here you go,' she said, bringing Leanne's coffee back out, and placing it on the reception desk as Mrs Gallagher was paying. 'I'm going to carry on cleaning in the back while I drink mine. Give us a shout when my Paddy gets here, will you?'

'Will do,' Leanne replied. Then she grinned at Mrs Gallagher. 'In fourteen and a half minutes and counting ...'

Forcing herself to ignore it, Vicky returned to the back room. Leanne was okay, really. Just a flirt and a bit of a know-all – which was fair enough, Vicky supposed, since she'd been there two years, and knew so much more about everything than Vicky did; she'd reached that precious milestone – she was even allowed to cut and perm now. And Vicky enjoyed it for the most part, particularly on those days when it was just the girls in, the boss, Francis, being a force to be reckoned with – he ruled the salon like a dictator.

The washing machine whirred to the end of its spin cycle, so she pulled towels from the drum and began folding them. No, on balance, working here was just fine. And who knew? Once she and Leanne got to know one another better, perhaps she'd have a new friend as well.

Or maybe not. She emerged with a fresh pile of towels to find Paddy leaning casually against the counter. On the other side of which was Leanne, busy cashing up, apparently, but clearly busier laughing at something Paddy had just said to her, and in that simpering fashion every girl knew so well.

Vicky marched across to the cubbyholes the towels were stored in. 'I thought you were going to call me,' she said to Leanne as she pushed the pile in. Then, because she couldn't stop herself, 'but you're clearly too busy.'

The words dropped out of her mouth and felt heavier than she'd intended.

Paddy laughed, then, as if specifically to wind her up, leaning across the counter. 'I told you she was jealous to death,' he said.

The towels safely stashed, Vicky stalked across the salon to fetch her jacket. 'You're such a *div*,' she told Paddy, who was now standing grinning at her. 'As if *I'm* bloody jealous of *you*!' It was pointed. It was meant to be. Paddy's jealousy was legendary. A bloke so much as glanced at her and he could turn caveman in a second. She swung her coat around and pulled it on, smiling sweetly at Leanne. 'Take no notice of this idiot, Lee,' she said, regaining her composure. 'He fancies himself as a bit of a ladies' man.' She then turned to Paddy and slapped him on the back. 'Come on then, loser. Let's get home and ready to party.'

Paddy winked and saluted as Vicky shoved him out the front door. 'Don't hate me, Vic,' he pleaded, while ducking another slap. 'I can't help it if the birds all love me, can I?'

'Don't kid yourself,' she huffed, even though she wasn't even cross with him anymore. Possession, after all, was nine-tenths of the law and, as Vicky so often reminded herself, it took two to tango, and her Paddy, much as he loved to flirt with girls, had never expressed any desire to tango with anyone else but her.

Paddy had parked his latest old banger down on Ivegate. It was a bright blue Ford Capri with naff go-faster stripes down it, and despite looking like it belonged in some ancient 1970s TV cop show, it was his pride and joy. Though that was mainly down to the fact that it had a brand new Pioneer tape deck installed in the dashboard, which meant that, coupled with the speakers he'd installed front and back, he could play his beloved Northern Soul music whenever he was driving. Well, blast it out for all to hear, more accurately. He was a bit like the crocodile that swallowed the clock in *Peter Pan* – you could always hear him coming before you saw him. Not least because he was fast becoming a dying breed – apart from her (and Vicky knew that it was only because of him anyway) Paddy was the only person she knew who still listened to it.

And looking at him now, as they made their way down Ivegate towards the car, she could see he was hoping they'd be playing it at Vikram's party. Despite the heat, he was wearing his long leather trenchcoat, over baggy black trousers and a white Fred Perry T-shirt. And as ever, she conceded, he carried it off.

'What should I wear, Pad?' she asked, once they were both in the car and the music was blaring at the max. She'd learned over time that it was always worth getting his input, in part because she liked to look good for him, obviously, but also because you never knew what 'good' might comprise. Sometimes he liked to show her off, and have her dress to the nines, but others – if he was in one of his periodic grumpy moods, he'd tell her she looked slutty if she turned out like that, telling her to tone down the make-up and cover herself up, reminding her that she was his, and his alone. What she'd never quite worked out was what either mood was based on. Mercurial, that's what her mam called him. Changeable, like the weather. She wasn't sure quite what that meant but she kind of got the gist of it. He was unpredictable. Which was probably why he still excited her so much.

However, anything for a quiet life. Which apparently tonight meant the black mini-dress she'd bought the previous weekend. Her first well-deserved purchase as a full-time working girl. 'And those shiny high heels,' he added. 'Give 'em all something to gawp at, eh, babe? We'll be the best-looking couple there, that's for sure.'

Not that any of that mattered to Vicky, and she was just about to say so, when he added, 'Not that your dopey mate and her fucktard of a boyfriend are any sort of competition. Gurdy tells me they're invited, more's the pity.'

'Paddy!' Vicky complained. 'It's not a frigging competition!' She swivelled in her seat. 'And please don't start tonight, babes. Promise me, okay? I want to make up with Lucy – not cause another frigging row. It's a party, so let's just all have a laugh, okay?'

He looked offended. 'Me? Start anything? Like *I'm* the one who has anything to prove?'

'No, I know,' she said, reaching between her legs for her handbag as Paddy parked up outside her house. 'But I also know *you*. Couple of drinks …'

'Cross my heart,' he said, pulling the key from the ignition. 'Come on, let's get you in and get you out of that work gear.'

'And *straight* into my party gear,' she added. 'You can stay downstairs with Mam. She's got some cider in. You can have a drink with her. She'll enjoy the company.'

Even as she said this, Vicky knew it wasn't going to happen. 'Alright, Mrs Robinson?' Paddy called as he followed her into the hall. Then, in Vicky's ear, as he grabbed her arse fondly, 'I'd much rather watch you strip out of that apron …'

Which meant it would take her twice as long to get ready. And it did. Two hours later, after a slow undressing, an obligatory romp on the bed and then a hurried re-dressing, she was finally ready for Vikram's party, albeit slightly flushed.

* * *

It was a nice place, the Coach House, where the do was being held, but, for some reason, it had always been known as Mucky Willy's. Not that anyone she'd asked could ever tell her who Willy even was, let alone in what sense he'd been mucky. Still, tonight it was all looking tarted-up and elegant, with Vikram, Gurdy and their parents looking equally festive, standing in the foyer, all togged up for the occasion.

Vicky could have kicked herself, watching other guests ahead of them, bearing elaborately wrapped gifts. She'd written a card, and popped a tenner in it, but why hadn't she thought to bring an actual present? She had to make do with gushing about how beautiful Gurdy's mam's sari was and telling Vikram they were looking forward to buying him a couple of birthday drinks. Though as soon as she'd said it she could have kicked herself again at the look on his mam's face – the senior Banerjees were both teetotal.

Paddy seemed to have no such concerns. With Gurdy's mam and dad busy chatting to some elderly relative, he shook hands with Vikram and pulled him in close. 'Now then, me little Paki mates,' he said, grinning at both brothers, 'point me to the bar, my son – this one has proper worn me out.' Ah, so he was in *that* sort of mood, then.

She slapped Paddy in the stomach with her handbag, as was her usual response. A small part of her loved the way he alluded to her being so sexy, but the larger part – the *much* larger part – hated it, and made her squirm. And she could see Gurdy squirming too, so she threaded her arm through his. 'Take no notice, pal – he's all talk,' she whispered as they walked inside. 'More importantly, are Lucy and Jimmy here yet?'

Gurdy nodded and pointed. In fact, it looked like *everyone* was here. Vikram not only had a family that seemed to stretch from Bradford to Leeds, he was popular too and had lots of mates of his own. Most of which, Vicky guessed, were his fellow workers from Fields Printers, the large factory between Clayton and Lidget Green where he worked, which was famous for printing cigarette packaging.

And despite the relative earliness of the hour still the party was in full swing, the dance floor packed and throbbing and long queues at the bar, and, with the curtains closed and the disco ball scattering the room with coloured diamonds, Vicky felt a surge of happiness, despite the ache in the balls of her feet. This was going to be a great night, she just knew it.

But Vicky's confidence looked like turning out to be short-lived. No sooner had she spotted Lucy and Jimmy, and raised a hand to wave a greeting, than she felt Paddy's hand grip her arm.

'Hey, you're with me tonight,' he hissed at her, while still smiling at the barmaid. 'Let's do the sensible thing, yeah? Leave the fucking numpties where they are.'

Vicky shook his hand off, and he didn't resist, thankfully. 'Oh, Paddy, for God's sake, don't start! I only want to go say hello to Luce. She'll think I'm being funny if I don't.'

'Then she can come talk to you here,' he said firmly. 'I mean it, Vic. You've got to let her come to you. That's the way to play it. And if she wants to, she will,' he added. 'Won't she?'

Vicky wished she'd never mentioned her and Lucy's last conversation. Why had she done such an idiotic thing? She should have realised she was only giving him ammunition against Lucy. She made a mental note never to do it again.

She looked at Lucy again, making what she hoped was enough of an apologetic face for Lucy to understand how her hands were tied, but not so much that Paddy would notice and think she was taking the mick. Lucy made a face back, and this time it was entirely unmistakable. She'd seen Paddy stop her going over and it was clear how she felt about it. Her expression said, *Yeah, I get it, you're a doormat and your boyfriend is a dick.*

Well, sod it, Vicky decided, stung. It was all so bloody childish. Were it not for the fact that it would probably turn into a fist fight, she'd like to bang her best friend and her boyfriend's bloody heads together. So she turned instead to the drinks Paddy was lining up on the bar. Perhaps getting something down her would chill her out a bit.

As was his way, he'd got a row of shorts lined up on the bar – three whiskies for him and two vodka and limes for her. 'Come on, Vic,' he said nudging her, 'get them supped up.' He downed his three in turn. Three tips of the head, three bobs of his Adam's apple. He then picked up his pint. 'Can't have you lagging behind, can we?'

Vicky felt her spirits sink. Paddy liked his drink, but unfortunately it didn't like him much, and she could already spot the tell-tale signs that he was going to be in the mood for bother. Not least that he kept glancing across the dance floor to where Lucy and Jimmy were sitting, despite his earlier reassurance that, because they weren't worth the effort, he intended to ignore them.

He downed the pint, too, and immediately held the empty glass up, after another. It would only take another couple of drinks before he was well and truly pissed. Great.

'Slow down a bit, babes,' Vicky said, stroking his arm. The last thing she wanted was for him to show her up in front of everyone. 'Tell you what, forget the pint – why don't we go have a dance?'

It was always touch and go, such a suggestion; Paddy never like being told what to do. But he was still just on the right side of belligerent. Plus he did so love to dance, and here he had a big audience.

'Good idea,' he said, grinning as he set the empty glass down on the bar. 'But first,' he said, grabbing her hand and tugging her out onto the edge of the dance floor, away from the bar queue, 'I'll go get that DJ to put something decent on, seeing as I'm all dressed up in my best dancing gear.'

Vicky groaned inwardly. That meant Northern Soul, of course. And much as she loved him, and loved dancing with him, too, this would go down like a lead balloon. If the DJ agreed – which he would, because Paddy would charm him – the dance floor was likely to empty in moments, leaving only the hard-core Soulies stomping around.

She watched disconsolately, her eye naturally travelling from Paddy over to Lucy, making an automatic connection. Lucy would know exactly what she was thinking right now and would probably sympathise. But she didn't appear to. In fact, her own gaze seemed to sweep right over Vicky. Preoccupied by something else, she clearly hadn't seen her, and, later, when they unpicked everything, she'd regretfully – so regretfully – know this to have been true.

As it was, Lucy's non-look was immediately followed by her dipping her dark head to Jimmy's blond one, and whispering something in his ear, which made him laugh. And at exactly the point when Paddy returned to her from his visit to the DJ. *From such tiny sparks*, she thought wretchedly, watching his gaze following hers, *do whole bloody infernos explode*.

'What's that fucker laughing at?' Paddy demanded. He'd let go of her arm now and was staring straight at Jimmy.

'How the hell should I know?' she said, trying to distract him. 'Come on, "Nine Times Out of Ten" – great choice. It's my favourite.' She grabbed both of Paddy's hands and started to try and swing him to the rhythm. Unfortunately, right at that moment, Jimmy decided to laugh even louder. And now she caught *his* gaze, which seemed to ask, 'What the hell?'

'No, fuck that!' Paddy said, and his tone made Vicky's gut clench. 'He's taking the fucking piss.' He stalked across the floor of dancing couples which, as she'd predicted, was already thinning, heading straight for Lucy and Jimmy's table.

Jimmy stood up as Paddy reached him, Vicky hot on his heels. Paddy was big and imposing and could intimidate pretty much anyone if he wanted to, but Jimmy was big too. And he could handle himself, even if in a less obvious way – as a copper's son, he'd had to learn to since he was small.

And it looked as though he was in just as much of a mood for trouble as was Paddy, because as he closed in, Jimmy was already rolling up his sleeves.

And in they went, nothing said, both girls looking on helplessly, while, almost as if choreographed to go along with the music, fists began to fly and connected with faces, then both of them falling to the floor in a rolling heap of knuckles, legs and hair.

It would take a brave man to separate them, but a determined female was in with a shot, at least, and when Lucy moved forward that was exactly what Vicky thought she *was* doing – trying to haul her boyfriend off and stop the fight. But, to Vicky's consternation, she was actually having a go at Paddy *herself*, kicking at him and calling him a bastard as he writhed on the floor.

Vicky was stunned into paralysis for a long, long moment, unable to quite accept what she was seeing. 'What the fuck are you *doing*?' she finally screeched at Lucy. 'Stop that, for fuck's sake!'

But since Lucy made no sign of taking the least bit of notice, she waded in too, grabbing a fistful of Lucy's mop of hair, and yanking it back so she could better press her point home. She then slapped her, an unexpected rage coming over her from God knew where. Slapped her hard – shockingly hard – across the face. 'Grab your fucking *boyfriend*!' she yelled at a now startled Lucy. 'You kick my Paddy again and I'll rip your head off, you hear?'

But there was no need. By now Gurdy and Vikram had hurried over and between them had already half-hefted Jimmy away. Vikram looked daggers. Like he was an inch away from slugging Paddy himself. 'You just couldn't help yourself, could you?' he yelled, as Paddy spat blood from his mouth. 'You fucking *imbecile*. You cretin. Showing yourself up as usual!'

Paddy wiped the back of his hand across his lips. Then, to Vicky's dismay, he didn't apologise – he grinned. Even jogged on the spot slightly, arms swinging by his side, his attention not on Vikram, but still very much on Jimmy. 'Teach you to be a clever little bastard, won't it?' he spat.

'Get him out of here,' Vikram said to Vicky, yanking a thumb in the direction of the entrance. 'It's my fucking birthday and I'm not having you idiots ruin it.'

Vicky started to apologise, but again Paddy's hand was on her arm. 'I see how it is,' he said to Vikram and a visibly shaken Gurdy. His voice was ice. 'Be my absolute fucking pleasure.'

Chapter 5

There was really nothing for it but to leave. Despite Vikram assuring both of them that he knew it had been Paddy who'd started it, Lucy couldn't countenance staying a second longer. She looked a complete state, for one thing. Her tights were laddered, her white court shoes now had a red polka-dot pattern, and her hair, she could feel, was like a rat's nest. But it wasn't just how she looked. It was how she felt: she felt shame. She'd felt everyone's eyes boring into her. Everyone judging her. As well they might have. What had she been thinking, wellying in the way she had? Was her hatred of Paddy Allen that strong that she could no longer contain herself?

She felt tears prick in her eyes. She was shaking still. Jittery. All that unspent adrenalin still coursing through her veins. She jumped in shock as Jimmy banged the pub door open with his foot. Followed him out into the car park, where it wasn't even dark yet. Looked around anxiously. No sign of Vicky and that bastard Paddy, thank God.

'Oh, babes, I can't believe this,' she cried, only now taking in the full, horrible extent of it. If she looked a state, Jimmy looked like a car crash. His trousers ripped, his shirt streaked with red, buttons missing. His best white shirt, too, the one she'd bought him for his birthday. She knew Paddy had belted him hard – Christ, she'd heard it – but it had obviously been even harder than she'd thought. The blow – or blows, the bastard – had split both his nose and lip open. And just as red raw now was Jimmy's anger.

'*You* can't believe it!' he barked, his fists still clenching and unclenching. Thank God Paddy hadn't decided to wait outside for them. She could see it would have all started up again out here. She took a step towards Jimmy, the tears really flowing now. Wanting only to comfort him and be comforted in return. But Jimmy was in no mood to either hug her or be placated. 'Luce, he's showed us both up to fuck, and for nothing! *Christ*, he's a prick! A first-class one, at that. Always has been.' He rounded on her now. 'I don't know how you expect me to tolerate him, I really don't. And frigging Vicky! What the fuck was she doing, threatening you like that? Some fucking friend she is!'

Lucy reached for Jimmy's hand, but he'd half turned away from her. He was still too wired up to stand still. And he had a point. She'd been shocked too when Vicky had turned on her. After all, she was only sticking up for her bloke. That bastard Paddy had just bloody punched him! And for nothing. For what? It had come out of nowhere. Jimmy had done nothing to provoke it. So what did Vic expect? That she'd just stand there and *let* him?

Though Jimmy clearly hadn't seen the way she'd flown at Paddy. But though a part of her was relieved at that

– Jimmy had no respect for brawling girls – a part of her felt bad for her friend.

But, at the same time, looking at Jimmy's battered face, she felt vindicated. Of *course* she'd kicked out. Vic would have done the same. And *she* would again. It was no more than Paddy Allen deserved. Lucy shrugged, conscious that they probably needed to leave it. 'Just sticking her oar in because I was trying to help you, I imagine.' Now she did take hold of his hand. 'I'm fine though, Jimmy, honest. It's you that's—'

'You're *not* though,' Jimmy said, pulling her in to him, kissing her hair unthinkingly and then yowling at the pain. 'Shit! Look at the state of us both. God, that fucking *shit*! I swear to God, hand on heart, Luce, I'll have that cocky bastard. He might have won this battle, but you mark my words, he will not – he really *will* not win the fucking war!'

It was enough to raise her spirits a notch. 'You sound like Winston Churchill.'

'That right? He was a sweary fucker too, was he? I must have missed that. Come on, babes, no point in hanging around out here. Let's go home.'

Not that the walk seemed to calm Jimmy any. In fact, the more they walked, the more he seemed to wind himself up, ranting on about what a twat Paddy Allen had always been, and about how Vicky was insane for having anything to do with him. About how Lucy should wake up and see things for what they were. That though they'd been mates for years, she should see what was in front of her – that the Vicky they knew now was not the same Vicky she used to be. That she'd been brainwashed by Paddy, and that the process was ongoing, and that the best thing she could do, the only thing she *should* do, was to cut Vicky out of her life now.

And Lucy had to concede there were elements of truth in what he said. 'I'll certainly be giving her a wide berth for a bit,' she agreed. She was still smarting at the memory of the expression on Vicky's face. It was one she'd never seen before, ever. 'And you never know,' she added, 'maybe if she doesn't have me to fall back on, she'll get tired of Paddy and see him for what he really is.'

Jimmy huffed. 'I wouldn't hold your breath,' he said dryly. 'She already *knows* what he is. A twat. And she doesn't care. She's with a twat who's always hated that she has anything to do with a copper's son – even if it's just by association. That's what it is. He wants an end to your friendship. And he won't stop causing trouble till that's exactly what he gets.'

Not for the first time, Lucy wondered at how different she and Vicky really were. For years everyone had said they were so alike. At school the teachers had called them the 'terrible twins', or the 'gruesome twosome', as they had always been inseparable. Then Paddy had come along and everything had changed. Vicky had changed almost overnight, in fact – like she was under his spell.

It shouldn't be like that, should it? 'I wish she'd met someone like you,' she said wistfully. 'Someone normal, and nice, and bloody *decent*.'

'Steady on, babe,' Jimmy said. 'You make me sound about as interesting as a fucking knitting pattern model.'

'You know what I *mean*,' she chided. 'Someone who isn't a twat. So we could all be friends, as couples, like every-frigging-body else. God, I despise Paddy. I really hate him.'

'Well, she didn't, and we can't,' Jimmy pointed out firmly. 'And she can't say we haven't tried, either. Now,' he said as they neared his house on Pasture Lane, 'are you coming into mine for a bit? Might as well. Dad's on a late shift and he won't mind us raiding his booze cupboard.'

That was true. In recent months, since she'd turned sixteen, Lucy had been spending more and more time at Jimmy's. And she knew Jimmy's dad was okay with it. It had been just the two of them since Jimmy's mam had left them twelve years back, and he often commented how nice it was to have a girl round the house. He liked Lucy, she knew, and she liked him too.

Jimmy tugged on her hand and grinned. 'Maybe even stay over? Give your mam a quick ring and tell her not to expect you home?'

'I already told her I was staying out,' Lucy said, answering his unspoken suggestion with a smile. 'Anyway, there's no point worrying them. Mam'll only want to know why I'm not at the party, won't she? Not that they won't know soon enough. You need to see the state of your face.' They'd arrived now, and she inspected it more carefully in the light from the porch. 'You know, you might even need a couple of stitches.'

Jimmy shook his head. 'It doesn't feel that bad. Couple of plasters'll do it. What I need now is a bloody drink and some serious TLC. As do you, babes,' he said, as he put his key in the front door. 'You look like you've been dragged through a bloody hedge.'

Careful inspection up in the bathroom revealed two positives. That all Lucy had lost was a pair of tights and some pride – the stilettos, happily, scrubbed up a treat. And, after cleaning up his mouth and nose, she was able to agree that Jimmy probably didn't need stitches. 'It's already swelling, though,' she observed. 'You'll be puffed up like a giant Sugar Puff by the morning. Just as well it's a Sunday ...'

'And it'll probably be black and blue by Monday. Great. So, of course everyone at work will want to know how I got it—'

'Like they won't already? With all Vikram's party guests looking on?'

But it was his shirt that angered Jimmy the most. 'That fucking twat,' he growled disconsolately, as he shrugged it off. 'I've a good mind to send him a bill.'

'Babe, it's just a shirt,' Lucy soothed, seeing his agitation levels rise again. 'I'll buy you another one. An even better one. I'm on a salary now, don't forget.'

Jimmy bundled the shirt into a ball and shoved it angrily into the little rattan litter bin by the bath. Then he sat down on the side of it, bare-chested, sheeny with sweat, his hands clenching and unclenching once again.

'Look, let's just forget it,' Lucy said. 'How about we go down and get that drink? I'm parched. Didn't even finish half of mine at Mucky Willy's.'

'God,' Jimmy said, locking his fingers and cracking his knuckles, 'what a fucking shower. I'm going to have to go round and see Vik tomorrow. Apologise. His poor parents, they must have been terrified.'

'And I'm thirsty, like I say,' she said, grabbing both his hands and pulling him upright. 'And you need to *chill*.'

A thought occurred to her then, thinking of Vikram and, by extension, of Gurdy. 'Babe, can I ask you something?' she said, as he followed her back downstairs.

'What sort of something?'

'Have you ever tried dope?'

He stopped on the stairs, and so suddenly that she fell against his naked back. He carried on then, reached the bottom, then turned around. 'Why?'

Lucy knew Jimmy well enough to read him like a book. She read him now. 'I just wondered, that's all. Only when I was out with Gurdy the other weekend he mentioned it.' Mentioned it, yes. And had then produced two fat joints. Things Lucy had never seen before. She didn't know where he'd got them and she didn't want to ask him, because she knew the answer would in all probability be Rasta Mo.

'As in suggesting *you* do?' Jimmy finished.

Lucy shook her head emphatically, having continued to read her boyfriend. There was no way in the world now that she was going to tell him that he'd not only suggested it but lit one of them as well. And suggested she try it. Which she had.

Though it hadn't done much. Just made her feel giggly and a bit sleepy. But Gurdy had told her that that was what often happened – first few times you tried it, at any rate.

And it wasn't that Lucy was into drugs or anything – that had never been her thing, really. But it was like everyone said all the time, wasn't it? Like Gurdy said – and had been amply proven this evening. It was the booze that caused the trouble, and all the fights. Everyone knew that. People who smoked dope never fought. That was fact.

'As in saying I *might*, but only if I *wanted*,' she told Jimmy now. 'Which I didn't. But it struck me that we should try it sometime, together. You know, to chill us out properly. Everyone does, don't they? Why not?'

Jimmy's answering 'huh' left no room for doubt. 'Because it's *illegal?*' he pointed out. 'And my dad's with – knock knock, Luce – the vice squad?'

Lucy shook her head. 'I wasn't suggesting we light up here, you div!'

'Oh, div am I?' he said, snaking his arms around her middle. 'Stick in the mud, law-abiding, thoroughly decent div?'

He moved his hands down her flanks and pulled her against his pelvis.

'No ...' she began. 'I wasn't thinking that at all.'

'Good,' he said firmly. 'Because I wouldn't want you to think that. No, seriously, babes – and this is between you and me only, right? There's no way I'd even get within ten feet of a joint. Because ...' he paused. 'Let's just say that I have pretty decent reasons. You know what I said about winning the war? Well, I will. *We* will. My dad's got him in his sights.'

'Who, Gurdy?' she asked, alarmed.

Jimmy laughed. 'Course not fucking Gurdy! No, a bigger fish.'

'Paddy?'

'Bigger than that, Luce – Mo. Paddy'll just be collateral.'

'Collateral?'

He grinned and moved his hands again, pressing her hips against him. 'Collateral damage. That cocky cunt thinks he can get away with murder. Always has. But as of now, I'm going to make it my personal mission to make sure he gets away with fuck-all.'

'You mean you're going to grass on him?' she asked, as he started undoing the buttons on her blouse. 'Because that would look a bit bad, wouldn't it, with your dad being a cop?'

Jimmy smiled and touched his finger to the undamaged side of his nose. Funny, Lucy thought, he looked strangely sweet with his face a bit roughed up. Perhaps she was feeling maternal. No, not that. No – she caught her breath. Suddenly, *far* from maternal.

He leant to whisper in her ear then. 'There are lots of different ways to skin a cat, my love. Now, come on,' he added, slipping the blouse from her shoulders. 'The night's young and my dad won't be back for hours. I can think of *much* better ways we can chill out …'

Chapter 6

Vicky felt anger welling up in her like bile. It sometimes felt as if there'd never be an end to it. Not while she and her mam inhabited the same house. She watched her staggering towards her now, shocked at how powerful was the temptation to slap her – just as her mam had slapped *her* so many times this past couple of years, every incidence of which she remembered like it was yesterday.

She pretended not to, of course, because that's what you did. When her mum, the next day, all sobriety and snot and snivels, always sobbed her apologies for being the way she was. And all the promises – no, just the one promise. That she'd stop drinking. That yes, she understood that Vicky wasn't her father. That no, she had no right to take her shit life out on her. After all, it wasn't her who'd upped and left, was it?

God, but how Vicky wanted to. Sometimes she just wanted to walk out of the door and never come back.

Vicky's mam was far from sober now, of course. So drunk that she could hardly weave her way across the living room – cannoning off bits of furniture like they were the bumpers in a pinball machine.

'When I was a fucking kid,' she roared, 'I tipped up *all* my bleeding wages to *my* mother, you hear me? And if I didn't, I'd get a good bloody hiding!' She lurched close enough that Vicky could smell the cider fumes hanging in the air between them. Her mam burped then. 'You're a selfish little get, that's what you are!'

Vicky dodged, so that her mam didn't actually fall into her. She was now swinging the almost empty cider bottle in her face. 'Mother, look at the state of you!' she barked back, disgusted. 'Just sit down before you fall down! I gave you a tenner yesterday, and I only get paid twenty-five quid! I've told you that. You know that. What the hell am I supposed to live on? How do I get lunch? Pay for my bus fares? I've got fuck-all left as it is!'

Too drunk to formulate a response to this, her mam did as instructed, landing heavily in the closest armchair, and banging her elbow as she did. Thank God, at least, that it was Saturday night, and Vicky could escape round to Paddy's till Sunday.

Paddy's home, increasingly, was her haven. A haven from her own bloody mother. One she increasingly needed, as well. It had been like a switch had flipped once she'd left school and started work. As if something had happened to her mother, something Vicky couldn't quite get her head round. She'd become so much more needy. So much less inclined to do anything but lie on the sofa. So much more inclined to drink herself into a stupor. So much nastier.

Leanne at work had a theory, of course. Leanne had a theory about everything. 'She's frightened,' she'd suggested.

'Because she's losing you, isn't she? You've got your independence now, haven't you? Full-time job, your own money. Not to mention that bloke of yours. She probably realises you don't need her anymore.'

Vicky thought what Leanne said had a lot of truth in it. But if that were so why did her mam keep doing such a good job of pushing her away? Like she was doing now, in fact, glaring up at her with a face like a slapped arse. 'I'm not surprised you've got fuck-all left, madam,' she said, waggling the bottle like it was a stick to beat Vicky with. 'Because you spent it all on them fancy knickers and lacy bra, didn't you? Anything for that fucking lover boy of yours. You'll see your mam go without fags and a fucking drink just so's you can dress up like a bleeding whore for him!'

'That's it!' Vicky railed at her mam, grabbing her overnight bag from the couch. 'I've listened to enough. I'm going outside to wait for Paddy. He'll be here any minute,' she added, hefting the strap onto her shoulder. 'And if he hears you talking to me like that,' she added, the thought having suddenly come to her, 'he'll have a few words to say to you, I can assure you!'

'Oh, you *assure* me, do you?' her mam yelled at her back as she stomped out of the living room. 'I've heard that cocky bastard call you a lot worse. A *lot* worse. You think I don't have working ears? Go on, piss off to him then. See if I care.'

Slamming the front door didn't have quite the satisfying effect Vicky had hoped for and, out on the doorstep, shaken and tearful, she took in gulps of warm air. She didn't want

Paddy seeing her in a state; he really would kick off at her mother if he thought she'd been giving her grief. And rightly so – it was all so *unfair*.

A month she'd been working now, and it had been the same every frigging week. She'd pay her mam her board money every Friday, but because she'd found out – God knew how – that hairdressers got tips on Saturdays, she'd start again, for more money, every week, without fail. And Vicky couldn't see an end to it, either. Her mam would no more get a job than fly, even assuming anyone would give her one and, where once Vicky had thought that, in time, her mam might start getting over having been left by her dad, it was like it was going in the opposite direction. Like a scab made worse every time she picked at it.

Leanne was right, she decided. Right about her mam being scared of her leaving and about the fact that leaving was the thing Vicky most wanted to do. Leave and move in with Paddy, and his mam and dad – his mam and dad who were always civil and sober and nice to her. And, better still, almost never there. Like this weekend. She doubted she'd see them at all. So it would just be the two of them. Her and her Pad. She smiled at the thought. Like a regular married couple. Like they were practising.

As if conjured by the force of her very thoughts, he turned up moments after, his arrival heralded as ever by the thump of the music as much as the roar of the Capri. She hurried down the path and out of the gate so she could make a quick getaway, just in case her mam had decided she hadn't said enough already.

'Alright, gorgeous?' Paddy greeted, winking at her as she climbed in. He helped her push her holdall onto the back seat, commenting that she'd packed the kitchen sink with her like she always did, then, as they roared away again, nodded suggestively at his crotch. 'I'm packing too,' he said, looking at her in the way that made her melt. 'And if you play your cards right, I've got a package down here just for you.'

Vicky groaned, despite secretly loving it when he said things like that to her in private. 'Honestly, Paddy, is that *all* you ever think about?'

'Pretty much,' he conceded. 'Though it'll have to wait for a bit. I'm going to drop you home so you can start making us a bit of dinner, while I go and see a man about a dog.'

Vicky huffed, because that was the required response, obviously. 'What am I,' she said, twisting to face him, 'your frigging wife, or something?'

The thing that, increasingly, she most wanted to be.

'Fuck, no,' he retorted, smirking. 'Thank God! *Wife*? Can't think of a bigger turn-off.'

Lads always said that, of course. That was just the way they generally were. So Vicky's mood, now so much brighter, wasn't dimmed too much by this assertion, and though she wished he'd find some other time to do his bit of business (whatever that was, she'd never ask) one thing she did know was the best way to lure him quickly back.

They were at his house not long later and, as he put his key in the front door, she unzipped the holdall. Fishing around briefly, she then pulled on the white lace of the expensive French knickers. 'I'll only be wearing these until ten o'clock, Paddy Allen, so if you want to make use of them, you best not be home late.'

Paddy grinned as he pushed the door open, and stepped aside to let her in. 'Very nice, but love, I couldn't give two fucks really. I'll have 'em off you in about ten seconds anyway.' He kissed her. 'And, no, I promise I won't be back late. Two hours tops, okay? Keep it warm for me.'

Vicky knew full well that Paddy hadn't been referring to the dinner, which was apparently going to be pizza. But as he'd taken a couple of frozen ones out of the freezer, she spent some time getting everything ready, enjoying the freedom of his parents' posh fitted kitchen and pushing guilty thoughts – ever present – about her mother away.

She could see herself here, she decided. Somewhere like this, at any rate. A better life. A fuller life. A life Paddy could provide for her. She sliced a couple of tomatoes to put on top of the pizzas, added some extra cheese, spread some oven chips on a pristine baking sheet and lit the oven, and finally laid the little table for their romantic dinner for two.

But one hour very quickly became two, and then more, and, bored with the usual dire Saturday-night television offerings, Vicky decided, on a whim, to phone Lucy.

It had been two weeks to the day now since the fight at Vikram's party, two weeks in which she'd several times considered phoning her friend to make things up. But the memory of their call before kept staying her hand. Surely it was Lucy who should be doing the apologising? After all, she'd been the one to start it, lashing out at Paddy the way she had.

But the later it got – two hours tops he'd said, hadn't he? So where the hell was he? – the more Vicky wondered at the validity of her stubbornness. And perhaps Lucy was thinking the same. That it was Vicky who ought to be doing the apologising. After all, she'd been the one who'd slapped Lucy round the face.

Feeling increasingly agitated – not to mention slightly adrift now, in Paddy's empty house, and thinking *still* of her bloody mother, which her friend would understand – Vicky picked up the receiver and punched the familiar numbers. Not that she was that hopeful that Lucy would be home. It was Saturday night, after all.

But it turned out she was. 'Oh, yes, she's in,' said Lucy's dad, sounding genuinely pleased that she'd called. 'So nice to hear from you, love. I'll go call her now for you.'

And then, not long later, came Lucy herself, sounding puffed-out, having hobbled down from her bedroom to take the call. She'd been in the middle of giving herself a pedicure, she explained breathlessly, then began chattering away, for the best part of a minute, about anything and everything but the one thing that mattered, almost as if she didn't dare leave any silence in case Vicky used it to leap in and slap her again.

Which wasn't like Lucy at all.

'I'm sorry,' Vicky said, seizing on a pause in her friend's ramblings. What was the point of them speaking if they didn't talk about why they hadn't been? 'That's why I called you. To apologise. Luce, I really *am* sorry ... I should have called you before. I just couldn't ...' She hesitated, struggling to find the words now to finish. 'I just ... well, I was just being pig-headed and stupid. I'm really sorry. Can we let this all go?'

There was definitely a silence now, albeit a small one.

'God, of *course*,' Lucy gushed at her, brightly. Too brightly. 'And me too. Honest, Vic, I've nearly called you *that* many times. You know what I'm like. Much too stubborn for my own good.' She chuckled. 'It's history. Stupid blokes. Bloody boyfriends. We shouldn't let them come between us, should we? It's not like we don't both have minds of our own, is it? Anyway, what you up to? Look at the pair of us, in of a Saturday, all on our lonesome ...'

And it felt like that, suddenly. Despite talking to Lucy – no, no, in fact, almost *because* of – Vicky felt exactly that. Lonely. She glanced at the clock on the living-room wall. 'Oh, Pad's home soon,' she said. 'He's just out—' She faltered again. 'Just out, for a bit, with a couple of his mates. And I'm knackered. Been on my feet all day. I need an office job like you've got ...' She chuckled too, politely, still confused by the exchange. 'Anyway, what about your Jimmy?' Christ, this was becoming such a weird conversation. 'He out too?'

'With some of his workmates,' Lucy confirmed. 'Someone's stag night, so goodness only knows what time he'll get home ... so ...'

'So look,' Vicky said, increasingly anxious to make some kind of proper connection, 'how about you and I going out one night after work, in the week? You know …'

'Oh, I'd love that,' Lucy answered. And quickly. Too quickly. 'Shall we talk tomorrow, maybe? Sort out which day works best for us both? You do a couple of lates in the week down there, don't you?'

'Yes, but—' Vicky paused again, hearing the sound of a key in the front door. 'Look, that'll be Paddy,' she said, anxious now. He was the last person who needed to hear her on the phone to Lucy. 'I'd better go. Speak tomorrow then, mate, yes?'

'Course,' Lucy said.

It was only when she'd hung up that Vicky realised that Lucy hadn't just said 'course'. She'd actually said 'course you had', and her meaning was clear. Course you had, as in 'course you had better go'.

Because of Paddy.

But it hadn't been Paddy. It had been Paddy's parents, home from the bakery. Home from the bakery a good hour or two earlier than Paddy had led her to believe they would be, sending her into a flat spin of embarrassment and self-consciousness, and cursing him inwardly for leaving her in such a way.

'Oh, don't you mind us,' Paddy's mum gushed as she came in, smelling of recently applied perfume and pastry. She smiled indulgently at the preparations that had been laid out in her kitchen. 'We'll be off in the living room, out of the way, don't you worry, love. You know,' she then told Vicky, as she stood at the sink, filling the kettle, 'it never ceases to amaze me how that lad of ours has managed to hang on to a girl like you.' She laughed then. 'Or deserves one, for that matter. One of life's enduring mysteries, eh?!'

Vicky knew full well that Mrs Allen thought no such thing. Quite the opposite. They might not be around much, but one thing was still true. They thought the sun shone out of Paddy's backside. They positively doted on him, especially his mam. Still, she was grateful for her sweetness in saying so.

Though she was still quick to excuse herself and go and wait for him upstairs – there to sit up disconsolately in bed in her new underwear, variously wondering where the fuck Paddy had got to and chewing over her strange call to Lucy.

Vicky knew she must have dozed off but when Paddy flumped down onto the bed, she was shocked to see, by the light of his digital alarm clock, that it was 3.00 in the morning. He was pissed. Or, at least half-pissed. He was at least making a stab at extricating himself from his clothing.

'What the *fuck*, Paddy?' she hissed angrily as she tried to budge him across the bed. 'Have you seen the fucking time? Where've you been?'

He said nothing. Too busy growling in exasperation at his belt buckle. Vicky lay and watched him, growing increasingly irritated. Where the hell *had* he been? She then felt anxiety begin to crowd her mind. It was so late.

Way beyond chucking-out time. And he'd not gone out dressed for clubbing. So more to the point, who had he been *with*?

She sat up straight. 'Come on! Where've you been, and who've you been with? You've been *hours*!'

She'd been prepared for some narky response to this – he'd been drinking, so that was always a possibility – but not for the way he twisted round on the bed and grabbed her. Grabbed her none too gently, by the wrist, and yanked her towards him. 'Just shut the fuck up, will you?' he growled at her, nose to nose now. 'Don't push it, okay? Just don't fucking *push* me!'

He let go of her then, and returned his attention back to getting undressed. She could smell the night air on him. See the tension in his shoulders. Perhaps she'd misread things. Perhaps his business, whatever it was, had been more complicated than he'd thought, and he was stressed. And the last thing he needed was a needy, jealous girlfriend.

Chastened, she reached out a hand and touched his back. 'I'm sorry, babes,' she whispered. 'I've just been worried about you, that's all. Wondering if you're okay ...'

'Yes, I'm okay,' he replied shortly, his back to her, a wall. Then he stood and stamped his feet out of his trousers.

'Come to bed then,' she said, pulling the covers back on his side. 'I kept it warm for you, like you wanted ...' She let the sentence hang.

Paddy crossed arms and peeled his jumper over his head, his shoulder blades moving sinuously under his skin. Then he turned around and, for the first time, he smiled. Vicky felt the anxiety drain out of her in a welcome rush, all thought of where he'd been, and what the hell he'd been up to, gladly extinguished by the loving glint in his eyes.

'Oh, go on, then,' he said, slipping into bed beside her.

It felt as if she'd only just gone to sleep when she first heard the commotion. And, at first, it was simply a part of her dream; a logical extension of the jumble of images and sounds that, on waking, she clung onto, confused.

But it was real. It was coming from downstairs and getting louder. Shouting – Paddy's mum? – followed by a sound she recognised; that of many boots, running heavily up the stairs.

And then a shard of white light, which quickly became a blaze, which made her eyes, barely open yet, shut again by themselves. So she was still squinting, shielding her eyes against the sudden glare, when the silhouettes in the doorway finally resolved themselves. Coppers. She counted them – one, two, three, four of them. Then she started. The first of them was Jimmy's dad.

Mrs Allen was right behind them, in a short jersey nightie, attempting to push her way into the room. 'I want to see the frigging warrant!' she was yelling at them. Mr Allen was there too, trying to hold her back.

Paddy sat up then, naked and confused. Then rubbed his eyes, flung the covers off and leapt out of bed, seemingly not remotely bothered that his mum was in the room and he was showing all he'd got. 'What the fuck's going on?' he demanded, now face to face with DI Daley. 'Has that fucking pussy son of yours reported me for giving him a fucking slap?'

Of the three other coppers, Vicky belatedly noticed, one was a female. Mid-twenties, Vickie estimated, slim and smirking. 'Patrick Allen, we're arresting you for taking a vehicle without consent and related crimes,' she monotoned at him. 'You have the right to remain silent, but anything you say, can and will be ...'

'Save it, bitch,' Paddy replied, cutting her off. He glanced across and grinned at Vicky, then started to swing his bits in the female officer's direction as he made a show of bending down to pick up his trousers. 'Mother,' he said, still bent over, 'you might want to go wait downstairs. Because the way this one is looking at my dick, I think she might want to do a body search.'

Vicky cringed. Why was he so intent on making everything bloody worse? 'What's he supposed to have done?' she demanded of Jimmy's dad. 'Tell us! You can't just barge in here like this!'

'I'd shut it, love,' the female officer warned. 'Or you'll be the next one to be arrested. I'm sure lover boy here will put you in the picture. If he ever makes bail,' she added dryly.

'I'll see you tomorrow, babe,' Paddy reassured Vicky, as, dressed now, after a fashion, he allowed himself to be led roughly out of the room. She scrabbled to free herself of the covers, not even caring that she was wearing little more than nothing. Though thank God she'd at least put on Paddy's T-shirt to nip out earlier and use the loo.

She grabbed his hand and squeezed it, and he turned around, his eyes almost black in the shadow. 'Don't you worry about me, babe,' he reassured her. 'You just get your-self some kip while I give these tossers some grief down the nick.'

'Shut it, Allen,' Jimmy's dad said. They were the first words he'd spoken. And the way he spoke them chilled Vicky to the bone.

It had taken less than five minutes. Couldn't be more. Probably less. Vicky stood on the bright landing, her bare legs sprouting goosebumps. Listening to Paddy's mam yelling at DI Daley's retreating back all the way down the stairs.

Chapter 7

Gurdy had heard about Paddy being arrested. Who hadn't? It had been all over – pretty much the only topic of conversation outside the Percy when he'd arrived there at just after twelve. News travelled fast in Bradford – and in this case at warp speed; it was Jimmy who'd told Gurdy first, perhaps unsurprisingly, phoning him to pass on the news almost as soon as he'd got up. Then, on his walk to the lock-up on Manningham Lane (where he'd planned to sell off some of the dope Paddy had given him) he must have been told by another half dozen others.

But it was at the Perseverance, or the Percy, as it was known to the locals, that the person who had most need to catch up with him found him. Namely, his boss and nemesis, Rasta Mo.

As always seemed to be the case, Mo had seemingly appeared out of nowhere, like a superhero in a blockbuster movie. Though hero he wasn't. Unless you liked your heroes to be dreadlocked, and in cahoots with the devil.

Gurdy could smell how expensive Mo's leather jacket was as he approached. 'The boy Paddy,' he said to Gurdy, having ambled up alongside him, 'he's been lifted,' he said, 'as you probably know.'

He poked Gurdy then, hard, in the shoulder, with his finger. 'And you're his boy, so now you have work to do, got it? You have a set of keys to my lock-up, yes?'

Gurdy nodded nervously. He was absolutely shitting himself, not to mention being painfully aware that the punters in the Percy, now milling outside with their drinks in the summer sunshine, were all witnessing his discomfort. He wasn't daft. He knew everyone knew what the score was. In this pub, in Arthur's Bar, and even the Mayflower – the curry shop on the corner – they all knew he'd become a running boy for Paddy, which ultimately meant he was owned by Mo.

Mo flashed his famous grin, displaying his set of immac-ulate white teeth, and shook the dreadlocks that framed his fearsome face. 'Good boy,' he said, clapping Gurdy on the back now, like they were mates. 'The pigs will be sniffing around now, obviously, so you need to do a clean-up, you understand? A proper clean-up. The boy won't squeal,' he added, 'but, you know, just in case.'

Gurdy didn't think Paddy would 'squeal' either. Given a straight choice, between the rule of the law and the wrath of Mo, he imagined he wouldn't squeal either. 'The cars too?' he asked, not yet sure what Paddy had been arrested for exactly. Drugs presumably. The precise details hadn't yet filtered through; Jimmy had been that elated when he'd phoned earlier to share the news that he'd neglected to mention what the arrest had actually been for. He felt the weakness in his sphincter increase. Would he be next?

Rasta Mo looked at Gurdy like he was mad. '*Yes*, the cars, man! Of course the cars! That's why he's been lifted. You need to hide the plates, the obvious tools, all the papers, *everything*. Just leave it set up like a tyre yard until they've done with us, okay?' He flashed another smile, gazing around at his audience. 'Don't fret, boy, the other business will go on as usual.' He lowered his voice, though for the life of him, Gurdy didn't know why. Did anyone *not* know who Mo was? What he did? 'But tonight you'll meet with either me or Irish Pete to collect your gear. Outside Arthur's, seven o'clock. Don't be late.'

Mo then turned and walked away, without another word or even gesture, and, out of nowhere, a black BMW pulled up on the lane and he got into it without a backward glance.

The car out of sight, and the chatter outside the pub starting up again, Gurdy pulled at the collar of his T-shirt to stop it sticking to his back. It was more than the midday heat. He was out of his depth with all this, and for about the tenth time that day he contemplated, and only just shy of hysterically, the merits of blowing what little he'd saved up, getting a flight to Karachi and going in search of one of the many elderly relatives he had there; the ones that lived in the middle of nowhere, far from civilisation – and danger – and eked out the sort of living his parents had come to Bradford to escape from.

Oh, if only. Because it was all getting just a little bit too real. While he just dealt with Paddy, it was largely okay; he could easily convince himself he was just doing stuff for an old school mate. Yes, illegal, but still just doing a bit of what loads of other people did – earning a bit of cash to help him on his way. But the reality he was forced to face now was very different. Rasta Mo was a seriously dangerous man. Everyone knew that. He had literally got away with murder, and on more than one occasion. Two dealers in the last ten years had been bludgeoned to death for trying to rob him, and though the police had been convinced that Mo had been responsible – everyone knew that as well – they had never found any evidence to put him on trial for it, and never once been able to break any of his alibis.

He could only hope that tonight he would be meeting Irish Pete. That Mo would have other, more important things to do. Pete was fine; just a big, friendly bear of an Irishman, with nice twinkly eyes and an equivalently twinkly smile. Far better to deal with than the intimidating Rastafarian, even if he knew deep down that Irish Pete, if crossed, would crush your balls between his hairy fists just as readily.

He needed a drink, he decided. One with a little more clout than the pint of lemonade he'd opted for as a nod to the time of day. He left it on the bench, all too aware of how everyone lowered their eyes as he passed them on his way to the bar.

He was just pushing the door open when, to his dismay, he saw Vicky making her way towards him. Even from a distance he could see what a state she was in. Eyes red and swollen, dressed in a pair of baggy trackies, she hurried up to him, looking on the verge of fresh tears. He bundled her inside, got them both a pint of lager, and, fearing the attention they'd attract given the Paddy situation, bundled her back outside, but this time through the side door.

They'd be okay here, he reckoned, given everyone was out enjoying the sunshine. The sun didn't make it round this side till gone two so he was confident they'd have the area to themselves. No, there weren't any chairs, let alone tables to sit at – just some grass and a couple of boulders. But what kept cars out could easily double up as seats.

He sat down on one and indicated for Vicky to follow suit. 'Now,' he said, passing her a brimming, slopping glass, 'have a swig of that and tell me all about it. So, Paddy's been arrested. And he's still at the nick, is he?'

'Oh, Gurdy,' Vicky sobbed, after taking a large slurp of her lager. 'I just don't know what to *do*. It was *awful*. They said it was taking a vehicle without consent. Or something – so that's, like, stealing cars, isn't it? Is that what he was doing? I mean, I'm not stupid – I'm really not, Gurdy, but he's a bloody *car thief*? Is that it? I mean, d'you think he has? I mean, is that what he does when he's off up to fuck knows what? I mean, *seriously*? I mean, how would I even know? He just fucks off and leaves me out of *everything*. So I never know, do I? Where he goes, who he's with, what he does … Tell me, Gurdy, what the fuck is he up to?'

Gurdy buried his nose in his own pint to give himself a moment to think. Vicky clearly knew nothing about anything very much, which left him in something of a quandary. It wasn't as if she was naïve – well, not to the point of complete ignorance, anyway. But she clearly knew almost nothing of what Paddy did for Rasta Mo.

He lowered his pint. And she didn't really need to know the half of it – didn't need to know *any* of it. Yes, it might come out at some point – and possibly sooner rather than later now, but Paddy wouldn't thank him for being the one to enlighten her that, yes, twocking – as in taking without consent – formed a substantial part of Mo's and Paddy's business.

Nicking cars, and then altering them beyond recognition – including removing all identifying numbers and markings – was precisely what they took vehicles without consent *for*. Not that Paddy was involved in the nicking part, as it happened. He was just the one who did the 'redesigning' part. Which thought caused a connection to be made in Gurdy's brain. So how come the plod had nicked him for that, then?

He smiled at his friend in what he hoped was a reassuring manner. 'Course he hasn't done that. Pad, a car thief? Never.' He shook his head with emphasis, happy that at least that part was true. 'No, you know as well as I do,' he went on, 'that Jimmy's dad's got it in for him. Specially now, after that fight – after what he did to Jimmy's face. Mate,' he said, leaning across to place a reassuring hand on Vicky's leg, 'he hasn't done fuck-all, I promise you. Listen, he was with *me* all last night. Up here on the Lane. So I'm his alibi if they try to suggest he did.'

Vicky sat back on her boulder. '*What*? He was with *you* last night? So why didn't he tell me? Doing what, then? He told me he'd only be a couple of hours – and that was before seven. And he didn't get in till three. What the hell were you *doing*?' She began sobbing again.

It was too much of a stretch to put his arm round Vicky's shoulder, so Gurdy stood up, then squatted down beside her rock, taking a slow draught of his drink to give himself a bit more thinking time. Three a.m.? What the fuck had Paddy been doing since he'd left him? Which had been nine or thereabouts – six whole hours earlier. His brain whirred. What would sound like a plausible explanation?

Scrabbling around desperately while Vicky sniffed, he eventually found one. 'You know Irish Pete?' he said.

Vicky shook her head. 'Not really.'

'Well, no matter,' he said, flapping his free hand. 'You don't need to. Only that he's got these pallets of video recorders from a factory that went bust. Top fucking notch, they are, and dirt cheap an' all. So me and Paddy was gonna store them for him, up at the lock-up, yeah? But then we had this idea to make an offer for them instead. The lot of them. Worth a fair bit, we reckoned. Anyways, we met up with Irish Pete last night, and it took us a good few hours, but he eventually made us a deal, and,' he paused to beam, 'they're ours now if we want them.'

'But 3 *a.m.*, Gurdy – you're telling me you were out till 3 *a.m.*?'

'Yes,' he said firmly. 'We were. You know what it's like, Vic. We ended up in the Mayflower – you know, to discuss how to get the money. And, you know what it's like. There's a lock-in and next thing you know … honest, Vic, you've got nothing to worry about, mate. I put him in a taxi myself.'

'*Really?*' Vicky said, looking far from convinced. 'He was in such a *mood* …'

'That's the drink,' Gurdy said. 'You know Paddy. Fight his shadow, he would, when he's that tight. You *know* that.'

'I suppose,' she said. 'But why didn't he just *say* so, for God's sake?'

'Because that's the way he *is*, Vic. You know that better than anyone.'

Gurdy took a breath then, ready to embellish his tale a little further – bring in some small altercation with the cab driver, or something, but Vicky was already nodding, and he saw she'd probably swallowed it. As could he, he thought, privately pleased with his invention. If only momentarily, because hard on the heels of his fiction came grim reality, thundering up like a herd of fucking wilde-beest. He had work to do. Work he had to do pronto.

'Oh, Gurdy!' Vicky said, 'I can't tell you how *sick* I've been feeling all morning. I haven't known what to do with myself! And I can't tell my mam, and I don't know what's happening – Paddy's mam and dad went down the station, and that's been the last I've heard of anything. And it's been going through my mind – what if they don't let him out? But they'll *have* to let him out now, won't they?' She smiled a thin smile. 'Oh, Gurdy, no wonder he never said anything to me. He's been saving … we both have …'

She looked dreamily into the middle distance. 'Oh, thank God,' she said again, draining her own pint, visibly happier. 'I'm so glad I came and found you. They'll have to let him go now. They will have to, won't they? Will you go down?'

Gurdy frowned. Go *down*? What, him instead? 'Go down where?'

'Down to the station, to give him his alibi.'

'Er, yes,' Gurdy answered, re-grouping again. 'Course. Heading there now as it happens.'

'Shall I come?'

No! He shook his head. 'No, no – you'll only muddy the waters. And what would Paddy say? Seeing you down there?'

'No, no, of course,' Vicky said. 'You're right. I'll head home then. Tell him, yeah? Tell him that's where I'll be?'

'What, you're going to walk?' It was a long way from the Percy back to Vicky's. 'Don't be daft. Let's get you a cab, yeah? Get you back home.'

Thankfully, apart from a pithy rant about how home wasn't fucking home anymore, she didn't argue and he was soon able to wave her off. And, watching another car head round the corner, he felt leaden. He had a garage to go and sort out and clean down, like, *now*. Which would take hours – possibly till late into the evening, he knew. Yet he was also supposed to be at bloody Arthur's Bar at seven.

He set off up Manningham Lane under the unforgiving sun. If only it *were* as simple as knocked off fucking video recorders.

Chapter 8

Vicky thought she might burst. It was really that physical. A kind of pulsating presence, sat high in her stomach, a constant pressure which she couldn't force down.

Heartburn, her mam had said. Which she knew all about, obviously. Vicky sometimes found her swigging milk of magnesia out of the bottle in the mornings, like she was some pisshead on the street and it was meths.

But it wasn't that. It was nothing amenable to medicine. It was as if her body was protesting about the stress she was under, and constantly bitching at her to sort it. And work didn't help. It just grated on her nerves. Not the work itself – she could do that on autopilot, mostly – as much as the need to be constantly smiling when all you really wanted to do was curl up and cry. Talking shit to the clients, and all the while smiling and smiling. Nice weather we're having. Any plans for the weekend? So, where are you going on your holidays this year? How about Armley nick?

Paddy had been released on bail mid-morning on the Monday, just over twenty-four hours since he'd been taken from his bed. He'd been in front of a magistrate, told he'd have to report weekly to the police station, and be available for his court date a couple of weeks hence.

'And you're surprised?' Vicky's mam had said when she'd blurted it all out to her. 'He's a rogue, always has been. Always will be, come to that. This day's been coming for a long time, as you well know.'

But that was the problem: Vicky hadn't known. And, despite the increasing weight of 'facts', she still couldn't quite accept it. She wasn't stupid, she knew Paddy was no angel – who didn't? That he had a long string of 'previous', as her mam liked to call it, to his name. Fighting, possession of weed, being carried in stolen vehicles – but that was no different from half the lads in their part of Bradford, was it? No, not really. And it wasn't like he'd ever been to prison, or anything. He'd never be so stupid as to let that happen.

And what everyone else knew, and Paddy had been at pains to tell her now this had happened, was that Jimmy's dad has always had it in for him. Had hounded him remorselessly, trying to pin something on him, however much Lucy might protest otherwise.

And that was another thing; when she sat down and put everything together, she felt sure Lucy knew something about what had gone on that Saturday. Why else had she been behaving so weirdly when they'd spoken? Why else had she been silent ever since?

And that was fine, because perhaps she didn't want to know. So she'd stopped short of asking Paddy too much about it. He was innocent, Gurdy'd said so. And that would all come out eventually. And in the meantime, she needed to support her man as best she could, whatever lie they were peddling about him actually having been in Derby that night, trying to pass on a cut-and-shut car to some apparently unwitting punter.

It wasn't true. Gurdy had said so. It wasn't true.

But, two weeks on now, the supporting bit was taking its toll. She felt like shit. Like she was walking round with a cloud over her head and a stone in her stomach. Because who knew? If Jimmy's dad really hated Paddy that much, who knew what other kinds of tricks he might get up to? What tricks he might have already got up to. She knew as well as anyone how bent the police could be when they wanted to. And, when it came to Paddy, they clearly wanted to very much.

Vicky looked miserably across to the other end of the salon. Then there was Lacey. The new girl. Who, despite having been nothing but friendly and helpful since she'd started, got right on her nerves. Yes, it was good to have another apprentice come and work there – God knew, since the schools went back, and the boss had buggered off on holiday for a fortnight, she and Leanne had been rushed off their feet. But did it have to be someone so relentlessly cheerful? So chirpy and giggly and little-miss-ray-of-sunshine? So Barbie-doll pretty and so *nice*?

Vicky could hear her now, while combing out one of their elderly regulars, Miss Read. 'And holiday plans yet for next year?' Christ, Vicky thought, as she folded the latest batch of washed towels. Miss Read had been coming in for, what – thirty years? She was at least pushing eighty, not at all steady on her feet, and even Vicky already knew how stupid a question that was, given that she was an agoraphobic who barely left Bradford.

The only small light in her dark mental tunnel was that Leanne had her reservations about Lacey as well.

'Comes across as *too* nice,' was her considered opinion when they found themselves together at the back of the salon. 'You know what I mean? Trying too hard. Till it grates. Sucking up to everybody. Never has a bad word to say about anyone, you noticed that? Something unnatural in that if you ask me.' She grinned. 'Still, she'll get worn down eventually, you'll see.'

Vicky wasn't sure that getting worn down was necessarily a good thing. She felt worn down, and it didn't have much to recommend it. 'You mean become a bit of a bitch, like we are?' she asked Leanne.

'Hey, speak for yourself!' Leanne huffed. 'Seriously, Vic. You really don't seem yourself this past fortnight. Are you okay?'

Was she okay? Now that was a question and a half. A question she wasn't sure she wanted to answer, not since Paddy had warned her how it was tongue wagging that had got him into trouble in the first place. He meant Jimmy, of course, but she wasn't sure she could trust anyone. But this was Leanne. It wasn't like they hung out together or anything. And since Lucy was off-radar and her mam was so full of bile, the urge to talk to someone, share her fears, was strong.

It wasn't long to break time, so she followed Leanne into the back room, lifted the kettle and filled it, before switching it on. 'I'm okay,' she said, suddenly decided, and feeling better for it. 'Look, shall I nip next door and get some sausage rolls or something? I'll update you on my dramas over a coffee.'

Half an hour later, as Leanne slipped the bolt across and changed the sign in the door to 'CLOSED', Vicky set out some plates for the sausage rolls and strawberry tarts that she'd bought from the baker's. No Lacey, though, which was a plus. She had some boyfriend, called Roger, who apparently worked at the Market Tavern, so most days she'd take herself off down there for her lunch.

'So?' Leanne said, once she'd taken a bite of sausage roll. 'Spill then. What's been going on? Let me guess. Judging from your face something to do with your Paddy.'

Vicky nodded. 'Well, he's definitely a part of it,' she conceded, 'but it's just everything at the minute – one fucking thing after another. My best mate still barely speaks to me – too busy being loved up with fucking Jimmy.' She sighed. 'Who's turning out to be a right frigging snake in the grass. Then there's my mam, whose only fucking aim in life is to see how fast she can get to the bottom of a bottle of cider, and who expects me to hand over any spare cash I have to fund it. I'm sick of it all, Lee, I really am.'

Leanne wiped shards of flaky pastry from her lap. 'And Paddy?'

Vicky considered her own sausage roll. Now it was in front of her she couldn't face it. She could hardly be arsed eating lately. 'And Paddy,' she agreed. 'My not-so-white knight in shining armour. Well, as you probably know – as everyone knows, thanks to the fucking *Telegraph & Argos* – he got pulled in for twocking – cutting and shutting and all that. Again, and we don't know for sure it's not a fit-up, but we think Jimmy had something to do with him getting grassed up. But anyway, even though they didn't find anything up at the garage, they had all the evidence they needed to put him on trial for selling a stolen vehicle, then driving said vehicle down to Derby. *And* knowingly working on the car that had stolen number plates on it. As well as the obvious stuff – no insurance, no MOT and no fucking tax,' Vicky sighed deeply. 'So he's definitely looking at a stretch.'

'Has his solicitor actually said that?' Leanne asked. 'That he'll go to prison?'

Vicky nodded, putting her sausage roll back down on its bag. John Cordingley, solicitor to every bad boy in Bradford, had told Paddy that although he'd do his best to get some of the charges dismissed, the magistrates would have no option on this occasion but to give him some time. Paddy had been let off too many times in the past, apparently, and was finally due his comeuppance. 'He'll plead guilty to whatever they tell him to,' she told Leanne. 'That way, it stays with the magistrates and he gets a lighter sentence.'

'Really? How's that?'

'Because if he goes with a not guilty plea it'll go to a proper court. And that Judge Pickles is a proper bastard apparently – if Paddy gets him, and there's a good chance he would do, he's cracking down and would make him an example.'

'Fucking hell, mate,' Leanne said as she slurped on her coffee, 'that sounds serious. You poor thing,' she soothed. Then her expression changed. 'And I'll bet he's none too happy about it, either.'

'Course he's not.'

Leanne shook her head. 'No, I mean about *you*.'

'About me?'

Leanne sat back. 'Cat's away and all that.'

'What d'you mean?'

'Well, how's he going to keep tabs on what you're up to if he's banged up in prison?'

'Lee, don't start. He knows I wouldn't look at anyone else—'

'More's the pity. You know, mate, you could do a lot better than him.'

Vicky felt her hackles rise. Confiding in Leanne had been a mistake, clearly. For all that she simpered round Paddy when he came in (and ditto bloody Lacey now, too, Vicky had noted) she obviously had a pretty low opinion of him. Or did now. Now she knew he was in trouble.

Oh, she didn't know *what* to frigging think. 'Don't say that, Lee. You don't know him. He knows I'd never leave him.'

'Made sure of it, more like. Look, Vic.' She leaned forward. 'Open your eyes. He's a bad lot.'

Vicky leaned back, frowning. 'Do you know something I don't, or something?'

'Vic, I don't *need* to. I'm just telling you to take stock, that's all. If he goes inside, you'll be better off out of it, believe me. Get some freedom back in your life – remember what it *feels* like. Enjoy doing what you want to do without him breathing down your neck.'

For the second time that day, Vicky wondered if she talked too much about Paddy. Wondered, too, despite wishing she wasn't *having* to wonder, if Leanne's words didn't hold an element of truth. She'd never say so but Paddy had already said as much to her. That if the worst happened, he was going to be sick as hell wondering what she might be up to.

But that was because he loved her. Because he'd *miss* her. And – hell, how would it be if the boot was on the other foot? She saw girls moving in on him twenty-four seven. And she didn't like how it made her feel, did she?

'Listen,' Leanne went on, 'I'm not trying to stir things up between you. I just think he's far too controlling, that's all. Just an observation. From a friend.'

A friend, Vicky thought, who didn't *have* a boyfriend. So how could she possibly understand how complicated it all was? 'I know,' Vicky said, knowing there was no point in arguing. 'I know, but I'll be fine.'

Then she stood up, grabbed their mugs and busied herself at the sink, so she could continue the conversation with her back turned. 'And if he's done, then I'll wait for him. That's the plan. *We* have plans. One day at a time, that's the way I'm going to play it. And when he comes out,' she added, turning round and clocking Leanne's cynical expression, 'who knows – he might have missed me so much that he wants to get engaged.'

'Yeah, and pigs might fly, mate,' Leanne answered.

Lacey was just arriving back from the pub as Leanne unlocked the salon door again. 'Shall I make us all a coffee?' she asked brightly as she shrugged her jacket off and reached for her apron. And, smarting still from Leanne's cynical assessment of not only Paddy but her future prospects with him, Vicky willed herself to respond nicely to Lacey's kind offer. She was glad of the distraction, if nothing else.

'Go on, I'll have another one,' she said, making an effort to smile. 'Nice lunch?'

'Lovely, thanks,' Lacey answered as she headed for the back room. 'Oh, and I've an invite,' she called back. 'To Roger's party, next Saturday week.'

Vicky and Leanne exchanged glances and raised their eyebrows. 'Ooh, that sounds interesting,' Leanne said. 'What kind of party would that be, then?'

Lacey stuck her head out from the back room, coffee jar and teaspoon in hand. 'His birthday party. Well, sort of. It's not at a venue or anything. Just a group of us having a night on the tiles, really. We thought it would be nice, you know, if you're free. And Paddy, of course.' She smiled at

Vicky. 'It would be nice to get to know the famous Paddy a bit better. I mean, it's fine if you don't want to – we just thought, well, that it would be nice, now we're all working together. But only if you want to. No pressure!' She disappeared into the back room again.

The famous Paddy? Did she really drone on that much about him? Or, more accurately, given recent developments, the *in*famous Paddy. Vicky wondered how much Lacey really did know. Perhaps Roger had filled her in, over lunch at the Market Tavern. About how Paddy might not even be around for his little party.

Unless her prayers were answered, anyway. That the dickhead from Derby who reported the car might suddenly die of a heart attack or something. That there'd be no court case. That Paddy would, as he kept promising her, get off. That everything could get back to normal, of a kind.

But then again, yes, pigs might fly.

Chapter 9

Vicky entered the Caverns nightclub with all the enthusiasm of a condemned man being marched to the gallows. She'd always felt this would be a mistake, pretty much since the moment Lacey had suggested it. And the famous décor did nothing to dispel the feeling.

Like any self-respecting nightclub, the Caverns was gloomily lit, bathed variously in deep red or watery blue light, which lent it a subterranean air. The theming didn't stop there, either, because the place was arranged as a series of caves; all low-ceilinged nooks and crannies, where you could tuck yourself away, each separated by rough sloping walls and pretend stalactites, which also formed pathways between a series of dance floors.

Vicky looked around her, trailing the already noisy group. The place was heaving, and she doubted there'd be anywhere to sit down. Which she was dying to, having been on her feet all day at work and, then, since it was Saturday night, in the packed pub. Paddy, in contrast (and, Vicky felt sure, fuelled by coke) was almost bouncing off the ceiling. Having established that he and Lacey's Roger had a few mutual (and dodgy-looking) mates, he'd been holding court at the pub, milking his new celebrity status for all that it was worth.

Worse was that Lacey was being seriously annoying, her constant giggling – at pretty much anything Paddy uttered, Vicky had come to realise – beginning to grate like a finger scraped down a blackboard. And it wasn't even as if there was anyone else in the group she could chat to. Leanne had gone home now, as had the only other girl – Roger's sister – leaving her and Lacey the only girls in the group.

It had turned out to be a large group, as well. Much larger than she'd anticipated from the way Lacey had described it at work. And being mostly lads, who were mostly single and on the prowl, she knew that within minutes they'd be all over the place. And this very much seemed to include Paddy, as she'd anticipated, him having made it clear, more than once, that if he was getting banged up the following week, then he was going to make the most of his night out.

'There you go, babes,' he said, handing a vodka and lime back to her from his place at the crush at the bar. The glass was hot. It had obviously just come out of the dishwasher.

'No ice?' she asked, frowning.

Paddy shook his head. 'Not tonight, Josephine,' he told her. 'The ice machine's broken.' He must have caught the irritation in her face because his own expression changed. 'And tell you what, how about you get yourself a bloody smile to go with it instead? If it won't crack your make-up, that is.'

'Ha bloody ha,' Vicky said, glaring at him. He was already too drunk and too punchy for comfort and, with little appetite for getting pissed herself, she really noticed. He'd be off on the dance floor at any minute, no doubt, keen to impress his doting audience, or – and you never quite knew which way it was going to go at this hour – he'd see some slight in some look that some random bloke might give him and, as night followed day, start a fight.

'You okay?' Vicky turned to see Lacey beside her, having wormed her way out of the squash of sweaty bodies. She had a half of lager in her left hand and a glass of water in her right. 'Rehydrating before it's all too late!' she finished brightly.

There had never been any doubt in Vicky's mind, nor Leanne's, but it was nice to confirm it anyway: Lacey was even more irritating when she was drunk. Vicky had to push down the thought that she'd like to wipe the inane grin off her face. Since when had she got so mean-spirited? But there was just something about Lacey, something about her relentless, girly niceness. Something fake, that was it. Like a handbag bought off one of those blokes in the market.

'Yes, I'm fine,' Vicky reassured her, having to half-shout over the thud of the music. 'Just not really in the mood tonight – you know how it is sometimes.' Yeah, as in times when your world's about to fall apart around you, and, as a consequence, you just can't get in the mood to go clubbing, because you've been sat in the pub with a bunch of virtual strangers and, try as you might, you can't get past the horror of it all – that your boyfriend might be in prison this time next week.

In prison. Because that was it, really. That was why she felt so down on smiley bloody Lacey. Just the sheer weight of it all pressing down on her. How could Paddy be so bloody bouncy and full of it and cheerful, knowing how likely it was he was going to *prison*? Not that she planned on sharing any of that with Lacey. She nodded towards the bar, where the lads were all joshing each other about something, Paddy once again centre stage. She was aware of Lacey following her gaze. 'Still, he's in enough of a party mood for both of us, eh?'

Lacey smiled. 'He's quite something. How long have you two been together?'

'Long enough,' Vicky said, not much liking that 'something'.

Lacey opened her already wide eyes even wider. 'You're *kidding* me. Really? God, I don't think I'd be in such a rush to kick him out of bed!'

'I didn't mean like *that*—' Vicky started, as some of the lads arrived to join them. 'I meant long enough to know that—'

'I need a piss, love,' Roger said to Lacey, thrusting his newly poured pint out. 'Look after that for me, while I'm gone, yeah?'

Since Lacey didn't have a hand free, Vicky took it automatically. And it was at that point, she thought later, when she should have acted differently, because it was at that point that she heard 'The Snake' come on – a song Paddy loved – and, moments later, saw him fist-punch the air. 'Yesss!' he yelled. '*Get* in. Who's dancing?'

And as night followed day, it felt almost inevitable that Lacey would squeal 'me!', along with most of the rest of them and, somehow – and she'd later wonder what the fuck she'd been thinking – she'd volunteered to mind not just Roger's drink, but everyone's, so they could head down the little path and take ownership of the dance floor. Paddy didn't so much as give her a backward glance.

It took all of a few minutes for Vicky to lose track of everyone. Roger returned, and politely took over drink-minding responsibilities, so that Vicky could go and use the loo herself. But when she returned to the little side table – well, more accurately, the crowded ledge in the cave wall they'd now occupied – both Roger and the drinks had disappeared. At first she panicked, albeit mildly, and more in irritation than anything, but it didn't take long to track him down. He'd nabbed a table in another nook, and was waving wildly at her, but, much more to the point, she had mislaid Paddy. He certainly wasn't on the dance floor she thought they'd all gone to, and, more anxious to find him than to finish her warm drink, she motioned to Roger that she was going to go and look for him.

Finding him took a lot longer. The club was not so much cave as bloody rabbit warren, she decided, as she pushed and shoved her way through the sea of resistant bodies, all too aware that just as she was casing the joint in one direction, he could be doing likewise in another.

But there was a bitter appropriateness to the way she finally found him. Via the sound of a particularly irritating giggle.

She made her way to the sound as if a moth drawn to moonlight. They weren't dancing. In fact, when Vicky first saw them, they didn't seem to be doing much of anything. Just standing in a random corner, apparently chatting, in that way people generally have to do in a noisy nightclub, by alternately bending their lips to the other's ears. Or in Lacey's case, obviously, lifting them.

Of more interest, however (and Vicky absorbed all this slowly) was that Paddy was perched on the edge of a table, legs splayed, Lacey almost standing between them. And as she watched her boyfriend lift his hand and place his beer on the table behind him, Vicky knew – knew as surely as that 'long enough' she'd mentioned to Lacey meant she *would* know – that the hand that had held the beer was going to snake round behind Lacey, cup her right buttock and pull her against him.

The kiss came out of leftfield, however. Mostly because Lacey – *fucking* Lacey – was the one to instigate it. And for just a moment – a precious moment – Vicky thought she knew what would happen. That Paddy, taken aback, would naturally pull his head back, the flirting being one thing, but the kiss – *any* kiss that wasn't from her – being a step *way* too far. And he did pull his head back. She exhaled her relief.

But it was apparently only to grin. 'Well, well,' he mouthed slowly. She couldn't hear but she didn't need to.

She could lip-read it perfectly. Then his mouth was on Lacey's, his black hair striped with blue, and then red, and then blue, and then red again.

Vicky felt something physical heave in her stomach. Not quite nausea, no, *worse*, something much worse than that. And for a moment it rooted her as firmly to her viewpoint as if she'd been set there in stone. It was only when someone barged her, in a rush to get past, that she was jolted from her paralysis.

'What the fuck?' came a bark. 'What the *fuck?*'

Belatedly, she realised it was Roger who was barging past her. Roger squaring up to Paddy. Paddy proclaiming innocence. Lacey feigning it too. Roger telling Lacey – shouting, spittle flying from him – that she was lying. That he saw what he fucking *saw.* Paddy going, 'Look, mate, it was nothing. Look, cool it, *okay?*' Going, 'Christ, it was *nothing.* Just a fucking peck. *Nothing!*' And then a couple of Roger's mates pitching up and joining in. One saying, 'Mate, it's not worth it,' the other, 'Come on, we're all pissed'. Then Paddy looking past him, his eyes scanning everyone. Seeing Vicky. His mouth opening. Then forming her name. Then him moving towards her, and being pulled back again. A hand slamming down on his shoulder.

Oh, Paddy.

She turned, blind with tears, and began to push her way out then, knocking a glass off the edge of a table she passed and hearing ice cubes go skittering across the floor.

Ice cubes. They *did* have fucking ice cubes. *Bastard.*

* * *

Out on the street, Vicky took in great gulps of air. It was dry and chilly, the clear air crisp and scentless and cold, and she felt the breeze whipping around her bare legs. Bar the pair of bouncers on the door, there was no one on the street now, the conga-line of chattering people waiting to get in now having vanished, and those already in there still a long way from being turfed out.

Bastard. She scanned the empty street, a worm of pain turning inside her, the memory of what she'd seen causing it to writhe in her gut. And, for a long anguished moment, she was incapable of coherent thought, choked and broken – and to a degree she wouldn't even have thought possible. How could he *do* that? Just let that little bitch kiss him like that? Kiss her back. Touch her up. Like it didn't even matter. What about her? What about *them*? What the fuck was she supposed to think now?

Vicky turned a circle on the pavement, unsure what to do. He'd be coming out after her, surely; the expression on his face had said so. But was he even now getting a pasting from the luckless Roger and his mates? What a bitch, she thought again. What the frigging hell was she up to? She had a fucking *boy*friend! What the hell was going on?

Her thoughts racing away in directions that she didn't want to contemplate, Vicky realised she needed to get away. She didn't want to see him. She didn't want to hear so much as a word of his bullshit. But where could she go? She was supposed to be sleeping over at his – *bastard* – and there was no way in the world she was going home. Christ, she'd rather spend a night on a park bench with all the winos than listen to her mother's drunken litany of 'I told you so's' and slagging off of Paddy. Even in her anguish, she thought wretchedly, she couldn't stomach that. She knew she'd find herself too moved to defend him.

And what did *that* say about her? She filed the thought away, unable to face it. No, she needed to escape. But where the hell *should* she go? It was gone midnight – the thought of being out alone so late suddenly gripped and held her – so what the hell was she supposed to do now? How dare he – how fucking *dare* he – put her in a position like this.

Rage forced its way to the top of her consciousness, and was an altogether preferable emotion. Rage fired her muscles and propelled her tired legs, made her arms swing, her heels click, her mind – thankfully clear of a debilitating level of alcohol – become resolute. She had already left Thornton Road and was heading up Bradford Road towards Clayton before anything other than rage could get a grip.

Thank God. Or she knew her legs would buckle under her.

Chapter 10

Lucy woke with a start, but had no idea what had woken her. Thinking it must have been a dream, she lay still with her eyes closed for a few moments, and was just drifting back to sleep when the noise came again. Someone knocking – knocking on the front door downstairs. Very softly, but knocking nonetheless. She checked the display on her alarm clock. At *this* time?

She threw her duvet off and swung her legs out of bed. There was no *way* she was going to go down and see who might be out there, but at least her bedroom window (she had the small bedroom that looked out onto the front garden) gave her a view of the gate and street beyond, if not the actual doorstep.

She was just peering down the road, satisfied that she couldn't actually see anything – or anyone – dangerous-looking, when a shape resolved itself, walking a few steps backwards up the concrete path. A shape that then looked up, and which then waved at her with both arms.

Lucy blinked in surprise. Good God – *Vicky?*

'What on earth are you *doing* here?' she hissed, once she'd pulled on her dressing gown, padded downstairs and let Vicky in. 'Come on, come back up to my room.

Be safer than going in the kitchen. And for Christ's sake, be *quiet*.'

Not that Lucy was concerned that her friend would start shouting. Even the short glimpse she'd managed to get of her friend in the dark hallway told her that Vicky was as sober as she was. Or at least almost. So this clearly wasn't some mad, impulsive, drunken thing. And it didn't look like she was round to kick off about Jimmy either. If she was angry – and, judging by her body language, it seemed so – it didn't appear to be at her. Thank God for that too.

Lucy followed Vicky upstairs, both of them treading on the edges of the risers, where they knew they'd be safest from creaks; the legacy of many a previous giggling late-night return home. Not that Lucy was worried that her mam and dad would go off on one or anything. If Vicky genuinely needed her (and it seemed as though she did, because she certainly wasn't giggling) then, of course, there'd be both a shoulder and a bed for her. Always. Her mam and dad knew as well as she did what Vicky's mam was like.

But there was no point in waking them if she didn't need to – not at this hour. Which she didn't, and with their own bedroom at the back, across the landing, there was little danger that they'd even so much as stir. When Jimmy had dropped her home an hour back and they'd spent a while smooching on the sofa, they could hear her dad snoring through the ceiling.

Vicky sat down on the bed heavily, and Lucy reached for the bedside lamp switch. 'What's happened?' she asked, seeing her friend's evident distress. Her cheeks were smudged with dirt, evidence of tears having been roughly wiped away, but other than that, Lucy was relieved to note, she looked as though she'd not come to any harm.

Well, at least not physically. '*Everything*,' Vicky said, her voice tight with emotion as she poured a handful of change back into her bag. 'Oh, Luce, I'm so sorry. I wouldn't have come here, but I just didn't know where else to *go*. I just got in a cab and—' She spread her hands. 'I just … I just came here. I'm so sorry.'

It was a sad reality, Lucy thought, that she hadn't been Vicky's first choice. An even sadder one that she felt the need to apologise for bothering her. And all down to that dickhead of a boyfriend of hers, no doubt.

'Stop saying sorry,' she said sternly. 'So, come on. Why are you here? Something to do with Paddy, I presume?'

She regretted her tone as soon as the words had left her lips. She knew from experience that Vicky would surely only leap to his defence even quicker, particularly now, with Jimmy's dad in the picture. But there was no fiery riposte forthcoming tonight. Her friend's eyes simply filled with fresh tears.

And out it all came. What he'd done. What she'd seen. What that bitch Lacey had started. And what she hoped her boyfriend and his friends were going to finish. Were finishing even now. 'I frigging hope so. I hope they kick the shit out of him,' Vicky finished.

'Lacey?' Lucy asked, confused. 'Who is Lacey?'

'The new girl. The *bitch*.'

'What, at work?'

Vicky nodded. 'And she's already *got* a frigging boyfriend. What a bitch! Got a boyfriend and she didn't even care!' A fresh sob escaped her. 'And nor did *he*!'

Lucy nodded. That, to her, seemed entirely in character. Particularly now, with a prison spell looming. 'Sounds like a case of *carpe diem* ...' she said thoughtfully.

Vicky frowned. 'What?'

'It's Latin,' Lucy explained. 'It means "seize the day". I got it off one of the solicitors at work.'

'Does it? Well, she was certainly doing that. And seizing my fucking boyfriend while she was at it, for that matter. Well, if she wants him that badly, she can bloody have him.'

Lucy knew Vicky didn't mean that, so she clamped her mouth shut. They were the words she had longed to hear from her friend for such a long time, but she knew Vicky didn't mean them now, any more than she ever did. Where Paddy was concerned, it was like she was immune to reason.

She reached instead for the box of tissues on her bedside table, snug in its cerise crocheted cover. 'Here,' she said, nudging her friend, 'have a blow.'

'And that's another fucking thing,' Vicky hissed as she plucked at the petal of pale tissue poking from the slit in the top. 'My mum's shit, Luce. You know that? Just *shit*. Why me?' She scrubbed at her cheeks with the tissue as she spoke. 'Why me? What did I do? What did I do in a past life to get a mum who's so fucking useless?' She poked a finger at the tissue box. 'I want a mum who makes covers for tissue boxes for me, like your mam does. I want a mam who'd even bloody *think* about *buying* a box of tissues to put in a fucking home-made tissue box fucking holder in the first place! I want a mum who'd think about me for a single fucking minute! Like, fucking *ever*! Just a single bloody tissue-box holder of my own. Honestly – is that *so* much to ask?'

Lucy couldn't help but smile, and her smile was infectious, because soon Vicky was smiling too, and then the pair of them were laughing – having to stifle their giggles in the same way they'd done countless times before, back when life was much simpler.

But it was never going to last, and, in a matter of minutes, Vicky's laughs had turned into the sort of wretched, shoulder-shaking sobs that Lucy knew were unlikely to stop any time soon. She pulled her friend close to her and stroked her hair while she cried, keen to offer comfort but wary of offering anything in the way of comment, much less proffering any advice. Whoever the girl was – and she certainly sounded like the bitch Vicky had called her – Lucy doubted she'd have meant anything to Paddy. Though, oh, wouldn't it be wonderful if there *was* a bit more to it; if Paddy – soon to be out of Vicky's life, at least temporarily – could be forcibly expunged from her heart at the same time? By going off with whoever-she-was, and setting Vicky free.

But it was a wish Lucy knew wasn't going to be granted anytime soon. Because Paddy didn't just have a long string of convictions for petty crime. If gossip was to be believed, and Lucy had no reason to disbelieve it, he had a long string of petty infidelities behind him as well. Vicky didn't know the half of it, and Lucy wasn't about to tell her, because, without evidence, she might as well be pissing in the wind – as her Jimmy had so eloquently put it. Not to mention being ever heedful of the advice in her magazines – that she'd simply be shot as the messenger.

And every time, every single time, he came right back to Vicky anyway. Like he owned her. Like, however many other girls he toyed with, it came back to the same thing. That he didn't actually want anyone else. That she was *his*. The thought creeped Lucy out.

So she said nothing. She simply listened as her friend's crying lessened. She knew Vicky was weeping as much for the thought of losing him to prison in a matter of days as to some girl he'd snogged in a club, after all. And, in a while, Vicky stopped, and declared herself to be exhausted, and was only too happy to be mothered by Lucy, in the way she almost never was at home; to be undressed and gently shepherded into Lucy's warm bed, with the duvet tucked round her and the bedside light extinguished, murmuring her undying gratitude as Lucy left her, for a few hours on the sofa again.

This time alone, under a throw.

Which turned out to be no more than a matter of minutes.

As before, Lucy woke and didn't know what had woken her. But this time, her senses keener, she soon guessed.

And this time, her reactions were as swift as they were anxious. She knew exactly what she'd heard. The slamming of a car door. And it was now being followed by another familiar sound. Of what she felt certain was another taxi heading off back down the road. And she could guess right away who it had dropped.

She wrestled the throw from her, grateful that she'd left on her dressing gown, and sprinted angrily to the front door before he was barely through the gate. Then, her thoughts almost in overdrive, to match the thumping of her pulse, flicked the button on the door so it was on the latch. This time, if need be, she *would* wake her parents.

Then she stepped outside, barefoot, the front step freezing beneath her soles. 'Don't even think about it, Paddy,' she said. 'You hear me? Just turn around and go home. She's not here.'

He turned to fasten the gate, which immediately struck her as a ridiculous thing to do, and when he turned around again she could see that he too had been crying. *For Christ's sake*, she thought, temporarily disarmed by this realisation, despite knowing his penchant for turning on the taps. '*Oh, Luce. You should have seen him. He was really so upset ... how could I not forgive him? How?*'

Blah, blah, blah. Lucy knew how all that worked as well. For Vicky, at any rate, who was susceptible to his mindgames, but definitely not for her. She studied his face as he turned back and approached her. His 'butter-wouldn't-melt-but-female-hearts-always-will' face. She could also tell by his expression that he knew she was lying. 'She's not here, okay?' she said again. 'Gone home. Half an hour back. So how about you just do the same, Paddy?' She cast her gaze up and backwards. 'Before my mam and dad wake up.'

Still he continued to approach her, looking pale and contrite, and as he neared her she could see that he had a weal on his cheek. And a stain on his jeans, and another on his shirt. Good. So perhaps the girl's boyfriend *had* given him that pasting. And perhaps, knowing the fate he'd already been warned to expect come his court date, he'd not even put up much of a fight.

There was certainly no fight in him now. 'Look, Luce,' he said, once he was near enough that she could smell him; the same pungent aftershave he always wore. 'Whatever Vic thinks she saw, she didn't, okay?' His voice was wheedling. 'Look, I just want to talk to her ... to explain to her ...'

'To say *sorry?*' Lucy couldn't help but spit the words out. 'As per usual? Well, you can't. Because she's not here for you to grovel to, okay? I *told* you. Go home, Paddy, okay? Go home and sort it out with her tomorrow.' *Or not, if I had my way*, she thought but didn't utter. 'Because you know, I really, really don't want to get involved.'

Lucy clocked the way he winced when she used the word grovel. It was hard to judge just how pissed he was – let alone what he'd taken. And for a moment she thought he was going to do as she'd asked.

'Look, I know she's in there,' he said, still appeasing, still sounding reasonable. 'So can't you just ask her for me? Please, babes? Let her decide, yeah?'

Lucy shook her head, knowing from long experience not to trust him. 'No, I can't. Because she isn't here. I *told* you. So you can stand here all night, and it won't make any difference. It's—'

'God, for fuck's *sake!*' The change came out of nowhere. 'So that's what I'll do, yeah? Okay? That's the plan then. I'll fucking stand here all night.' He was bouncing on the balls of his feet slightly now. 'That's what I'll do. I'll fucking stand here all night and there's fuck-all you can do about it, either.' He loomed closer, and now the alcohol on his breath eddied between them. 'Pissing "don't want to get involved" crap. You fucking love it! Little miss filth-lover. You just fucking *love* being involved.'

Lucy stood her ground. If there was one thing she believed without question it was that Paddy Allen would never dare lay a finger on her. Which didn't make it less scary, just kept her on the spot. Plus she was angry. 'Right,' she said, and now she did move, to turn her back on him. 'Have it your way. I'll just go and call the police.'

'For fuck's sake,' Paddy hissed at her. 'On what grounds, exactly? Like I'm doing anything wrong.' She heard a sound and turned around again. He had run back and, to her astonishment, simply vaulted the gate.

'Oh, just go *away*,' she tried again, emboldened by the distance – and the gate – between them now. 'Sod off back where you came from. You think Vic even wants to clap eyes on you again? Surprise, surprise. No, she *doesn't*. And guess what?' She smiled at him. She couldn't seem to help it. '*That*, Paddy Allen, is like music to my ears.'

He banged the latch on the gate down and stomped back towards her so fast that she heard herself gasp. And had taken hold of her arm before she could get away from him, putting paid to her previous confidence. He was almost nose to nose with her now, tall, dark and swarthy. Like a gypsy out of some romanticised Hollywood film.

'You know what, love?' he snarled. 'I get you. You know that?'

She glared at him. 'You *think*.'

'No, I do, Luce.' His face inched even closer. 'Trust me, I do. I can see right through you. You know why you hate me? Because you're jealous of what Vic's got.'

Lucy pulled her head back, incredulous. What was he *on*? 'Jealous? Of Vic having you? You *really* think that? Then you'd better speak to whoever it is you get your drugs from. *Seriously*. And take your hand off my arm.'

To her astonishment, he did so. Immediately. Shook her arm away, almost. 'Always *so* fucking clever,' he said, grinning nastily. 'And it's my pleasure, love. Wouldn't touch what you've got on offer with a bargepole.'

'That right?' Lucy taunted him, realising, with some pleasure, that she'd hit his Achilles heel. 'Don't you mean couldn't? Would *like* to, but couldn't? There's nothing I've got that's on offer to *you*, Paddy. I've always set my sights a *lot* higher.' She spread her palms in mock apology. 'Sorry.'

She clamped her mouth shut then, slightly in shock at her own boldness. Where had *that* come from? Perhaps she'd had just signed a warrant for her imminent demise. The second stretched, and as it did so she found herself shaking. First a little, then a lot, her naked legs in a tremor. She hoped he couldn't tell. She hoped she was wrong. Then, for one horrible moment, she thought he was going to kiss her. That he was going to stretch a hand round her head, grab her hair, crush her to him. Exert his power and masculinity, and address the change in power-balance. Tough it out. It would be such a Paddy thing to do.

But in that instant she saw she had pierced something in him. Found that sweet spot – that soft spot. The thing that made him hate her most of all. The truth that here was someone, a female, who he couldn't own, ever. And she knew that excited him as much as it infuriated him. He'd always loved a challenge, after all.

She saw his fists clench. The war that was raging in his head. She raised her chin a notch, almost challenging him to strike her or grab her. He did neither – he was all sorts of things, but not stupid.

'You know what, bitch?' he said instead. 'You won't win this battle.' He glanced up to Lucy's bedroom where, she hoped fervently, Vicky was still sound asleep. 'She's mine, okay? Mine,' he said, 'whatever you think. And you slag me off to her at your peril.'

He turned around then and began loping back towards the gate. He didn't seem half so drunk any more. Lucy was just about to speak when he turned back again. '*And* hers.' He waggled a finger at Lucy. 'You *got* that, sweetheart?'

'Just piss off,' Lucy told him. And, now, at last, he did, proffering a thumbs-up and a grin as he headed down the road.

She watched him all the way round the corner before going back in. And only then, once the door was locked, the house dark and silent, did she fully realise just how terrified she'd felt.

But strangely powerful. And more resolute than ever.

Chapter 11

Vicky looked down at the blue line on the stick in her hand and stared. It was a busy Thursday, and she was already a good ten minutes late for work. But, though she knew that, she couldn't move: she was transfixed.

In the fairy-tale scenario she'd fashioned for herself, the baby had been conceived on a Monday. The Monday night before Paddy had been led away and taken off to prison, which made it a child that would be born of love. Of commitment, and passion, and also of promises. That they would love one another always. That they would always be together. That she would wait for him, like a wife torn from her husband by war. That he would do right by her. Return to her. Stay with her.

She had walked home on the Sunday morning, carrying her slingbacks by their straps, having borrowed a pair of Lucy's old pumps. And despite her assurances to her friend that she was done with him completely, she'd still felt a pang when Lucy told her he'd come to find her, and a similar rush of unwelcome emotion as she rounded her corner to see his Capri parked outside.

She tried to steel herself, even so, calling to mind – which wasn't hard – what she'd seen in the nightclub, with Lacey. And, as she approached, she was heartened to see that he'd not ventured into the house. It would make it all the easier to tell him to sling his hook.

She saw him first, walking silently in the old Dunlop plimsolls, and, as always happened (and perhaps always would, more was the pity), she felt the fluttering of butterflies in her gut.

He was half-sitting, half-standing on their gate, smoking a cigarette in the watery sunshine. He was so beautiful, she thought, even though she didn't want to think it. And she wondered just how he would cope if – when – he got incarcerated. She'd heard the stories. And she'd seen documentaries on the telly, too. He was a good-looking man – but only *just* a man, really. In prison terms, eighteen was no age at all, was it? Yes, a world away from sixteen – to Vicky, Paddy was a man through and through. But in prison ... She shuddered. There would be men in prison – older, harder, *stronger* men in prison – who'd feel the same attraction to Paddy as she did.

And when he saw her – when he turned to flick his spent cigarette into the kerb – that sense of his vulnerability was even stronger. Just his face, his swollen cheek, his look of shame, his look of *love*, were sufficient to make her completely rethink her decision, and consider going with her feelings after all.

But she held firm. There was too much pain and anguish to bear. She stopped on the pavement, and nodded towards the car. 'I don't want to talk to you. I don't want to see you. So, please, just go away, Paddy, and leave me alone.'

She was surprised by the calm way she'd managed to get the words out. And mindful, which made her resolve that bit stronger, that what Lucy had said about her naivety wasn't true. She *had* been here before. She might be here again. Probably would be, if she didn't end it now.

'Vic, babe, *please*,' he began, opening his walnut-brown arms out to her.

She walked around them, eyes down, and started up her path.

'Please, Vic. I *love* you. Vic, *please* hear me out.'

She ignored this as well, and reached into her handbag for her key.

But it was her mother who opened the front door.

She heard Paddy mouth 'Fuck'.

Vicky took in the sight. The haystack hair. The old trackies. The frayed jumper. But her mam looked reasonably sober, which was something, at least. But she shouted at Paddy, even so.

'Just piss off, you little pipsqueak! You hear me? Bugger off!' Then she yanked Vicky roughly over the threshold and slammed the door.

'Spoke to Lucy,' she explained. 'Once you'd left.'

That had been that. Even Paddy – local bad boy and hard man that he was – wouldn't want to get embroiled in a set-to with Vicky's mum. Not because he couldn't pulverise her, either mentally or physically, but because he had a reputation to protect. An old lady? You just didn't go there.

So he called. She never answered. But the phone rang incessantly. Till, by teatime, her mam – Vicky had pleaded that she didn't – picked up the receiver and roared down that at him as well.

And then silence. Till around eleven, when Vicky went to put a note in one of the milk bottles, and found the most enormous bunch of deep, blood-red roses. A couple of dozen, at least. And on a Sunday. Where on earth had he found them?

Her mother, half way down her second bottle of cider, squinted at them through her cigarette smoke.

'Undying love?' she slurred. 'Yeah, and I'm the bloody pope.'

He'd called again then – had he been waiting somewhere, watching to see she'd got them? And every inch of her, angry and full of hurt though she still was, wanted to rush into the hall again and answer the phone.

'I mean it, girl,' her mother said, though Vicky had made no actual move to pick the receiver up. 'You do that and I'll cut the fucking cord.'

So it was Monday before Paddy was able to pin her down finally. After work. And on a day when – surprise, surprise, surprise – Lacey had called in sick. There'd been flowers there, too, another big blowsy bunch of them – this time gerberas and chrysanthemums and tiny pearls of gypsophila, driving Leanne into a frenzy of speculation.

'Come on, spill,' she kept saying, knowing nothing about Lacey apart from her apparent illness. 'What's he done? Come on, *tell* me – he must have done *something*.' But, determined not to air the whole humiliating episode in public, Vicky held her line – that it was just because he might, almost certainly would, be going away tomorrow, and wanted to send her flowers while he still could.

The irony of her fiction wasn't lost on her. Because Paddy *only* made such gestures when he'd wronged her in some way. 'You got *me*. *I'm* your gift,' he'd always joke. 'What other presents do you need?'

And then, eventually, it was Lucy who did for her. She called in her lunch break, as any caring best friend would, to check she was okay, to check she'd stayed firm. To check she hadn't 'caved in, like you know you always do, in the face of his pathetic floral offerings'.

It might have been the words she'd used. It might have been the looming court case. But, either way, when Leanne found her later, after Lucy'd left, and between clients, she was sobbing her heart out in the back room.

And of course, Vicky told her what had happened.

'The fucking *tart*,' was Leanne's considered opinion of Lacey. Then she shook her head. 'So that'll mean we're an apprentice short again, won't it? I doubt she'll show her face again here, will she?' She grinned, and clapped Vicky on the back while she snivelled. 'Still,' she added, 'you can do lots of overtime, can't you? You'll have a bit of time on your hands after all ...'

She grinned at Vicky. 'That's a *joke*. To make you *laugh*. You dozy mare! But seriously, Vic, you want my honest opinion?'

Vicky nodded.

'Well – and don't hate me, but if the poor sod's being carted off to the nick in the morning, shouldn't you at least give him the benefit of the doubt? He's clearly sorry. Bloody hell – and that's my kind of sorry!' Vicky had already told her about the roses. 'And he obviously loves you. Why else would he go to such lengths? And it's not like you have to do anything other than listen. That's what I'd do,' she finished, crossing her arms across her chest. 'Though chance would be a fine thing, of course.'

So Vicky did give him the benefit of the doubt, even though there had never been any, when he arrived at the salon ten minutes before closing, exactly as she'd always known he would.

And there was a certain power in being so desperately needed, so she not only listened, she let him take her back to his house where – his mam and dad being up to their elbows in flour down at the bakery – she allowed him to apologise, and apologise, and apologise, and then, because no one understood him like she did, she allowed him to make love to her, as only he could.

And forgave him, as only she would.

But that night of passion ten days back, though she'd love it to have been so, had not been the one that had resulted in this fairy-tale conception. She knew it hadn't. Well, it might have, but that was academic now anyway. She'd known she might be pregnant for a good three or four weeks before that, because she'd already missed one period and the next one hadn't happened yet, hence the realisation. And the purchase of the test.

She'd still kept her fingers crossed, of course, and a part of her, albeit a tiny one, had still believed she might not be. Not just because Paddy was always so careful, but also because she knew periods didn't always happen when they were supposed to. Specially when you'd not been having them that long. Her mam's didn't settle down till her twenties, she'd said. God, her *mam*. Having to tell her mam she was pregnant ... She couldn't even *think* about that right now.

Then there was Lucy. Lucy's periods were all over the place and always had been. She never knew when to expect them, and she missed them loads, too. It had gone on so long that she was even under the doctor about it. They were trying her on the pill now – about which Vicky had been pretty jealous – just to see if they could get them sorted out.

God, how she wished she could talk to Lucy about it. But she couldn't – well, couldn't have up to now, at any rate, since she'd decided not to tell Lucy about her reconciliation with Paddy. What would be the point in getting her all cross again, after all? Because the following morning (they'd said their goodbyes that night) he'd been sent to Armley Prison, as promised. And Gurdy had since reported (Gurdy had been at the magistrates' court, giving evidence) that he was expected to serve nine of the eighteen-month sentence he'd been given.

Nine whole months. The time it took to make a baby. Which was apparently already growing inside her. Vicky wiped the stick with some loo roll and shoved it in her handbag.

She felt sick. Though she now had a reason for all that. But most of all, heady, intoxicated, strangely brave.

Now she *would* have to tell Lucy. It felt like a relief.

There was a client already in and having a hood dryer lowered over her rollers when Vicky flew in. Leanne looked across, her expression first one of predictable irritability – Vicky was rarely late, but with only the two of them in the salon today, Leanne was obviously cross.

Her expression changed though, seeing Vicky's flushed cheeks and addled expression. 'You alright, love?' she asked. 'What's up?'

'I'm so sorry, Lee,' she said, yanking off her jacket and hanging it on the hook. 'I'll make it up, I promise. I'll work through my lunch.'

Leanne gave her client, one of their elderly regulars, a copy of *The Lady* to read while she waited for her curls to set. 'And I'll bring you a cuppa and a custard cream,' she shouted to her, over the noise of the hood. She then nodded at Vicky. 'Come on, you,' she said, heading towards the back room. 'You're looking terrible. You sure you don't want me to give the boss a ring? Sure he can get one of the Saturday girls to come in and help me if you want to go home again.'

Leanne's kindness made Vicky feel tearful. Was that how it was going to be now? Because that was what pregnancy hormones did to you, wasn't it? Made you emotional and faint, made your boobs hurt, made you nauseous, made you burst into tears for no reason. God, how she needed to tell someone. But it should be Paddy first, surely? He had the right to know first, didn't he? Then Lucy, no question. But she was just so full up with it all.

Full to bursting. She shook her head. 'I'm okay,' she said, 'Just been a rush today. Better after a coffee though.' She added a third mug to the two Leanne had already put out.

'You don't *look* okay,' Leanne said, scrutinising her minutely. 'You sure you're not going down with something?' She put a hand to Vicky's forehead. 'Are you feeling hot?'

It was such a sweetly maternal thing to do – not that she'd ever had much of *that* – that tears instantly welled in Vicky's eyes.

'Hey, Vic, *what*? What *is* it?' Leanne said, putting both arms around her. 'What's happened?'

Vicky couldn't stop herself. 'I'm *pregnant*,' she whispered.

'You're what?' Leanne let her go and inspected her again. Then pulled her close again. 'Oh, shit, Vic. Bloody hell. No wonder you look like you've seen a bloody ghost!'

She let her go again. 'You just found out? Jesus – how far are you gone? Does Paddy know?'

'He has no idea. I've literally only just done the test.' She reached for her bag and pulled the stick out. 'That's why I was late.'

'Shit,' Leanne said again, perching on one of the chairs. 'Christ, Vic.' She frowned. 'Christ, what will your mam say?'

Vicky didn't give a shit what her mam might have to say. That maternal boat had long since sailed. She said so.

'But what about Paddy?' Leanne said. 'I mean, are you even going to tell him? I mean, under the circumstances …' She stood up again, to fill the kettle. 'I mean, have you even decided what you're going to do?'

Vicky was confused. 'What do you mean, what I'm going to do? Do about what?'

Leanne blinked at her. 'Well, you aren't thinking about keeping it, are you? Shit, you are, aren't you?' she said, presumably reading Vicky's expression. 'Fuck's sake, Vic – *really*? God, you're too *young*! Seriously,' she added, 'you have to think about this, Vicky. Who knows where you'll be … what you'll be doing … who you'll be with … It's odds-on you won't be with Paddy, that's for sure. And what then?' She spread her hands. 'Who'll want you with a kid as part of the package?'

Vicky was more stunned than she'd been when the blue line had begun appearing against the white. The thought of getting rid of it had never even occurred to her. Should it have? *No.* She couldn't even countenance such a thing. 'Of course I'm going to keep it,' she said. 'I'm a Catholic, for one thing. And for another, it's Paddy's, and as far as I'm concerned, we *are* going to be together. Why wouldn't we be? Christ, Leanne, I'd *never* abort his baby!'

Leanne shook her head, then sighed. Then patted her arm. 'Alright, calm down.'

'I *am* calm.'

'And, look, I didn't mean anything by it – just, well, you know, I didn't realise you felt like that, honest I didn't. I mean, you know, what with him going to prison and that. D'you think he'll feel the same though? D'you think he'll actually *want* the baby?'

Which was a question Vicky hadn't even allowed herself to think about. She stuck her chin out. 'Of course he will,' she said.

Chapter 12

Vicky wished she'd had the foresight to get some travel sickness pills. The journey from Bradford Interchange to Leeds wasn't only interminable, it was like sitting on the axle of a go-kart, as the bus wheezed and strained its way to Leeds. Not that it was hilly, or particularly windy – just stop-start, stop-start, in the endless traffic. The thought of doing this every fortnight weighed heavily.

And she wouldn't even be there when it reached its destination, either. She still had to find a taxi to take her the rest of the way to the prison.

'Best way,' Gurdy had told her. 'Or you'll be faffing about with another load of buses. And it won't cost you much. It's only a couple of miles or so from there.'

He'd spoken with great authority – authority he really didn't have. Or, at least, shouldn't have. Since when did Gurdy know all about this stuff? Vicky knew he'd asked around for her – he'd said as much, sweetly. He'd been so anxious to help her out – had even offered to go with her, even though she knew that, at least this time, she must go alone. But it niggled at her that dear, sweet, *good* Gurdy seemed to have such ready access to the sort of information she required.

It sometimes felt, lately, that she was being sucked into a world she wanted no part of. Or, rather, catapulted – headlong. It had all happened so quickly. It was one thing to turn a blind eye to whatever 'business' Paddy got up to (something – as Lucy had always been quick to point out – that she'd been managing to do nicely these past couple of years), but here she was, on a bus bound for another, distant city – a city which housed the prison in which her boyfriend was now incarcerated. Her boyfriend, the convict. Her boyfriend, who had a record. And now she – and she couldn't help but cradle her still barely visible bump with her hands – had become a prison visitor.

They'd stretched out on Paddy's bed that last night before the trial, both looking up at the ceiling, Paddy drawing on a cigarette, defiant to the last, in the face of his mother's fury when she came into his bedroom the following morning and could smell he'd been smoking in there.

'Why should I care?' he'd said, flicking ash into the ashtray which was nestled among his chest hairs. 'I'll be out of here, won't I? And they'll fucking disown me anyway.' They since had, pretty much. 'So it's you and me, kiddo,' he'd told her tenderly. 'You and me against the world.'

They were words that she'd clung to while she'd cried into her pillow every night since. Him, her and their *baby*, against the world.

And he'd explained everything to her, carefully, as if to a child. That, once he'd arrived in the nick, he had to apply to the governor for something called a VO, which apparently stood for visiting order. That he'd be allowed two a month (unlike Gurdy, who'd needed to ask, Paddy knew exactly how prison worked), and that since his 'lousy fucking parents' obviously wouldn't want one, he'd request both for her, which meant she could go and visit him once a fortnight. 'Keep an eye on what you're up to,' he'd said then, teasing her, running a proprietorial hand over her naked breasts. 'Make sure you're not getting up to anything you shouldn't be.'

And Vicky had laughed then – as *if* – feeling secure in his embrace, all thoughts of him snogging the likes of bloody Lacey, or any other random slapper, spirited away. So she'd sought to reassure him – both in word and, for another languid hour, in deed.

And when it could no longer be in any doubt that she was carrying his baby, she had felt a welling of something approaching joy. No, it wasn't the best timing. Yes, she was obviously far too young. No, she wasn't sure how he'd react – he had a lot on his plate, didn't he? And, yes – yes, of *course* she was scared. But she was carrying Paddy's child. Which meant she was carrying a part of him inside her. Which, since he had been taken from her, felt exactly as it should be.

Or would seem so, once the small matter of her telling him about the baby had been dealt with. She'd pretty much decided now that she wouldn't. Had decided that almost as soon as she'd spoken to Leanne, in fact. After all, she should wait till it was properly confirmed, shouldn't she? By the blood test she was going to get down the doctors this coming week. Though, in reality, she knew she was simply looking for reasons to put it off, because it was such a momentous thing she had to do. She rehearsed it constantly in her head – how she'd broach it, the way she'd look, the exact words she'd say to him. But every time, she stalled at the next bit of the conversation, because she simply had no idea how he'd react. Having a child together wasn't something they'd discussed, ever. Not even in jest. Not like Lucy had with Jimmy, who apparently talked about such things all the time. Well, so Lucy said. She only had her word for it.

But her and Paddy, never. So it was uncharted territory. He might be in raptures or he might go apoplectic – even if (and she told herself this constantly, to reassure herself) he would, without question, come round in the end.

And strangely, so strangely, the one other person she *had* told had reacted in a totally unexpected way. She'd expected Lucy (who she'd rushed to tell, feeling guilty she'd told Leanne first) to rail at her, fume at her, drag all sorts of Paddy-avoidance promises from her. Yet she hadn't. She'd gone misty-eyed. Lucy! It had been surreal. Her friend had even cried with her, seemingly overwhelmed by the enormity of it all. It was like being braced for a whack by her mam and not getting it – all her emotional muscles had been stiff with disbelief.

'Of course you must keep it,' Lucy had told her. 'It's your *child*. Doesn't matter that it's *his*' – this word being hissed, so no change of heart there – 'it's *your* child. How could you possibly even consider getting rid of it? Be rid of him, yes, but, never, *never*, your baby. How'd you know this isn't your one shot at being a mum? How *could* you know?'

And when Vicky had pointed out that she'd never once considered getting rid of it, even if her mam kicked her out on the street, *that* had been when Lucy had spilled all those tears. 'And I'll support you, you know that, don't you?' she'd promised. 'Sod your mam – *I'll* support you. Money. Time. Anything you need. Blood sisters, remember? I'll help you look after it. Her … him.' She'd wiped her tears away then. 'I wonder what you'll be having?' her eyes all shiny.

And they'd hugged and they'd hugged and it had all been so lovely (not to mention reassuring) but still all so weird.

Vicky gazed out of the bus window now, trying to breathe through the constant waves of nausea, seeing the leaves turning on the trees and the fields and hedgerows slowly greying – almost as if to match the city looming darkly ahead. And she was struck by the thought that by the time Paddy was returned to her, the winter would have come and gone and it would once again be spring. And she'd have had her baby. There was absolutely no doubt about that now. There couldn't be. Nine months minimum, the solicitor had said. And the baby due in about seven. The baby Paddy didn't even know existed.

She'd written daily. Long letters. Since the day he'd been taken. Long chatty letters, full of day-to-day minutiae and, because she was mindful that her letters would be read by other people, only very lightly sprinkled with coy references to sex. In return, despite him having all the time in the world, she was in possession of just the one reply. Which had at first upset her, it being full of self-pity and recriminations, and the sort of 'me, me, me, me' stuff Lucy was constantly pointing out to her. And very little, bar a crude 'I hope you're keeping it warm for me', in the way of wondering how she was getting on.

But when Vicky read to the end she understood things a little better. Paper and stamps both cost money (a prison reality she'd never thought about) and why would he need to be the one writing the letters to her anyway? He was stuck in a prison, with nothing to tell her, so why waste money on paper when he could at least buy a few cigs – anything to help him get through the endless grey days. And Paddy'd never been much of a one for wearing his heart on his sleeve. Why would that suddenly change? And would she want it to? She'd never been one for wet lads, after all.

No, her letters to him were the things that most mattered. And now, in a matter of less than half an hour, she'd be seeing him in the flesh, the thought of which gave her butterflies. And made her heart leap, as if anxious to get there quicker.

HMP Armley looked like a castle, Vicky thought. Not a fairy-tale castle – it could never be that – but with its towering stone walls, its giant doors and its turrets, the sort of castle you'd see in a film about the olden days – you could almost imagine it being stormed by knights on horseback.

As it was, it was being stormed – albeit quietly and politely – by a small army of visitors, mainly women and children, some with babies hooked around their hips, many done up to the nines for their men. (Keeping it warm? The phrase couldn't help but return to her.) But most of them wore the same sombre, almost defeated expressions of people who had to be somewhere they didn't want to be.

Joining the queue for entry, and clutching her vital piece of paper, Vicky wondered at the way the next few months were going to go. The curious business of her being ordered here once a fortnight (it was a visiting 'order' after all) in much the same way that Leanne had told her she'd be summoned to the baby clinic to check on her and the baby's progress.

'First time?'

Having been silent for so long now, and still trying to take everything in, Vicky started at being spoken to. It was by an older woman – in her thirties, perhaps, and accompanied by two whey-faced children – who was behind her in the signing-in queue. The woman smiled. One of her front teeth was missing, and Vicky found herself wondering if the man she had come to visit had been the one to knock it out. She'd been studying everyone with the same ghoulish fascination, wondering what the men they were visiting were in for. Whose partner was a murderer? Whose son was a burglar? Whose brother was convicted of rape or assault?

'Thought so,' the woman said, seemingly pleased at her deduction. 'You got that look about you. Don't worry though. The natives are friendly. Well, mostly!' She nudged Vicky's arm and laughed. 'My Don has his moments,' she added brightly.

The woman's words struck a chord, and Vicky found herself looking into a future that she did not want to see. How often did these children get to see their father? Once a fortnight, for an hour? And for how long had that been? And for how long *would* it be? Half their childhoods? If she resolved anything – which was hard, because Paddy did what Paddy wanted – it was that she would do anything she could to ensure he was never locked up again.

Still, the woman, for all that her life seemed to be the one Vicky least wanted, was helpful and cheerful and reassuring in the face of all the strangeness. She explained that after signing in, being patted down and surrendering her handbag to a locker, she'd be given a number and shown into a waiting room. There, amid a batch – there were various concurrent visiting sessions – she'd hear her number called and a guard would take her in.

'They let you keep your purse, love,' the woman explained. 'You've brought some money with you, have you? There's vending machines, see. So you can have a cuppa together. They like to be a bit spoilt on a visit, of course.' She smiled. 'And there's usually home-made cakes and stuff, and all.'

As if it was a school fete, or something. As if all of this was normal.

The vending machine was the first thing Vicky did see – standing like a sentinel at the back of a room full of tables, at which of each sat a prisoner. The tables were set in rows, like exam desks laid out in a school gymnasium, except here, in place of invigilators in suits, who smelled of chalk, there were prison guards, unmoving, like stone pillars.

Her batch of visitors began to stream out around her. And soon the silence was replaced by a hubbub of noise. Chairs being scraped back. Throats being cleared. Greetings, exchanges of kisses, the whoops of excitable children. The sharp shushings of mothers and soft cooings of fathers. It was almost like Vicky imagined a reunion after a war.

She felt nervous and exposed, anxious to pick Paddy out in the sea of blue prison garb, but at the same time anxious about meeting his gaze, as well. Glancing around, watching women sitting down opposite their menfolk, she wished she'd decided to dress differently. Here, in the uniform world of the prison, the sense of occasion was only heightened further. Painted fingernails. Giant hairdos, glued in place by cans of hairspray, tight jeans, killer heels ... even in her best jeans and a little white broderie anglaise top Paddy liked her in, she felt she'd not made enough effort. Was that what you did, though? Tarted yourself up to remind them what they were missing? Had she read how you did this all wrong?

But there he was, and the look in his eyes reassured her. And his smile. It was just so obvious how pleased he was to see her. Perhaps absence really did make the heart – his heart – grow fonder. Perhaps this enforced separation would be good for them both.

'Alright, babe?' he drawled, as she hurried across to him and pulled her chair out. Then he half stood to embrace her, and kissed her hard, on the mouth. He smelt different. Clean, but still different.

Vicky took her seat, feeling embarrassed by the ardour of Paddy's kiss. She glanced across at two officers who were talking in low voices. About her?

'Ignore the screws,' Paddy said, his hands palm up on the table, ready to grasp hers. She placed hers in his. 'You look nice, babe,' he said softly. 'Like I remember.'

Like he was remembering. Remembering her *unclothed*. He didn't need to say it. 'It's only been a fortnight, babes,' she said. 'How much was I going to change?'

He squeezed her hands, sliding his thumbs back and forth over her palms. 'I'm just so glad you didn't plaster your face like the rest of the slappers that come in here. Bunch of tarts. Fuck me,' he added, leaning in towards her, 'I've missed you.'

Relaxing now, she smiled at him. 'How are you coping, babe? I miss you too.' And as he squeezed her hands again, so gently, she almost told him, but he spoke first, glancing from side to side, as if he was a spy or something.

'I'm fine,' he said. 'But I tell you what, babes, I've had time to do some serious thinking. And I've worked it out. It's all down to that fucking Jimmy Daley.'

'What is?'

'Don't be dense, babe. The reason I'm fucking *in* here. How else would his dad have known? I've worked it all out, babe, like I said. He's got someone on my case. And he grassed me up to his dad. It *had* to be him. Who else *could* it have been?'

Vicky knew she wouldn't have been the only thing on Paddy's mind. But even so, his insistent tone made her anxious. 'But *how* would Jimmy have known?'

She wasn't about to say so, but she knew Paddy had lied to her about that evening. And Gurdy too, albeit to protect her. She hadn't wanted to believe it at first, but she had proof that he'd lied about the video recorders, because she'd since found out that he'd pleaded guilty to some of the car-related charges. Why would he do that if he could prove that he hadn't even been there?

'Because fucking *Gurdy* knew!' Paddy said. 'Or at least he had half an idea, the little Paki fucker.'

'Gurdy? Grass you up? He'd *never* do that, babe, *never*.'

Paddy let go her hands, leaned back, and then leaned in again. 'He must have. I can't think of any other explanation, can you?'

'But he's your friend—'

'And his too. They're both up each other's fucking arses, aren't they?'

'No they're not. Paddy, Gurdy is *your* friend,' Vicky insisted. 'He wouldn't say anything, especially not to Jimmy. He knows how the two of you are. Honestly, babe,' she added, hating that she had come all this way – all this *fucking* way – and having to sit here and to defend bloody Gurdy. She still had to though. 'Babes, he just *wouldn't*.'

All the warmth seemed to drain out of Paddy's face. 'Why'd you do that?' he asked her.

'Do what?' she said,

'Do that.' He waved a hand languidly in her direction. 'Go against me.'

'I'm not going against you. I'm just saying—'

'Where's your fucking loyalty? Seriously, Vic. I mean, shouldn't you be on *my* side in this?'

'It's not a question of sides, Paddy,' she told him, feeling her hackles rise despite herself. 'I just think – no, I know – you are barking up the wrong tree. Gurdy adores you—'

'Yeah, but you don't.'

'Babes, you *know* I do—' She snaked a hand across the table. He withdrew his. Out of the corner of her eye she could see that the nearest guard was watching.

Paddy pouted now, and she knew he was tempering his response for their benefit. He stretched his hand out, then his other. She enveloped both, feeling ridiculously as if they were about to play that school game, where you kept pulling out the bottom hand and slapping it down on top.

'Well, you've got a funny way of showing it,' he said mildly. 'You think all your mates are such fucking goody two-shoes, don't you? But I'm telling you now, Vic,' he added, in the same incongruously mild tone of voice. 'None of them, *none* of them, can be trusted, you hear me?'

A different prison guard stopped by their table, making Vicky start. 'We're not having any problems here, are we?' he said softly. 'Only, you are looking a little bit agitated, Mr Allen, and we can stop a visit if it proves to aggravate a man.' He turned to look at Vicky. 'Hmm?'

She smiled at the officer. 'Everything's fine here, thank you,' she said politely. 'So,' she added, turning back to Paddy, 'shall I get us some cake?'

The taxis were lined up and waiting when Vicky emerged. Plenty for everyone who wanted one. A bumper profit day. And she was lucky to get a bus almost immediately once back in Leeds, for the hour or so's trip back to Bradford Interchange.

It had got better. A little better. He had calmed himself down. They'd eaten cake – something with poppy seeds that lodged in her teeth – about which they'd laughed, and which he'd tenderly got rid of. She'd hang on to that. The words he'd mouthed as he'd touched his nail to her tooth. The way he'd slipped it along her gum, mouthing things that made her blush. The way he'd told her how he physically *ached* for her.

Yes, she'd hang on to that. Not the stuff about her not going out. Not the stuff about how there were people on the inside who knew all about what happened on the outside. Not the stuff about how it would be best if she didn't hang around with Lucy – with any of them – not till he was out and he could look after her properly.

'I can look after myself,' she'd told him, chin up, defiant.

'You think you can, babe,' he'd said, 'but, trust me, you *can't.*'

No, she'd definitely stop trying to figure out what he'd meant. Just hang on to those last words. That he physically ached for her. And loved her. He'd been sure to tell her that.

And as they'd hugged, it had occurred to her that his protective streak was a good thing. He would surely feel the same about his baby.

Chapter 13

'So you haven't told him *anything*?'

Vicky's tone was incredulous. Lucy shook her head, feeling irritable and tearful all of a sudden. And all of a sudden wishing she had stuck to her guns and told Vic she'd prefer to get her results alone. It would be almost comical if it wasn't so awful. Sitting here, in the waiting area of the packed gynae clinic only a week after sitting in the antenatal one with her friend. Just a corridor and a whole world away.

'No, of course not,' she said now, feeling guilty for sounding snappy. 'There's nothing to tell him yet, is there?'

'No, but … you know. About your periods and that …'

'No, Vic. I *haven't*.'

'Alright, mate,' Vicky said, putting an arm around her shoulder. Which act of tenderness – almost maternal tenderness – just made it worse.

Lucy had never been one for horoscopes or fate or other such spiritual nonsense. There was a girl at the solicitors – an articled clerk, so no doubt pretty clever – who read her stars in the paper daily, and, since she'd begun there, Lucy's too. And Lucy (wondering how someone who had letters after her name could take any notice of such nonsense) would smile politely and agree that it would be nice to 'come into some money', or 'see a welcome shift in a special relationship', or whatever other guff was in the paper that day. And yet this morning – she'd taken the afternoon off for her appointment – astrology had warned her to be 'braced for bad news'.

'Though your natural Sagittarian optimism will help you overcome any obstacles,' Marie had continued brightly, before dumping the paper and returning to her work.

Lucy had picked it up and re-read it, trying to see it for the rubbish it was. And yet, was it?

It had been such a strange and disconcerting few weeks. Vicky pregnant. Vicky *pregnant*. Vicky going to *have a baby*. As her mam had commented when she'd told her the astonishing news, it seemed only yesterday that the pair of them were babies themselves. 'Running round the garden in your pants and vests,' her mam had finished. She'd sighed then. 'Where did all those years *go*?'

And it did feel exactly like that, despite everything. Despite the fact that they'd both been with their boyfriends for ages. Despite the fact that they'd both been having sex. God, was it really so astonishing that Vic should fall pregnant? That was the way nature had designed humans, wasn't it? To have sex and make babies while they were young and fit and fertile. Well, at least in Vicky's case, anyway.

'I'm so jealous,' Vic had wailed to her when she explained about the GP having put her on the pill.

'You know, Vic,' Lucy had said, feeling chippy about it all. 'There's nothing stopping you from going to the family planning clinic, you know.'

'Er, how about my *mam?*'

'Vic, you're sixteen. She doesn't even need to know.'

'Yeah, but you think I'd manage to keep it from her? Not a chance, mate. She's like bloody Sherlock!'

Which struck Lucy as a bit of a ridiculous thing for Vicky to say, since her mam could barely rouse herself enough to get off the sofa, much less start ferreting around in her daughter's sex life. No, the truth was much simpler: she just hadn't got around to it. That and the business of being brought up Catholic. And the 'fact' – if fact it was, and Lucy's doctor had said it wasn't anything like a given – that if you went on the pill you immediately put a stone on, and might get a thrombosis as well.

But it was that stone – that was the main thing. Lucy knew how Paddy's mind worked. He monitored Vicky's size like it was a project he was micro-managing. If she put on so much as an ounce he'd be on at her that she was letting herself go.

Oh, the irony. Vic would be putting on a lot more than that now. But would *she* be able to, ever?

So, no, she hadn't yet told Jimmy – not least because another piece in the miserable jigsaw that had revealed this potential picture had been that when she'd told him about Vic's pregnancy, that same evening, round at his, the enormity of everything she might now deny him had all become so painfully clear.

'Christ,' he'd said, shaking his head. 'Poor fucking baby.'

And just as Lucy had been about to leap loyally to her friend's defence, Jimmy had gone on to clarify that he wasn't being arsey – simply that it wasn't exactly the best start in life, was it? What with Vic being sixteen, and her mum being rubbish, and the kid's father being one Paddy-fucking-tosser-Allen, currently residing at Her Majesty's pleasure.

'She won't get rid of it,' Lucy told him, 'and I told her she shouldn't either. God willing' – like any God would have had anything to do with it – 'she'll see Paddy for what he is now, and finish with him. Who knows? It might happen anyway. For all that he thinks he owns her, I wouldn't be surprised if he drops her like a brick once she tells him she's up the duff.'

But Jimmy didn't want to even speculate about what Paddy might or might not do – didn't know, didn't care, didn't want to waste his breath. 'Far as I'm concerned,' he said, 'that twat is history.'

He'd then added 'or will be', but didn't explain further, because he was much more interested in Lucy and how she seemed. 'You're all emotional, aren't you?' he'd teased. 'Christ, don't tell me you're feeling broody.'

And that might have been fine – specially when they kissed and they cuddled, and, his dad working that night, soon went a good deal further – except that, afterwards, he'd whispered, 'Just think, Luce, one day we'll be at this lark properly – making our *own* babies. Christ, that's something to think about, isn't it?'

And she'd agreed that it was, because she'd been thinking it all the time lately, and when he went on – in that drowsy after-sex way he often did – about when they were married and how many kids they'd have, and how much it mattered to him to have a family, she'd felt as if her heart might break in two.

But Lucy didn't *know*. She didn't actually, conclusively *know* that she had something wrong with her that meant she couldn't have kids. It was probable, yes, and the doctor, like the horoscope, had told her to be braced for it, but even when she'd gone for the ultrasound and hormone tests, she was already expecting it. She'd read enough, knew enough, *felt* enough to know. Coming here today was just the confirmation.

A nurse came out and called her name and Vicky squeezed her shoulder before releasing her. Bright, blooming Vicky, with her small but present bump. Who, despite the fact that she hadn't dared tell Paddy yet, even though she'd been to visit him twice now, still exuded this aura of calm and equanimity, as if happy to be left in fate's hands now. That's what baby hormones did: they took you over.

Vicky offered to go in with her, but Lucy shook her head. 'They might, you know, want to examine me,' she lied, and Vicky nodded, obviously believing her.

'Good luck, mate,' she said. 'You wait, it'll be good news.'

But, then again, what else would she say?

* * *

The doctor – a woman in perhaps her thirties, with a long, swishy ponytail – indicated that Lucy should sit down. 'So,' she said, scanning a sheaf of papers in front of her, 'how are you today, Lucy? Okay?'

Lucy didn't know how to answer, since the answer should be so obvious. How the fuck could she possibly be okay? But she understood that this was just the usual exchange of niceties, and her job was to nod and say 'Fine, thank you' politely, so that, pleasantries dispensed with, they could get on.

And the doctor didn't waste any time. As if by a pre-arranged signal, her whole demeanour changed, to one Lucy knew she'd remember for years to come. That stern-but-sympathetic face, just on the right side of stern, so that she didn't dissolve into tears then and there.

'You have polycystic ovaries,' the doctor explained, her hands clasped in her lap, her eyes not leaving Lucy's as she spoke. 'As your GP has probably explained to you might well be the case, we now know they're the reason for the symptoms you've been experiencing – the irregular periods, the hair thinning, the skin problems and so on ...'

And on she went, talking slowly, but still too fast – there being just way too much information – for Lucy to take it all in. All but one thing, which sat there like a stone in her stomach. That no, PCOS (what they called it) couldn't be treated. Just managed. They would now help her manage her symptoms, like she had been left in charge of a particularly badly behaved child and couldn't possibly control it by herself. And that, no, she'd be highly unlikely to be able to conceive naturally.

'Which is not to say that you won't be able to conceive at all,' the doctor told her. 'There are all sorts of medical interventions that can increase your chances. Certain drugs, new procedures. You've heard of IVF, I assume? It's a field that is developing all the time.'

But Lucy didn't want to be in a field full of medical interventions. She wanted to be normal. She wanted to have babies. She didn't want to be one of the statistics you saw in the papers. One of those wretched women – those desperate 'six rounds of failed IVF' women. 'But is it likely?' she asked the doctor, feeling young and frustrated but, most of all, defective.

'The odds,' the doctor told her, 'are improving all the time.' And then she went back to explaining how they'd start 'managing' her condition. Like Paddy-fucking-tosser Allen managed Vicky's weight. Or used to. How could life be so bloody unfair?

'Oh, God, mate, I don't know what to say,' Vicky said, crying along with Lucy as they trudged back to the bus stop. 'Isn't there anything they can do? Isn't there an operation or something they can do to sort them out?'

Lucy shook her head. 'It's not curable.'

'But you said they said you might still be able to have a kid, right? You know, by drugs and that? So there's still some hope, isn't there?'

'Some,' Lucy conceded. *They.* What was this 'they'? Like there was some committee standing in judgement?

'So you've got to look on the bright side,' Vicky went on. 'Miracles happen, Luce, they do ...'

And then she started on about some woman her mam knew who spent years trying to have a baby and then, just as they were about to sign adoption papers, suddenly got pregnant. 'Just like that,' she was saying, 'after, like, six or seven years.'

Vicky was sniffing away tears as she spoke, tears that Lucy knew were genuine. Genuine love between mates, and understandable frustration. And, understandably, Vicky was only doing what anyone else would. Trying to find a positive. Conjure up a solution. But six or seven bloody *years*? That was really going to cheer her day up, wasn't it?

Try as she might, Lucy could not help the rage building inside her. What had Vic got to fucking cry about? She was having a baby. No effort involved. No particular desire to have one, either. Yet here was one, growing in her belly, even as they stood there.

And by that bastard who didn't deserve a fucking dog, let alone a child! Thinking of Paddy – that *bastard* Paddy – made her rage all the more. And even Vicky – the best mate, who she would stand by, like a rock, through the whole sorry palaver – didn't have the wherewithal to wipe her own arse half the time, and yet she would soon be changing nappies. It was all *so* unfair.

She had no right to rage at her friend. None at all. But she knew if she were to achieve the seemingly impossible, she would have to put some distance between them.

'Look,' she said, seeing the bus approaching in the distance. 'You get back. I'm not going to go home, not for a bit. I'm going to walk to Jimmy's. He should be just about home by the time I get there—'

'Luce, I'm not leaving you. Come on, let's go back to yours and have a cuppa. You can see him later.'

'No, I need the walk ...'

'Then I'll walk with you. I'm not leaving you, Luce, I'm not.'

The bus was almost upon them now. Lucy felt a powerful urge to run. 'Really, Vic ...'

'No, Luce.' Her voice was sharp. 'I'm not leaving you in this state.'

And she *was* in a state, even if she didn't quite acknowledge it. She could tell by the concerned expression on the face of the woman who'd now emerged from the bus shelter.

But she had to get away, and, as soon as the idea formed in her head, it wasn't so hard to say the words that were needed. Perhaps they had to come out in any case.

'Vic, just fucking get on the bus, will you? Look, I'm sorry, but you're the *last* person I want to be with right now.'

Then she turned tail and stalked off as fast as she could, so she wouldn't have to see the expression on Vicky's face.

By the time she caught up with Jimmy – it was a good hour's walk to his house, even using all the shortcuts – she had managed to regain sufficient composure that there was no concern in his face, just surprise. And pleasure, which made her wretchedness even more profound.

He'd obviously beaten her home by mere minutes because he was still in his work overalls. And must have been wondering why she was at his when she would normally have still been at work. She hadn't told him about her appointment at the hospital, just as she hadn't told him about the last one, on the basis that if it turned out there was little to worry about, there would be no point in dragging it all out. Besides, some things were not for a lad's ears, not really; that, as her mam had once told her, boyfriends and husbands shouldn't be privy to.

But as soon as he smiled at her, went 'Hiyah, babes, this is a nice surprise', went to kiss her, it felt like the dam she'd so carefully erected had been exploded into pieces. She fell against him, the sob she'd been holding back all the way there escaping from her throat on a massive outbreath, like a tsunami of emotion.

He crushed her to him, going, 'What, babe? What the fuck's up? What's happened?' But for an age she couldn't speak, only press tight against him, inhaling the cocktail of strange chemical smells on his overalls – sharp plumbing-related smells that were as familiar and dear to her as the shape of his nose, or the precise way his hair felt, or his laugh.

But finally, after he'd shuffled her into the front room, and sat down with her on the sofa, she managed to spew it all out.

Jimmy listened in silence, his expression changing as she spoke, one minute sad, another angry, another full of compassion, and locked as she was into the explaining of all her misery, she was alert to any expression that might confirm her worst fear. To any hint, however tiny, that once he had taken everything in, Jimmy would realise that he was with the wrong girl. He wanted a family so badly; to create the one his mother had taken away from him. And however much hope the doctors tried to instil in her, one she knew it was odds-on she could not provide, she wasn't stupid. A future without Jimmy seemed such a terrifying place. But she wasn't stupid – not about happy-ever afters. He might think – be completely convinced, even – that they could just make the best of it, *now*, but she knew better. It would eat at them. It was eating at her now.

'So look, babe,' she finished. 'I've been thinking about it all the way here. And, you know, if you wanted to finish with me, it's okay. Honestly.' She clasped his hands, trying to effect a lightness she'd could never feel. 'I wouldn't ...' she could hardly get the words out, she felt so scared. 'I wouldn't, I would never, ever hate you.'

Jimmy stared at her for a moment. Then pulled his hands away from hers. Then almost seemed to explode up from the sofa.

'Christ, Lucy – I can't believe I just heard you say that!'

She stood up too, shocked by the anger in his voice.

'But I wouldn't,' she said. 'Really, Jimmy. I just don't want to ruin your life, that's all. I can't bear it ...'

'*You* can't bear it! Christ, Lucy,' he said again. 'I don't know what to say to you. Really. I fucking don't. You really think I'd do that? That I'm the sort of shit who'd just fuck off and leave you over something like that?'

'No, Jimmy – I just—'

'Then why the hell would you even *say* something like that? I just can't believe you'd think I'd *do* that. I …'

He ploughed a hand through his blond curls, which were dulled by dust and dirt. And she realised why he'd stopped speaking. Because he couldn't speak.

He cleared his throat noisily and pulled her back into his arms. 'What kind of man do you think I *am*? I fucking love you, Luce. How can you say that? I fucking *love* you, you fucking idiot!'

'And I love *you*. I just …'

He kissed the top of her head. Almost roughly. Almost angrily. Could a person be kissed in anger? But that's how it felt. Like her mam had done that time when she'd lost her in the park, and when she'd finally found her, and was so cross and choked. Just like that.

'Then just don't,' he said. '*Fuck*.'

And Lucy felt safe again.

Chapter 14

Apprehension sat like a stone in Vicky's stomach. A stone that jumped every time Gurdy lurched away from junctions, the minutes ticking past till she'd have to face Paddy. As his officially pregnant girlfriend.

But why the hell hadn't he written back? To torture her?

'For God's sake, Gurdy!' Lucy huffed from the back seat. 'I'm going to throw up in a minute. You are the worst bloody driver on the planet. I mean, seriously. Did you *really* pass your bloody driving test?'

'It's not me, it's the car!' Gurdy protested as they kangarooed forwards. 'It's got some problem in the ignition chamber. Misfiring an' that. Or something.' He turned to Vicky and grinned. 'Probably "or something". I need Paddy, innit? He could fix it. I miss him, I proper do. Almost as much as you do, no lie.'

But *did* she miss him? Vicky wasn't quite sure. Not at the moment. Not with it hanging over her that she was shortly going to have to face him. Because his face would say it all. She still wasn't sure she'd done the right thing in writing to him to tell him. Lucy's idea. Lucy's plan. Lucy's 'best thing to do'. And Vicky supposed she was right. Better perhaps to break the news to him in a letter than risk him going off on one in front of everyone in that bloody visiting room.

And better for her, perhaps. Better in that it sort of let her off the hook. But had it? It had been almost a full fortnight since she'd written now, because she'd done so only a couple of days since she'd last been to visit. And not a word in reply. Which she might have accepted (he was no writer, and the same rule about the cost of stamps still applied), but when she'd told him something so momentous? When she'd specifically asked him to write back and reassure her he was happy?

Lucy laughed. 'You don't miss him like that, I hope,' she teased Gurdy from the back seat.

'Yeah, yeah,' Gurdy said. 'Ha bloody ha.'

That had been one positive thing, at least – the only positive thing lately. Well, depending on your viewpoint, and Vicky knew plenty who didn't share hers and Lucy's, but they'd found out Gurdy was gay – like they didn't already *know* that? – so now she was officially pregnant, and he was officially gay.

He'd told Jimmy, of all people. While pissed as a fart, down at the Old Crown. Pissed to the point of barely being about to speak, let alone function, when some girl had come onto him – he wasn't half bad-looking now he'd grown into his face a bit – and, according to Jimmy who had hardly been able to recount the tale for laughing, that she'd said, 'Want a bit of this, mate?', and he'd replied, in his usual polite-to-the-ladies fashion, 'Only if you have a penis in those pants, love!'

'How priceless is that?' Jimmy had said. And Vicky wondered if Paddy would be quite so accepting. 'Honest, bless him, I was so glad there was no one around to hear him.' (And that was another worry, Vicky thought, as the prison loomed greyly in the distance. It getting back to Paddy that she'd been out with Jimmy and Lucy at *all*.) 'Because he was off then, burbling on, all the fucking way home, on and on, about how much he wished he fancied girls, like his brother Vik did, but all he wanted was a bit of cock, and how I mustn't tell anyone.'

Jimmy hadn't been sure how he'd be able to keep a straight face when he next saw Gurdy, thinking it was a good thing that he'd been too pissed to be likely to remember. But Vicky and Lucy begged to differ. They had no intention of aiding and abetting any amnesia, and at the first opportunity – a couple of nights later, when they'd met up in the appropriately named Oddfellows – they reported what Jimmy had told them. And though at first Gurdy was mortified, they all soon agreed that they couldn't remember a time when they *hadn't* thought he was gay.

'So you knew even before *I* did? What's *that* about?' he'd admonished. Then he'd laughed and they'd hugged and it was all a bit lovely. And they'd talked about his parents and how they'd go absolutely bonkers. But they were too blind to even see it, thank God, they all agreed. And they were now on a mission to find him a boyfriend.

All of which was a world away from where they were now, Vicky thought. Which was good old HMP Armley: a place for grown-ups, and a very dark and charmless place.

There to leave her to her fate, while Lucy and Gurdy went back off into Leeds city centre, there to go shopping, for baby stuff, among other things. She wished she was going with them instead of through the prison doors.

Gurdy, ever the gent, leapt from the driver's seat and came around the bonnet. It was an old Mini, his pride and joy, in a rather unlovely shade of maroon. In an ideal world, he'd have liked to have taken temporary ownership of Paddy's Capri, but that was never going to happen. It was safely under a tarpaulin in the Manningham Lane lock-up, and though he had been tasked by Paddy with starting it up periodically to 'keep it sweet', Vicky knew he'd no more risk taking it for a joy ride than jumping off a cliff. The repercussions were just way too grim to contemplate.

But now he had his Mini (funded no doubt by shady dealings with Rasta Mo) and he cherished it. 'Mad-*arrrrm*,' he said, reaching his arm in to help her out of the front passenger seat. Like she was some delicate flower, or eight months pregnant rather than just a couple, and again with his new sing-song voice.

'Gerroff, you Noddy,' she told him. 'I'm not a bloody princess.'

'Yes you are,' Lucy said, as she pinged the vacated seat down so she could sit in the front now. 'Or at least you're supposed to be *his* princess, aren't you?' Her voice was understandably sarcastic. 'So don't you go taking any of his shit, okay?' She kissed her. 'Pie and pea shop. Hour and a half or so. Top market. Okay?'

'Okay,' Vicky said, as Gurdy nipped back round to jump in again. 'Drive carefully,' she called out as they pulled away.

And as she watched the car splutter back down the road towards Leeds she felt this powerful urge to run after it. No tax, no insurance, and Gurdy drove like a retard. But it wasn't quite that. It was just the sense of them both disappearing. And the knowledge that, Paddy aside (and it was a feeling she wanted to shake off but couldn't), all the love and security in her life were in that bloody rust-bucket of a lawnmower-on-legs bloody Mini.

Shaking her head to try and clear it of the sense of impending doom, Vicky made her way slowly up the gravel road to the iron gates that incarcerated the love of her life. This was only her fourth visit, and she was surprised by how quickly it had become routine. The queueing, the endless chatter of the other women and children, the handover of most of her possessions and the humiliating body search, but in her pregnant state it had begun to make her feel even more violated.

Still, at least she'd had company this time, and for that she was extremely grateful to her friends. Because it wasn't like it was easy – Lucy had had to book a day's holiday and though Gurdy mostly worked his own hours he was probably much shorter on work now that Paddy was inside, so it wasn't like he wouldn't miss the chance of a day's pay.

Yet they'd been insistent – not least because they all knew the score; that Paddy's reaction to becoming a father was a major unknown. Plus, as Gurdy had pointed out, the markets in Leeds were way better than those in Bradford – like he'd also come out as some kind of shopping guru.

The thought made her smile. She was probably panicking about nothing, she decided, as she raised her arms robotically in readiness for being patted down. And, good or bad, all the wondering would be over in a minute. Just as soon as she clapped eyes on his face.

Though it wasn't his face that first drew her gaze. No, as she made her way across the blue tiles of the visiting room, it was his arms she saw first. They were outstretched.

'Hello, Mum,' Paddy said, his smile wide and welcoming. And all at once, Vicky felt her fears vanish. 'Oh, babes,' she whispered, as he drew her into his embrace across the table. 'I've been so worried about everything. Why didn't you write to me? I've been on pins!' She felt ridiculously like crying. Well, not so ridiculously, given the emotion she felt, but she didn't want to break down in here. Not in front of all the bloody screws. Specially didn't want to mess up her make-up.

'What's the point, babes?' Paddy answered. 'Fuck me, you smell good. By the time I got your letter it was, like, why bother writing? I'd rather tell you – *show* you' – he managed to get his tongue into her ear – 'than write some stupid letter.'

'So you're okay with it?' she pressed, once he'd let her go and they'd both sat down. 'Honestly? You're not cross?'

'At the thought of a little Padster in there?' He gestured towards her stomach. Then he sat back. 'Nah, not at all. In fact, I like the idea. I mean, it's not the best timing, but, you know, what will be will be and that ...' And Vicky realised that he genuinely liked the idea – not least the idea that he was such a stallion. His face said it all.

'Oh, babes, I'm so happy. Because I couldn't begin to think of getting rid of it. I couldn't. I mean, people told me to—'

'What people?'

'Oh, just a girl ...' she stumbled. She'd almost said a girl at work. 'You know how it is. People always think you're too young. And what with you being in here ... But, Christ, I sometimes feel I'm older than bloody Methuselah. I feel like a mum already – to my *own* mum. And what with Lucy ...'

'What about her?' Paddy's mouth formed a frown.

'Oh, just that she's had the worst news from the hospital. She and Jimmy probably can't even *have* children.'

He raised his brows. 'Like I'd *care*?'

'Oh, don't be like that, babes. It's *sad*.' But sensing this was a conversational avenue she shouldn't even be going down, she laid a hand over his – big and hard, and more calloused than ever. Man's hands. Hard-working hands. *Her* man's hands. She squeezed them. 'I mean, it just made me think, you know? Realise that you can't take stuff for granted. I mean, I know it'll be hard but, you know, it's a life we've made, isn't it?' She touched her belly with her other hand. 'I still can't quite believe it's in here. I've got my scan booked though. I can't *wait*. I can get a picture to bring you.'

'Can you feel it?' he asked, stretching across the table to touch her stomach. 'She's preggers, my missus,' he told the nearest screw. 'Just copping a feel. Nothing to worry about.'

My missus. Vicky loved that. Though rather less so when he added, 'And it'll keep you out of mischief an' all.'

'Paddy! Will you bloody stop that!' she said, slapping his hand away.

He grinned and shook his head. 'Jesus, babe! Keep your hair on,' he said mildly.

She got tea and cake for them. Stewed tea. Some sort of fruit cake. And sat and ate it, almost like it was a tea party in a village hall. But it wasn't very long before Paddy being Paddy, he lost interest in hearing about the bump he could hardly feel, let alone begin to visualise as a person. And she got that; she knew lads were like that about babies. After all, it wasn't them pregnant, was it?

But despite her efforts to keep things light, and update him on all the gossip, he very soon returned to his favourite topic of conversation: why he was banged up and who'd put him in there?

'I hear things,' he said, when she told him for about the fourth time that he was being paranoid. 'And I keep coming back to the same bloody thing. Why am I in here and no one else, eh? Like that little Paki friend of yours.'

'He's your friend as well, Pad. Why d'you keep forgetting that fact? He even brought me here today.'

'What?'

'In his car. He's got a car now. An old Mini. Drives like a sewing machine. But at least it's something ...'

'A car? Where the fuck d'he get the money?' And his expression made it clear that, far from quelling his suspicions, it had only added to them. 'Where the fuck did that little twat get the money to buy a car? Rasta Mo?'

'It's not insured,' Vicky whispered, in case one of the screws could hear her.

'What's that got to do with anything?' He was beginning to look really cross now. 'I tell you what, since he's mister all about all of a sudden, you can tell him something from me. Just tell him he's not as clever as he thinks he is, okay? And to remember that there's always someone new joining me in here.'

'What are you *on* about? What exactly do you think he's been doing?'

The bell went then, and Paddy immediately pushed his chair back, and as the room was full of leaving sounds – the scrape of chairs, the crackle of coat zips, the kissing – he pulled her to him roughly, kissing her properly, hungrily, his hands tight round her biceps.

'Just always thought,' he said finally, once he'd released his grip slightly, 'that it was a bit fucking odd that I got collared and he was left untouched, that's all. Always assumed that fucking Jimmy had purposely kept him out of it, but from tales I've been told recently, I'm not so sure.'

'You're being paranoid,' she told him firmly, feeling flustered by his kisses. 'Gurdy loves you. He'd never grass you up, babes. Honest. *Never.*'

'Never say never,' he said darkly.

Then he smiled again. 'Anyway, babes,' he added, 'you keep that little one safe, yeah? For his daddy.'

She smiled too. She hated leaving on a bad note. 'How d'you know it's not a girl?'

He touched his nose and winked. 'I just *know*.'

She saw Gurdy first, waving manically at her, as she pushed her way through the crush at the pie shop. 'At last!' he said. 'We thought they'd banged you up an' all, didn't we, Luce? Where've you been, mate? We thought you'd never get here!'

Vicky said there'd been a long queue for taxis but, in reality, she'd walked a fair bit of the way before flagging one down on Armley Road.

The queue hadn't been that long – she'd just wanted to walk for a bit. She felt light. So much lighter than she'd felt in long weeks now. He was happy. It was still sinking in. He was *happy*. She didn't so much want to walk as skip back into Leeds, because the world suddenly felt a much more manageable place. She wanted to walk so she could bask in the joy of feeling happy. Before she met her friends and would have to be necessarily less excited. She had to think of Lucy and how tough all this must be for her.

But now her feet hurt and the cake was repeating on her mercilessly. 'I'm parched,' she said. 'Shall I go up and order?'

'You sit down,' Gurdy said, springing up. 'I'll go and do it. What'll it be for you?'

Bless him, she thought, how could anyone think ill of Gurdy? 'Oh, just a pork pie with mushy peas and a Coke.'

Lucy tugged at Vicky's arm as she sat down. 'Here, have a peek at all the stuff we've managed to get,' she said, pulling a wodge of bags from the space between their seats. 'Bootees and matinee jackets, oh and these amazing little babygros.'

'Blimey, mate,' Vicky said, touched almost to the point of tears. 'All this, and so early.'

She wished Paddy could see it too. Wished so much that he wasn't missing out on all this. Because it was important, wasn't it, that he felt involved? But she knew Lucy didn't want to talk about Paddy. As far as Lucy was concerned, Paddy could go straight to hell. Vicky knew, though Lucy tactfully stopped short of saying so, that she thought the best thing would be if she moved on from Paddy. That she wanted to hear Vicky tell her that he was angry to find out she was pregnant. Except he hadn't been angry. He'd been the opposite, and she wished things could be different. That she could tell Lucy that.

Gurdy obviously sensed it, though. 'You look like the cat who's got the cream, mate,' he said as he put her drink in front of her.

She couldn't help it. 'He was fine. He was *fine* about it. Happy. All that worrying …'

'Yeah, for *now*,' Lucy pointed out so quickly that she'd obviously already been thinking it. 'Easy to be happy when it's not actually born yet …'

'Oh, don't be like that,' Gurdy said. 'Anyway, more to the point, did he say anything about me?'

'You?' Vicky said, wondering quite what was behind this. Who had gone into Armley, and what exactly had they said?

'No,' she added. 'Why? Were you expecting him to or something? I mean, you know what he's like. Always paranoid, world's always out to get him.' Gurdy's frown only deepened at this and Vicky frowned back at him. 'Mate, what's up?'

Gurdy shook his head and shrugged. 'It's probably nothing. Just something Pete was saying the other day. Saying stuff about Paddy apparently blaming me for his arrest.'

'Blaming *you*?' Lucy said. 'It had fuck-all to do with you. And I know that for a fact.' She turned to Vicky. 'And so do you.'

Vicky nodded. And decided she should maybe start trying to find out. 'Course I know that. Everyone knows that. You know what he's like.' She smiled at Gurdy reassuringly. 'But no, he didn't say anything about you,' she lied.

Gurdy sat back, looking palpably relieved. 'Good,' he said, 'because if he thought that, he'd fucking kill me, I know he would.'

Lucy laughed. 'Now who's being paranoid? As *if*.'

Part Two

Whenever I saw those who ploughed wickedness
and planted misery, they gathered its harvest.

Job 4:8

Chapter 15

Clayton, Bradford, June 1988

It was a huge effort of will not to shout. To scream, even. Vicky certainly felt close enough. Today of all days, and her mother was being a total pain. Being useless, just like she had been, pretty much, since the day of Chantelle's birth.

Yes, she supposed she had made an effort to help out. But even as Vicky conceded that, it induced a fresh wave of anger. Why should she have to berate herself for thinking badly of her mother? For all that she'd acted promptly when Vicky had gone into labour, where had the love been? The support? The little murmurings of reassurance? It was more like some basic animal instinct had kicked in, and she'd simply gone through a tick-list of things to do.

Chantelle's birth had begun by the old twin tub in the kitchen; her cries of pain – and astonishment; astonishment as much as anything – blending seamlessly with its wheezings and chunterings.

At that point her mam had been in the other room sorting clothes out; some of Vicky's old romper suits that she'd brought down from the loft, and the exquisite babygros and little outfits Lucy and Jimmy had bought, and which had brought tears to her eyes.

At that point, her mam was like this wholly different person, leaping for the phone, calling the ambulance with such a sense of purpose and authority, picking up the last bits Vicky needed and packing them efficiently in her little case.

And, with no Paddy around to hold his 'partner's' hand (the young woman at the ante-natal clinic always called the men 'partners') her mam had lumbered into the ambulance with her, to go too. Not to actually go in, not to the birthing suite – that would have been a motherly step too far for both of them – but at least she'd been in the building. Been a presence. A reminder, particularly when the crunch came, that though it often felt like it, she wasn't completely on her own.

But just as Boxing Day followed Christmas – invariably gloomy and anti-climactic – so the reality of Chantelle (who she'd named after her dead maternal great-grandmother, having always loved the exotic-sounding name) soon spirited whatever instinct had driven her right away. Business as usual. Trackies and cider, while Vicky functioned like a pilot groping blindly in a fog. Like being a grandmother meant absolutely nothing to her.

She was doing it now. Just sitting there on the sofa, while her granddaughter screamed herself hoarse on the living-room rug, her only attempt to soothe her being to stick a bunioned foot out and intermittently poke her shoulder with her big toe.

Vicky bit down on her lip, hard, before speaking to her mam again. After all, what the fuck else had she honestly expected? 'Can't you just pick her up?' she said. 'Just take your eyes off the telly for one bloody minute? For God's sake, Mam, are you still pissed, or what?'

Her mother turned and glared at her, apparently unrepentant. 'It's your frigging kid, madam, not mine! And anyway, they just need leaving when they cry for nothing, otherwise they'll grow up soft.' She waved a dismissive hand. 'Go on, go back upstairs. Get yourself tarted up for bleeding lover boy and leave me *alone*! I know what I'm doing.'

Vicky scowled at her mother, all her nerves firing and jangling. They didn't warn you how your baby's crying could get to you the way it did. And with a mam like hers for a grandmother it got to her all the time. That and the fury. Her frigging kid indeed. Exactly! Which meant she shouldn't be having to run around after her frigging mother as well! Which she was *still* doing. Not to mention spending half her maternity money to keep her in bloody cider. Much as the thought of leaving Chantelle appalled her, a part of her was desperate to get back to work. She'd not spent so much time in her mam's company in years, and she was fast reaching the end of her tether.

But it wasn't just that. It was the thought of having Paddy home. The thought of him finally clapping eyes on his daughter. She was eleven weeks old, almost, and he'd yet to even meet her. He hadn't wanted to. Was adamant that prison was no place for a kid, and had been content just to look at the photos Vicky had brought in instead. Though not looked at with any degree of interest, if she was honest, despite what she'd kept on telling Lucy.

Today though, she was sure everything would change. Today she'd go and meet him, and bring him back home, and he'd take one look at his little girl (his own flesh and blood; and there was no mistaking the likeness) and his heart would melt. He'd be head over heels.

His little girl who was still sobbing her heart out on the rug currently. 'For Christ's sake, Mam,' she said, fighting against the urge to pick Chantelle up herself. She daren't. If she didn't get her skates on she'd miss the train to Leeds. 'I'm already late. Please at least warm her bottle and give her that. *Listen* to her, Mam. She's just *hungry*!'

'She is not,' Vicky's mum huffed. 'It's not been four hours yet. She's just trying it on, same as you used to.'

'Mam, she's just a *baby*. How can she be frigging trying it on? Look,' Vicky said, making a Herculean effort to keep her tone one of appeasement. 'I know you know best, but I have to get going. *Please?*'

Her mother finally relented. 'Go on, piss off then,' she puffed, hoisting herself off the couch and stepping over the baby to reach for the empty bottle. 'And I suppose I'm minding her till you get back, am I?' she added, which made Vicky cross all over again. Like she took it all for granted. Like she hadn't had to ask her mam so nicely. Like it was such a bloody inconvenience to spend time with her only grandchild.

'Mam, it won't be for long, honest,' she said as nicely as she could, through gritted teeth. 'And if you feed her she'll probably sleep till I'm back, won't she? If you don't have the telly on too loud, anyway.'

Her mam lit a cigarette then and with it planted firmly between her lips, finally picked up the baby – who stopped crying immediately – and took both her and the bottle into the kitchen, while Vicky belted back up the stairs.

It had been a conscious decision not to take Chantelle to meet her father. Much as she'd have loved to, Vicky knew all too well that it was *her* Paddy wanted to see waiting outside the gate for him. Her alone. And looking her very best for him. He'd made much mention in the final couple of visits before the birth of how much he was looking forward to her getting 'back to her old self' instead of the 'lumbering fucking pudding' she'd turned into.

She wished she hadn't shared that particular gem with Leanne. Most men, Leanne had said, really fancied women when they were pregnant. Thought they looked sexy. Vicky wasn't sure when Leanne had become the expert in such matters. But what she did know was that Paddy definitely wasn't one of them.

And even two weeks after the birth, when she'd made the long journey to see him – no small effort – almost the first thing he'd remarked upon (and way before he so much as mentioned Chantelle) was how he hadn't expected her to look so much like she was *still* pregnant. That had stung.

She'd worked so hard to lose the extra pounds, too. And how could she ever get back to 'her old self' anyway? She was her new self. A mother. A proud and happy mother. No longer a girl, but a woman and his daughter's *mother*. It never ceased to surprise her that she'd coped so well so far. And once he was home, he'd soon appreciate quite how well she *had* coped.

Though thinking that made her anxious because one other thing she did know was the thing her mam had drummed into her since she was old enough to hear it. That a lot of men were bastards, her own father included – they got you up the duff, then, when the baby came along and life got complicated, they scarpered.

She couldn't let herself believe that. Not all men were like her father. And she mustn't, wouldn't, let herself become infected by her mother's bitterness. Paddy wasn't like that. Paddy worshipped the ground she walked on. If a lad so much as glanced at her he freaked, didn't he? She was nervous about seeing him, even so. It was one thing for him to cherish her while he was banged up in prison. Quite another now he was once again free. So she'd made no small effort with her appearance in the scant time she'd had left to her – donning her gypsy skirt (pure white, and not to be worn around the baby) and the off-the-shoulder Bardot top he always loved her in. Not too much make-up – Paddy hated girls who slapped on too much make-up – and her best pair of flat winkle-picker shoes. It felt not so much an outfit, though, as armour. To do battle with the demons that couldn't help but harass her daily.

That kept reminding her that, however much he constantly told her otherwise, he might not fancy her new self anymore.

The complicated train and bus journey finally over, Vicky stepped down onto an Armley Road that was bathed in bright sunshine, her hair – which she'd styled into a bouncy half-pony – being stirred by a light summery breeze. And for a moment she felt a little like Sandy, from the movie *Grease*, off to claim her own John Travolta.

It was a big step. The first day of their new lives together. And as she covered the short distance to the hated iron prison gates, and glanced at her watch, she felt a surge of joy at the thought that, in a scant matter of minutes, she was going to have everything she wanted. Well, almost. It was irritating that she was still living at home, and that they couldn't yet be a proper family, but, as Paddy had pointed out when she'd broached the subject of getting their own home, how could he be expected to sort their lives out from a prison cell?

But that was all about to change now. She'd take him home, make him happy, show him how beautiful his little daughter was, and he'd melt, she just knew it. He would melt.

Vicky hadn't, however, anticipated just how much *she*'d melt when she saw him. But, when the heavy doors finally opened and Paddy stepped out into the sunshine, the unexpected butterflies in her stomach momentarily floored her.

She had forgotten just how handsome he looked in his own clothes. Having only seen him for the last nine months in drab blue prison garb, she almost gasped at the enormity of the transformation. He was in his court clothes, as he would be. They'd been stored there since his arrival. The smart black trousers ('Look decent, that's the way, lad,' the solicitor had told him) and the same, then brand new, white cotton shirt.

He wolf-whistled extravagantly when he saw her. 'You scrub up alright, babes!' he called, almost shouted, waving, and then glancing back to see if the guards were still there watching. They were. And still were when he jogged the last yards between them, pulled her tight against his body, which felt hard and lean and masculine, and kissed her hungrily, pushing his tongue between her lips. 'I hope you've kept it warm for me,' he whispered when he stopped for air. 'I tell you, babe, I'm like a fucking dog on heat.' He grabbed her behind. 'Just you wait till I get you home.'

She was wanted. So wanted. It was all the welcome she needed. Her fears dissolved. Everything was going to be okay.

Chapter 16

Lucy felt a pulse of anger throb in her temple as she watched Vicky snivelling on her knees on the living-room floor. She was trying to change the baby, plopping tears on her belly, fannying around ineffectually with the square of towelling beneath her. 'Oh, fuck, Luce,' she sobbed. 'What the hell am I doing *wrong?*'

It was tragic to witness, but Lucy resisted the urge to help. Right now she wasn't even sure where her anger was directed. Was it at Paddy Allen, whom she'd just encountered out on the pavement? Who'd shouted, by way of greeting, 'And you can fuck *right* off, you bitch!' at her, before she'd so much as opened her mouth?

In part, yes, of course. She could slap him as soon as look at him. But it was also, she knew (which was why she had yet to answer) an anger she couldn't help but feel at Vicky. When the frigging hell were the scales going to fall from her eyes? How much more shit was the stupid cow prepared to take off him?

But the shuddering of Vicky's shoulders made her heart soften a little. She joined her on the carpet. 'Come on, you ninny, you know how to do this. Get a grip. You take this corner first, then ...'

'Not the nappy!' Vicky sobbed. 'I mean, with *Paddy!*'

What a long and rosy honeymoon it had turned out to be. Sweet, but, like her mam had always been fond of saying, like a chewed-up bit of toffee. It was like they were thirteen again, and mooning over some pop star. Except it was just Vicky doing the mooning, and it wasn't about a pop star. Just the same Paddy Allen as always.

It had been sweet to the point of setting Lucy's teeth on edge. He'd showered Vicky with presents. A leather jacket. Diamond earrings. A fake designer handbag. A bunch of lingerie from Debenhams, all black and red and satin – 'Ooh, isn't it gorgeous, Luce? Though why he's bothering, I don't know! He has it off me the second I put it all on!' And other similarly edifying gems.

Then the stuff for the baby. The ridiculously enormous teddy bear. The overpriced baby clothes she'd grow out of in a matter of weeks. The garish expanding silver bracelet she'd be saddled with for years. The money, the money, the money, the bloody money. Ironic, Lucy thought, as she looked at her friend now. The money and the attention had been almost like a drug to her. Yet she was blind to the drug-dealing it had come from.

It was sickening. Or rather had been. But there was no satisfaction in the knowledge that she'd known it wouldn't last. No pleasure in saying 'I told you so' to Vicky.

She sighed as she took over the nappy-changing duties. Perhaps this, she thought – the business of the crappy terry nappies – would be the straw that might break the camel's back. No more Pampers, it seemed. Back to basics for Paddy's baby. And all because he'd finally had to go out and buy some himself and, so appalled had he been at the cost of the things, he'd decided (unilaterally) that since Vic was no longer working – and that was another thing – old-fashioned wash-them-yourself ones would be henceforth good enough.

Vicky blew her nose as Lucy deftly fastened the clean nappy. 'He barely even looks at her these days,' she snivelled. As if it had been a year since he'd been out of prison, rather than just over a month. 'He's like Jekyll and Hyde all of a sudden, and he barely even *looks* at her. Just like that. Why? And the slightest thing sets him off. Just, like, *anything.*'

'Just like now,' Lucy said, rather than asked. 'So what was that about?'

'He called me a fat pig,' Vicky said, a touch of welcome defiance creeping into her voice now. 'I mean, the *bastard* – Christ, I'm back to a frigging ten! What more does he want?'

'He's insane,' Lucy said, holding back the urge to point out that only a week previously, according to Vicky's breathless, all-too-detailed account, he'd not been able to get enough of her assets. But it was something she really didn't want to dwell on.

'That's what I told him,' Vicky said. 'I told him if he didn't like what was on offer he should fuck off out the shop.'

'So he did. And you're stupid to rise to it. He only does it because he knows it winds you up, you *know* that.'

Vicky's eyes filled with tears again. She nodded miserably. 'But I can't help it.' Lucy wasn't sure if she meant her
weight or being wound up. 'And he told me if I didn't hurry
up and sort myself out he'd go and find someone else who
appreciated him!'

'For Christ's sake, mate,' Lucy said, scooping the baby up
off the rug, and wondering if she'd got stuck between the
pages of a teenage girls' magazine. 'He's a total bastard, and
it's him who needs to appreciate what he's got. You, for
instance. And he *knows* that. So don't take any bloody
notice. And as for this one' – she jiggled the baby on her
lap – 'she's such a cutie. I mean, look at her. How anyone
could blank her beggars belief. And that's bloody rich, that
is. The way he talks about her down the pub, you'd think
he was dad of the frigging year!'

If Lucy had thought this would endorse her dim view of
the bastard in question, Vicky's expression soon put her
straight. 'He does?' she said, her face brightening noticea-
bly. She got up off the floor and reached for a baby wipe to
wipe her face with, leaving Lucy to get Chantelle back into
her clothes.

And that was *another* thing, Lucy thought, as she turned
the baby's vest the right way out. This sort of thing was
becoming more and more of an occurrence – this letting
her take over anything Chantelle-related. Like her arrival
always equalled a temporary end to Vicky's shift.

It had been a shock the way Vicky seemed so happy to
let her do so much. Lucy had expected her friend to turn
out to be such a brilliant mother – and while her bastard

boyfriend was still banged up, she'd been doing okay. Yet it seemed Paddy, now he was out, was even getting in the way of that – claiming first place to their daughter's poor second. Lucy had already babysat her twice just this week, much to Jimmy's annoyance. But how could she not, when the alternative was being left with Vicky's mum – and her bloody cider – while the pair of them were out till God knew what hour?

She looked up to see Vicky had moved to the window, where she'd pulled back the net to peer out. Something snapped. 'For God's sake, Vic, get a grip, will you?' Lucy said. 'Look at you! Gawping out of the bleeding window, hoping he'll come back and grovel. Fuck him, Vicky! You told him to sod off and he has.'

Vicky turned around and Lucy held out the wriggling, cooing baby. She didn't take her. '*This* is the person you're supposed to be looking out for,' Lucy told her. 'Honest, mate, you've got to think about your priorities. Don't let him spoil this for you. Trust me, you'll regret it forever if you do.'

Vicky's expression hardened. 'Oh, like you know all about what it's like, do you? I've got enough on my plate without you lecturing me as well. And he's not going to spoil it. It's just hard this, *bloody* hard. For *both* of us, okay?' She took Chantelle from Lucy finally. 'But he *will* sort himself out. He *will.*'

'Oh, hello, love.' Lucy turned to see Vicky's mam in the doorway. Still in her nightie, despite it being gone three in the afternoon. She crossed the room, slumped into an armchair and lit a cigarette. 'Who will? Lover boy? I heard the door slam. He gone on the missing list again, has he?' Her laugh turned into a low, phlegmy cough. 'Fucking big man he is, that one. Does fuck-all for this one. Fuck-*all*.'

Lucy caught Vicky's eye; a familiar expression. Start her mam off and she'd never stop going on.

Which would help nothing. Only entrench Vicky even further into defending him. It was like her default position. To wail on and on about all the ways he wronged her, then when you agreed with her, to defend him unto bloody death. It was almost like he'd re-programmed her brain. 'He's nipped off about some work,' Lucy said, while Vicky put Chantelle back into her pram under the window. 'You reckon that bottle's cool enough now, Vic? Shall I go and fetch it for you? Or, I tell you what,' she said, seeing the way Vicky was glaring at her mam now, 'how about we head off for a walk in the park? Take it with us. It's much too nice a day to be stuck indoors.'

'Nice day?' Vicky's mam growled. 'What's that when it's at home? Not been a nice day since way back fucking when.'

'Don't start, Mam,' Vicky snapped as she snatched up the baby's bottle and her own cigarettes. 'Don't forget, when Paddy sorts our flat out, *I'll* be out of here as well. Just wait till you see how nice *that* is.'

They walked up to the park, mostly in silence, while Chantelle guzzled on her bottle, holding it firmly between her splayed chubby fingers. 'I'm sorry,' Vicky said suddenly, as they approached the park gates.

'For what?' Lucy said. There could be any number of things, after all.

'For saying what I did. I didn't mean it. Course you know what it's like. You're more of a mother to her than I am half the time.' She smiled ruefully.

'Forget it,' Lucy told her, even though she knew she wouldn't. 'Ice cream,' she said decisively. 'We need an ice cream. My treat.'

'I—'

'Don't you even dare bloody *think* it,' Lucy commanded. 'You're having a bloody ice cream and that's the end of it, you hear me? If he wants a twig for a girlfriend he should go to the bloody garden centre!'

Which made Vicky laugh, and, for now at least, the afternoon felt a little brighter.

Well, for a while at least. Because no sooner had they bought and eaten their ice creams than Vicky was already on about having to get home again.

'What?' Lucy said, gazing around her at the pretty sunlit park. 'Why? Back for what? What's the rush?'

'Because I'm supposed to be going *out*?' Again the hint of defiance in Vicky's voice. But this time directed at *her*. No, not so much defiance, as defensiveness, Lucy decided.

'Out where? Out with who?'

'Out with *Paddy*.'

Lucy stopped walking, wondering how she'd come to be pushing the pram. Not to mention wondering if she was going slightly mad. 'But you just told me you'd told him to sod off.'

'I know. I did.'

'But you're still going out with him.'

Vicky frowned. 'Luce, don't start.'

'No, come on. Explain it to me, will you? You're in floods because he's called you fat, and you've told him to sling his hook. Yet you're standing here telling me you're going out with him this evening. How does that work? Did you make up by telepathy, or what?'

'Luce, you know what he's like. He just goes off on one, doesn't he? Because he's stressed. So—'

'So he'll be back round to pick you up in that lurid bloody car of his and it'll be like nothing ever happened? Is that what you mean? Or, no—' She raised a hand to stop Vicky from answering. 'More like you'll get yourself ready just in *case* he comes calling. Mate, you're beyond help, you really are. I tell you what you should do, you should make sure you're *not* in, that's what you should do. Keep *him* on the hook, not the other way round.'

'Luce, it was just a silly tiff. They *happen*. Come on, let's not have a row about it, *please?*'

'Vic, I don't want to row with you, but can't you see how mad this is all becoming? Yes, tiffs happen. But don't you think you should stand up for yourself a bit? The way he talks to you …' She tailed off. What was the point in going on? They'd be straight back to the same place they always got to with Paddy. He'd wind her up, make her cry, Lucy would pick up the pieces. Then he'd be forgiven. Defended. And round they went again.

And the worst of it was that Lucy knew it would be

exactly as Vicky'd told her. That he'd turn up and sweet-talk her, possibly bring her flowers. And though her mam would scowl and moan, being left with the baby, off they'd skip to enjoy their Saturday night, Vicky with a gormless grin on her face.

'So where you off to?' she said, feeling bad all of a sudden, for the contempt with which she'd viewed this scenario. This was her friend, who was in a dangerously volatile rela-tionship, and did indeed have a lot on her plate.

'Not sure yet,' Vicky told her, a spring forming in her step now. 'Depends what sort of deal Paddy manages to do today.' She turned and smiled at her friend. 'He reckons he stands to make a few hundred pounds today if it all comes off, so we'll probably end up down town. Fingers crossed, eh?'

All these 'deals' being 'done'. All these 'bits of work', and things 'in the pipeline'. Lucy wondered at what point Vicky might actually wonder what any of those words actu-ally meant. Cars, that was the line. That it was all about the garage. And Vicky – knowingly? – didn't seem to want to know more.

And Lucy, a conspirator too, didn't ask her. Truth was she didn't ask because she didn't need to. He was back working for Mo. And doing overtime, by the sound of it. Recklessly so. She blew a raspberry at Chantelle, who'd just woken up, and reflected on the genes that were running round her veins. Paddy's genes, God help her. Lucy could only hope she didn't inherit his bloody arrogance. Anyone with half an ounce of sense would lay low for a while after being released from jail. Not Paddy Allen. He was all about – like the last nine months had never even happened. No, he was probably, at this very moment, either buying a load of cocaine, or selling it, or (and, increasingly, given the changes in his behaviour, this seemed highly likely) shoving it up his own nose in some town-centre pub.

She couldn't quite believe that Vicky was totally oblivious to that side of her boyfriend. Could she really be that naïve? Or did she just not want to know? She'd said herself that he'd turned into this Jekyll and Hyde character, but did it never occur to her to wonder why that was? The possibility that it might be down to drugs?

Because it *was* drugs. No question, however much he denied it. And deny it he obviously did, because the one time Lucy had ventured to suggest it, Vicky had looked at her as if she was crazy. Paddy Did Not Do Drugs. Total shut-down. Even angry. So it seemed there was nothing for it but she find out for herself one day.

As she would. Lucy knew this because Jimmy had told her. And not just Jimmy; she'd also heard stuff from one of the junior solicitors at work, who was friendly with John Cordingley, who'd been Paddy's solicitor. Paddy was, it seemed, on increasingly shaky ground.

It just needed time. 'Nice work if you can get it,' she said mildly. 'But what about you? Bet you're itching to get back to work now, aren't you? You know – having a bit more of your *own* money?'

Vicky shook her head, just as Lucy had known she would. Which was *another* thing. The fact that Paddy would rather she didn't work at all. She'd be completely dependent on him for everything then, wouldn't she? Which must not happen.

'Not particularly. I mean, I will, for now. But, you know, in the longer term. Once he's back on his way, with Mo's garage and that, Paddy will want to look after me, won't he?' Lucy thought that was pretty debatable. 'And his mam and dad are loaded. And it's not like I want much. Just enough.'

'And the odd Saturday night on the town,' Lucy said, realising that now probably wasn't the time to remind her friend that before Paddy came out of nick she'd been counting the days till she could get back to work. How things had changed. 'I suppose it's not a lot to ask, really,' she finished.

'Exactly,' Vicky agreed. 'Anyway, what are you and Jimmy up to?'

'Probably just a few drinks in Lidget Green,' Lucy told her. Jimmy didn't like going into the centre of town much. Too much risk of meeting up with some of the criminals his dad had collared. Or, probably worse than that, their mates.

Vicky sighed. 'God, I *so* wish we could all go out together.'

'I know, mate. So do I,' Lucy lied.

As far as she was concerned, anywhere Paddy Allen might turn up was exactly where she *didn't* want to go.

Chapter 17

There was no reason to suppose Lucy would be bumping into Paddy either. For one, she remembered the look on his face when she'd seen him, and clung on to the vain hope that he'd stand Vicky up and head into town with his dodgy mates instead. Anything to hasten the demise of a relationship that she knew in her heart no good could come of. And for two, the last place she expected to see him these days was the Oddfellows at Lidget Green.

But as they stepped through the door – propped open to allow in the evening sunlight – there he was, with his back to them, at the bar. She felt Jimmy's hand tighten around her own as she glanced around, but of Vicky there was no sign. So perhaps – the thought cheered her – she wasn't here?

'Let's just go somewhere else,' she whispered. 'I don't trust myself around him.'

She really didn't. She'd been brooding on it all the way back from Vicky's, wishing she'd chased after him before she'd even gone into the house, and given him as good as she'd got. But her thoughts, as ever, turned to the depressing reality that, just as with her trying to get Vicky to wake up to reality, every barb she slung at Paddy just gave him further encouragement for him to take her on – in the business of ownership of what he saw as his property. She wondered, as she always did, what kind of twisted mind existed beneath that head of piratical hair.

'*You* don't?' Jimmy muttered under his breath. 'Join the bloody club! Come on, we'll go across the road to the Second West instead.'

Too late.

'Jimmy D! Hey, my man, how's it going?' It was Vikram, Gurdy's brother, peeling away from a group near the door, his voice ringing out across the still half-empty pub. He clapped Jimmy on the back and winked at Lucy, like he always did. As if they shared some in-joke that was known only to them. She'd never quite understood why that was.

'We're just off, mate,' Jimmy said, but Lucy already knew it wouldn't happen, because just as he did so, Paddy Allen turned around to face them, and made a big show of leaning back, elbows on the bar. Which, of course, meant that no way could – or would – Jimmy leave.

Not now. And even as she braced herself to loyally tough it out, a part of her cursed stupid male pride.

Vikram clocked Paddy too, and studiously ignored him. 'Let me get you two a drink, yeah?' he said expansively, ushering them in. Then 'Good to *see* you' as if they never went out. But she knew it wasn't just because Vikram wanted to be generous. Yes, he was generous, always, and there was absolutely no side to him, and Lucy knew how much he appreciated their friendship with Gurdy. But it was more than that. Vikram didn't involve himself in the murky world Paddy Allen chose to swim in, so, happily, their paths hardly ever crossed. But he certainly hadn't forgotten Paddy's behaviour at his party, and nor would he. And Vikram wasn't scared of the likes of Paddy Allen. So to snub him in favour of Jimmy would be fun.

Too much fun, perhaps. Lucy really wished he wouldn't.

But it seemed Jimmy, now he'd adjusted, was perfectly happy to snub Paddy also, pulling Lucy along as they headed for the far end of the bar.

'We'll just stay for a quick half,' he promised, obviously sensing her displeasure. But even as he did so she could see the change coming; sense that all too soon, a drink in, he'd revise that decision – because to leave the pub they'd intended to spend the evening in, because of Paddy, would feel too much like cause and effect for him to stomach.

And as if to endorse her gloomy premonition, Lucy then saw Vicky appear from the ladies. So she was here after all.

Her expression when she saw Lucy was immediately apologetic. And for a moment Lucy wondered if her friend had actually engineered this. Persuaded Paddy to come to the Oddfellows specifically in the hope that she'd see them. But would she really be so stupid? So naïve? Surely not. It was a nice thought, that the four of them could co-exist in harmony, but if she thought it could ever happen she obviously lived in la-la land.

But no, Vicky didn't think that. Lucy could tell as she approached, in the way she was glancing at Paddy, who was now busy chatting to one of his cronies – but whose eyes never left her – as she skirted round tables so she could come and say hello.

Vicky pulled a face and mouthed 'Awkward!', and she looked it, as well. Saying a breathy hello to Jimmy, politely declining a drink from Vikram, and, despite looking so cool in a flowery skirt and crop top, putting a hand up to the flush that was blooming on her cheeks.

'We're not stopping,' Lucy told her as Vikram passed her and Jimmy their halves of lager. 'You off as well? You're looking nice. Still going to town?'

She had her back to the other end of the bar now – a conscious decision – but even as she was beginning to relax, listening to Jimmy and Vikram chatting, Vicky's anxious glance behind her told her trouble was coming.

And it soon arrived. 'On the halves?' It was Paddy's voice, loaded with derision. 'You'll be asking for some blackcurrant in the fucker next.'

Lucy turned around to find him next to her. So close that she could smell the musky aftershave he went for, and which would forever be unpleasantly associated with him. Had always been – she even used to catch it in Vicky's bedroom sometimes. He was like an animal, marking his territory.

And by the bucket load, judging by the strength of it. He grinned at her, and she decided he might already be on something. But one thing was certain – that his words had been for Jimmy, rather than her.

Thankfully, Jimmy simply ignored him. As did Vikram, who hadn't even bothered to glance around.

'Leave it out, babes,' Vicky said, her own voice high with tension. She'd almost made it sound like a question.

'Alright, Luce?' he said, shaking off Vicky's hand on his arm. He was definitely high on something, Lucy decided. A snort in the loos? A joint? Some sort of pill? Something, at any rate. The pub was flooded with light, but his pupils were huge. 'You out, then?' he asked, his gaze sliding up and down her front. 'Out for a night on the tiles with your *man*?'

And she just couldn't help it. It was the way he was leering. She just couldn't stop the words bursting from her mouth. Just the two words, but the wrong ones. 'I *was*.'

'Oh, you *was*?' he mimicked, looking delighted to be challenged. 'Sorry, love, did I say man?' He raised his voice a touch. 'What's wrong with a fucking pint?'

Now Lucy did clamp her mouth shut, conscious of silence behind her. But Paddy hadn't finished anyway. He put his own pint on the bar. 'Mind you, Vic,' he said, turning to Vicky and nudging her, 'pints are for *proper* men, aren't they?'

'Paddy, *shut* it,' Vicky hissed. 'Just bloody *shut it*!'

Paddy put his hands up as if someone had just trained a gun on him. 'Sorr-eeeee,' he said. 'But I'm only telling it like it is, babes. You know, how some men aren't *real* men, on account of firing blanks. Just saying, babes,' he finished. 'Just saying.'

Lucy heard an intake of breath and realised it was her own. She glared at Vicky. Stared at her, open-mouthed, appalled. How could she? How fucking *could* she?

But before she could so much as order her thoughts, she saw a hand reach out – Jimmy's hand – and Paddy's glass being raised aloft, and before she could stop it happening, even in its grisly slow-motion, watched Jimmy tip the lot over Paddy's head.

A flailing of arms, a bit of shoving and they were on the floor in seconds, making animal noises as they ripped into one another. She felt sick. Sick and helpless. Like she really was going to *be* sick. And above it all, across the tangle of bodies on the floor between them, she saw Vicky. Her so-called friend. Who'd betrayed her. 'How the fuck does he *know*?' she screamed at her above the din. 'How could you do that to me? Why the fuck did you *tell* him?'

The landlord and landlady were out from behind the bar now, pushing both girls aside roughly in an attempt to pull the lads apart and stop half the tables going over. Vicky was crying now. Looking lost. Like a princess out of a fairy tale. Looking like she didn't have a clue how it had happened. Lucy hated her.

'You fucking told him!' Lucy said again, still stunned at her disloyalty.

'I didn't mean to!' she sniffed, as the lads were hauled to their feet, both still growling at one another. 'I never thought. I only mentioned it when I visited once. Yonks ago. I was sad for you ...' She wiped the back of her hand over her eyes and smeared all her mascara. 'I didn't mean anything by it, *honest*. It just came out!'

'Well, fucking thanks for that,' Lucy said, looping an arm through Jimmy's, as, kicking and bucking, he was now being escorted from the bar by one of the older barmen, followed by the landlady. Paddy, she noticed, was being similarly encouraged to leave the premises, though by the back door, only with enough of an entourage that she at least didn't have to worry on that score. There'd be no danger of a resumption of hostilities out in the road. It wasn't that sort of pub, and she knew they'd like that to remain so. She hoped they'd give him a bit of a kicking, out of sight.

But Vicky. God, *Vicky*. What the hell had she been *thinking*? Was she really so thick that she didn't even consider how much of a gift something like that would be for Paddy? How much pleasure he'd get out of her and Jimmy's pain? Mr Cock of the Walk, strutting around, like he was some sort of god. *God*, he'd probably cherished that bit of news like it was a valuable bloody gemstone. Had probably been waiting so gleefully for a chance to bloody use it. And the worst of it, the very worst of it was that it wasn't even *true*. It was *her* who was firing the fucking blanks!

Yet Jimmy hadn't said a word to put the bastard straight. But then, why would he? He made his point using his fists. She grabbed his hands now and kissed his knuckles. Kissing them better. Tasting dust.

'I'm alright,' he told her, splaying them. 'See? No harm done.'

'More'n can be said for my front bar!' said the landlady. She was brushing dirt from her blouse with swift, irritable movements.

'Oh, God, I'm so *sorry*,' Lucy said. 'I'm so sorry. It was all my fault.'

'*What?*' Jimmy said. 'No it fucking wasn't!'

The landlady touched her arm. 'Don't worry. You're not barred, love.' Lucy hadn't even thought to ask her, but was grateful nevertheless. 'Neither of you,' she added. 'That little shit was bang out of order. I just can't be having a brawl on a Saturday night, can I? Come back another time, you'll be fine.'

'That's good of you,' Jimmy said, standing as if to attention and ploughing his wayward curls back. Reminding her so much of his father.

He was silent then, as they both watched the landlady go back in. Standing stiff-legged in the empty road. Like a statue.

'You alright, love?' Lucy asked him. 'God, Jimmy, I feel *terrible*.'

He turned and smiled at her. Full wattage. Like none of what had happened had even happened. 'Do you?' he said. 'I don't. That cunt had it coming. Has *got* it coming.' He put an arm round her waist and smiled again.

'But what he *said*. God, I can't believe she *told* him. God, I'm sorry.'

He put his other arm around her waist. 'You really think I give a fuck what that cunt says?'

'But it's not even true!'

'Exactly. So why worry?'

He seemed odd. Strangely fired up. Like he was *glad* about what had happened. 'Let's go home, shall we?' she said. 'To yours, maybe? My mam and dad are home tonight, or else …'

'Fuck that,' he said. 'I mean, not that.' He grinned and kissed her. 'I mean, let's save that for later. Come on, let's go and have a proper drink, shall we? Somewhere decent. Trust me, Luce,' he said, as they set off down the sunset-dappled street, 'I'll have the last laugh in all this, you mark my words.'

'You keep saying that,' she said. 'Why? *How?* What do you know that I don't?'

'Stuff you don't need to,' he said firmly.

Chapter 18

Paddy leaned across the unfamiliar single bed and reached for the girl's cigarettes. She was still sleeping, curled up foetally, with her back to him, her hair, long and blonde, half across her face. She looked doll-like and he wondered idly how old she was. He had some recollection that she'd told him last night that she was sixteen but, looking at the array of posters on her bedroom wall, he doubted it. Wanted to believe it, but doubted it even so. Oh, well, he thought, striking a match.

It was the smell rather than sound that finally woke her. She'd turned over in her sleep now, and wrinkled her nose like a rabbit. A young one. But Paddy remembered the old adage he'd learned from Mo: if they're old enough to bleed, they're old enough to slaughter.

He shook her shoulder, 'Hey, sleepy head, it's time to wake up.'

She stirred, pushing the sheet back. She was brazen, no question. Then she rubbed her eyes, rearranging the last of her eye make-up. 'Morning, Paddy,' she said, impressing him by remembering. 'What's the time?'

'Half nine,' he said, letting his gaze rest on her tits. Which were small, but beautifully formed. Not like Vicky's.

Who knew having a kid could wreak such fucking havoc? Like a pair of saggy watermelons, they were, these days. Christ – how long had it been since he'd seen a pair this perfect?

He felt a familiar twitch between his legs and wondered if he had time for a quick shag before getting off, but immediately dismissed it. Not only because with the daylight had come sobriety – and a tiny amount of guilt – but mostly because he had to get to the lock-up to meet Mo. 'So you're going to need to shift your arse. Duty calls. Tell you what, though, my mouth feels like Gandhi's fucking flip-flop. I could murder a cuppa tea.'

Obediently – and he did love an obedient woman – she pulled the sheet off all the way and swung her legs out and onto the floor, then picked up a white towelling dressing gown and shrugged it on. Again the twitch, and he did a quick mental calculation. Tea or shag. No, on balance, the tea. Not least because the robe had her name embroidered on it – Jenny, that was it – which felt a markedly adolescent thing to do.

'But just you be quiet, okay?' she told him as she carefully turned the bedroom door handle. 'My mam and dad like a lie-in on a Sunday and the last thing I need is *you* waking them up.'

Paddy put out his cigarette in the ashtray, which he'd rested on his chest, nestled among the ever-increasing thicket there. Prison had put hairs on his chest – and in more ways than one. That done, he put the ashtray back on the cluttered bedside table, got up and stretched, then walked naked and curious over to her desk, picking up various bits and bats to have a nosey.

And soon found the evidence, in the form of a school exercise book, on which was written (in small writing, in purple biro) *Jenny Froggatt, A3. Science.* Fucking third year! Jesus, the lying little cow! Still, if she was okay about bringing blokes home for a quick romp while her parents slept, then who was he to argue?

Not that he wanted to meet her father on the landing, so he dressed quickly and quietly, with special emphasis on the quietly. Two gulps of the tea and he'd be off, he decided. No point pushing the bit of luck that had brought him this bounty, after all.

And it had been an unexpected bit of luck, as well. The non-starter of the fight – well, that had been an amusing enough diversion, and it had been good to trade some punches with fucking Daley. But Vic blowing up like that – that had been entirely unexpected. What had she expected him to do with the knowledge she'd given him (and completely willingly, for that matter)? Forget it? As if. Or perhaps, in her stupidity, she thought he'd accompany the pair of them down the adoption clinic, going 'there, there'. Was that it?

So for her to kick off the way she had was disingenuous at best, pathetic at worst. And that was another thing – since when was that loud-mouthed bitch of a friend of hers more important than *him*? They were a fucking couple, for God's sake – fucking parents of a kid! It was high time she started thinking about her priorities. So there was a kind of justice in her going off on one and telling him to go and fuck himself – because it gave him carte blanche to go into town and do exactly that.

Still, the twitch in the loins of lust couldn't compete with the jab in the ribs of guilt. He downed half the tea the girl brought back up to him in two thirsty swallows, answering her question 'Am I going to get to see you again, Paddy?' with a kiss (on her head, not her lips – class A fucking 3!) and the whispered explanation that, lovely as she was, he reckoned his bird might have something to say about it.

She looked genuinely shocked. 'You've got a *girlfriend*? Well, what the *fuck* did you come home with me for?' she hissed.

He bent to kiss her head again, but she darted away crossly. He raised his hands in supplication. 'Love, you wanted a bit of the Padster, did you not? And I'm afraid I can't say no to a pretty face.'

He then pulled on his leather jacket, responding to her teary-eyed 'You can fuck off then' with an apologetic grin, and heading quickly (and again, quietly) down the tastefully decorated staircase, past the door to the kitchen (again, decent, fitted kitchen) and out of the door, reflecting that some girls never learned, did they? Give it up in a heartbeat, and you'll get your heart broken.

Christ, the thought of his own daughter shagging on demand like that … He closed the front gate and glanced up at the front bedroom window. No, he'd be a *much* better dad.

* * *

Realising he was in Great Horton – it had all been a blur, last night, really – put an extra spring in Paddy's step. He was near enough to the town centre to be able to walk in and grab a pint, before heading up to the taxi office and getting a cab to the lock-up on Manningham Lane.

He could give Vicky a quick ring from there as well. And as he walked, thoughts of conciliation soon resolved themselves into anger, so by the time he'd arrived at the Old Crown, he was not only unrepentant about making the most of the opportunity she'd given him (not that she'd ever know about it) but also increasingly of the opinion that what she most needed was a bollocking, both for giving him so much grief when he pretty much had to fucking *keep* her, and for showing him up in front of everyone in the bloody Oddfellows.

He got himself a pint, which went a long way to soften the hard edges of an increasingly nagging headache, then went to call her from the payphone. 'Oh, baby, I'm so sorry about last night,' she said immediately she answered the phone. 'I've been going mad here, not hearing from you. I'm really, really sorry. I was just so upset – I just hadn't thought about it – you know, Lucy and that, and having told you about her not being able to have a kid and everything – just completely forgotten, and she was so upset, and I just lost it. And it was my fault in the first frigging place. I shouldn't have yelled at you. I didn't mean to stomp off like that.'

Her tone of appeasement momentarily floored him. He'd been expecting a rant and was up for a fight. All so much neater if she was still in a rage. Put shagging Jenny the randy schoolgirl in the right moral box.

Still, he'd stick to his guns. 'Quite bloody right! It's not on, Vic. I'm getting sick of you mugging me off at the slightest fucking thing. I was like Billy fucking no mates in town on my own. Like a div. And I'm not fucking having it.'

'I know, babes,' she gushed at him. 'And I'm sorry, I *really* am. Anyway, you coming up now? So I can apologise to you properly?'

He was sorely tempted, even though he knew he absolutely couldn't. She was good value for money when she was feeling apologetic. And despite everything, she still had that *something* about her. He'd never known a girl quite so sinuous and biddable. Perhaps because he'd been the one to deflower her.

Such an odd word that, he mused, as he took a sip of his pint. Surely, when you thought about the mechanics of sex, it was a lot more about her flowering?

But she killed it dead. Started wittering about the baby. Again. Oh, you should have been here! She almost rolled over! I can't believe it! So early! And so on. He rolled his eyes. This was getting to be too much of a regular thing these days. Her on about the bleeding kid all the time, like she was some kind of genius. Babies were just that: bloody babies. They cried, they crapped, they drank milk, they slept. This one, as far as he could tell, was no different from any other. Like his dad used to say when his mam had some cousin or neighbour's kid over to babysit, 'Show me again once it can actually bloody *do* something.'

Still, she was now on about cooking dinner, and she was a half-decent cook, so the prospect of heading over there after doing his bit of business with Mo wasn't without an element of appeal.

'Right,' he said, 'I'll be there when the pubs shut in that case. About half three, but don't think you can get round me that easily. A roast dinner doesn't make up for last night, babe.'

'Brilliant,' she twittered, as if she hadn't even heard that, but then maybe she already knew the subject was closed now. That, even if she didn't realise why, they were square. 'And I'll put our Chantelle in that new pink dress that I bought her,' she went on. 'And I'll try to keep her awake till you get here.'

Paddy shook his head as he put the phone down. Our fucking Chantelle? What was she like?

'Bird trouble?' the barmaid asked as she pulled Paddy another pint. He was obviously giving off some sort of aura today, because she smiled at him provocatively and made a big show of leaning right across the bar in order to give it to him. And in a top that left little to the imagination.

'Could be if you don't put those threepenny bits away,' he told her, winking. She was at least as old as his mother, but firm-looking, and she probably knew a trick or two.

'In your dreams, gorgeous,' she replied, winking back.

It's a hard life, Paddy thought, as he gulped down half the second pint. So many birds and so little time. But Rasta Mo would be royally fucked off if he wasn't at the lock-up to receive the next load of coke, so no time for flirting. Not today anyway. This lass would have to go in his 'to do' book.

It was – and would never be – a good idea to mix booze, dope and coke. The unholy trinity, Paddy thought, feeling pleased with his invention, though less pleased with the state of his head, bones and muscles, which were now in a state of mutiny, and refusing to work as a team. Sod it, though, he thought as he pushed Vicky's gate open. It was a pay day that was worthy of a celebration, after all. Why do all that graft and take all those risks if you couldn't splash some cash around now and then? And it wasn't like he was mean with his good fortune either. Sure, he could be, but almost as good as the money was the look on folk's faces when he pulled his wad of cash out and bought drinks for anyone who he talked to.

Irish Pete called it pathetic, being flash with your money, and if Pete hadn't been Pete, he'd have given him a slap for fucking saying that. What did Pete know about him? His life? The things that mattered to him? What did he know about the importance of respect? Pete just didn't get it. And he probably *would* never get it. He wasn't trying to buy it, he was fucking earning it, wasn't he?

He was also pretty generous with the blow. And he always had a stash of ready-rolled joints for his special friends; the ones who made a proper fuss of him like he felt he deserved. The ones he could rely on. His family, if you liked – yes, he liked that. He closed the gate with a clatter and walked carefully up the path. He hoped the fucking kid was asleep.

'Paddy, your dinner's ruined!' was the first thing Vicky said. So her good mood hadn't stayed the course then.

'It's not half four yet!' he pointed out, having consulted his watch.

'Yeah, but that's like an hour since you said you'd be here, and everything's ruined. Bloody chicken, too, and all the trimmings, which I made specially for you. And now it's all dried up!'

'A bit like you then, you mardy cow,' Paddy slurred. He wasn't sure if her anger was a pain or a plus. On the one hand she could rant like a banshee when she was riled, but, on the other hand, it made her all the wilder in bed. 'Just give it here,' he said. 'I'll eat the fucker, for fuck's sake. I'm bloody starving, I am. I could eat a cardboard box. Anyway, where's the dragon?' he asked, following her into the tiny kitchen, all steamed-up windows and chicken smells and unwashed pots and pans.

'Bingo,' Vicky said, her back to him as she pulled the plate from the oven. 'Just left. Lucy and all. I think we're okay now, thank God.'

Paddy found himself sparking with sudden anger. 'What d'you mean "okay"? What the fuck have you got to apologise to *her* for? Seriously, Vic, have you only got one brain cell?'

Vicky lifted off the plate covering Paddy's meal with gloved hands. Her back was stiff. 'I wanted to apologise for *upsetting* her.' She turned around now. She'd put her hair up into some sort of clip, and bits of it clung to her temples and neck. She looked suddenly so much a woman. An adult. 'Pad, she didn't *know*, did she? I never told her I'd ever mentioned it to you. I'd pretty much forgotten myself, it was so long ago. So she was bound to be upset, wasn't she?'

Paddy took a step closer to her. The food, dried up though it might be, made his stomach rumble. And for some reason – the weed, perhaps? Probably, he decided – he couldn't really be bothered to have a fight with her. 'So what you're saying,' he said, 'is that you were apologising for *me*. For what I said to her cunt of a boyfriend.'

She blinked at 'cunt'. Then she shook her head. 'I was apologising for having told you in the first place. Because I shouldn't have.'

'Your girly secret.'

'Our girly secret,' she agreed.

'So that's the way it goes, is it? You two keeping secrets from me?'

'Like you don't?' She sounded defiant. 'Like what you're up to? Where you go? What you do at that lock-up with Mo?'

He'd half expected her to add 'Where were you last night?' to the list. But she didn't. So that was good. He couldn't help it, he smiled. Must be the weed. *Definitely* the weed.

'It's not funny,' Vicky said, her face crumpling, 'and what have you been taking? You're acting all weird.'

He laced both arms around her waist. She smelt, not unappealingly, of stuffing. 'Don't start,' he said mildly. 'I just think … I just think …' What *did* he think, really? 'I just think it's them …' he decided upon. Yes, that was it.

'Them?'

'Him and her. Laurel and fucking Hardy. We only ever row about *them*, don't we? When we bump into them, or about them, or anything to fucking do with them. And we shouldn't. We're supposed to be a *family*, aren't we? You, me and Chantelle. She asleep, by the way?'

Vicky nodded, looking bemused now. 'Just gone down.'

'So I just reckon,' he said, making a calculation about the dryness of his dinner, 'that we're better off out of it. Away from them. Completely. Away from *her*, that means. You get me? *Right* away. She might be your mate, babe – and I know you go way back, and fair enough, I respect that – but her fucking boyfriend is dangerous, you get me? To *me*. To *us*. To our *family*,' he added. 'So I really don't want her around my daughter, you know?'

She nodded again, meekly. My *daughter*. He could tell that had got her.

Vicky glanced out into the hall. The baby was probably kipping in her pram in the living room. So be it. Paddy let her go and popped the plate back on the other plate. Then slid it onto a shelf in the still-warm oven.

'Come on,' he said, taking Vicky's hand and tugging on it playfully. 'Let's nip upstairs for a quickie while the dragon's down the Mecca dotting her numbers.'

She tugged playfully back.

Easy as one, two, three.

It had turned out to be quite a productive weekend.

Chapter 19

Seeing Gurdy sitting in the corner of the Italian café on John Street gave Lucy a little pang of something she recognised as regret. She loved her job. Liked the people – even the toffs she thought she wouldn't like. She also loved the salary, loved the fact that she had prospects for a different, better future. But it still struck her, all the time, specially since Vicky'd decided to blank her, that she was moving up in the world, on in the world, but away from her friends. In Vicky's case forcibly, but in Gurdy's case not so; it was more like he was being dragged from her by an invisible thread. Part of the fabric of his increasingly different life now.

She waved then pushed the door open, glad he'd suggested the place he had. It had been a brisk walk from the office but at least the service would be quick. The owner was such an arsehole the staff couldn't be anything else.

She also brightened at clocking the pleasure on her friend's face in seeing her, and wondered how much he knew about recent events. He was like a radar for trouble – emotional trouble, anyway. She wondered if he'd seen anything of Vicky. Or just Paddy. She hated that he still worked for Paddy. Hated that he seemed increasingly to work for Paddy. And, by extension, that monster Mo. She wished he'd stop.

'What d'you fancy?' Gurdy asked her, hopping up as she sat down. 'I'm guessing you don't have a lot of time, yeah?'

He looked skinnier than ever, though he was wearing an expensive-looking shirt.

'Just the hour,' she said, 'thank you. And just a plain omelette and salad, and a diet Coke,' she added, undoing the zip on her handbag to get a fiver out.

Gurdy pulled a face. 'Sure?' he asked, dubiously. She nodded. 'And don't worry about it,' he said. 'Lunch is on me today.' He patted his back pocket and then burst into un-self-conscious song. 'Moolah, moolah, moolah!' he warbled, rubbing finger and thumb together. 'Is a rich dude's world!'

Lucy couldn't help but laugh. Gurdy had this way of making everything seem better, and she felt momentarily guilty that her main reason for phoning and asking him if he fancied lunch was so that she could unburden herself about Vicky and bloody Paddy – whom she knew was behind everything – by dumping all her murderous thoughts on him.

Not that she was stupid – he probably knew that only too well. Almost definitely, according to Jimmy, who'd bumped into him earlier in the week, when his first question had apparently been, 'How's Lucy?'

Gurdy was back in moments. They'd done well to get in before the rush. He announced he'd ordered a burger and chips, as if to a waiting audience. 'If they could see me now …' he sang as he took his seat again, and handed her a can of Coke.

'If who could?

'Mummy and Daddy, of course,' he said, grinning. 'Christ, you'd think I was murdering a fucking cow in front of their eyes if they copped me eating that sort of stuff.'

'Must be odd, that,' Lucy commented, wishing she'd done the same now. Did it really make that much difference to her prognosis, all this healthy eating lark? Was there any science in it? She wasn't sure. It wasn't like she normally ate like a pig, was it? All she knew was that it didn't make her feel any better, and a lot of the time – now, for instance – it just made her feel sad. She didn't want to be thin and sad, she wanted to blossom with fertility.

Gurdy looked at her quizzically. 'Odd?'

'You know, having all this stuff you're not supposed to eat.'

'Could be worse,' Gurdy said. 'Could be a Muslim, couldn't I? No bacon sarnies then. Now that really *would* be torture.'

True to form, the food arrived in less than five minutes and as they started eating, having dispensed with the usual catch-up pleasantries (yes, work was fine, no, he hadn't yet found a boyfriend) she launched straight into how Vicky had dumped her.

'Well, I say dumped – it wasn't quite like that. More "just best if we don't see each other at the moment, because it's coming between us". As in her and that bastard. And how she had to realise where her priorities lay now. I mean, fucking hell, Gurdy, when is she ever going to see him for the control freak he is? He is *such* a bastard!'

'That lunch of yours doesn't look any too pretty either,' Gurdy observed, pushing his plate closer to her. 'Go on, help yourself to some chips before you die of salad poisoning. And, erm, not anytime soon, I reckon, don't you?'

Lucy leaned forward. 'Look, I know you're stuck in the middle of all this, mate, but has he said anything to you? Only I keep veering between one thing and the other. Do I keep trying to speak to Vic? Or her mam? She can't stand him. Or do I speak to Paddy?'

'You're seriously thinking of doing that? What would *that* achieve?'

'Oh, I don't know … I just keep thinking of the baby … What's happening with her now? How the hell is Vic managing without me to help with the childcare? I just, oh, I don't know … I just can't do nothing, can I?'

Gurdy put down his burger and wiped his mouth delicately on his paper serviette. 'He'd love that, of course.'

'Who, Paddy?'

Gurdy nodded. 'It's like a game to him, you and Vic.'

'Well, that's clear enough …'

'No, I mean, in keeping you apart. He likes winding you up. I reckon he likes winding you up more than he likes winding *her* up. Because he fancies you.'

He sat back, clearly pleased with his little bit of detective work. Lucy was tempted to tell him he was talking rubbish. It wasn't the sort of thing she wanted to articulate – definitely not the sort of thing she'd like said around Vicky. But there was no getting away from the fact that it might be true. To a point. She'd make a good scalp. A good notch on his bedpost. He was such a shit.

She said so. 'Not to mention the fact that he also hates me.'

'They reckon there's a thin line between love and hate, Luce,' Gurdy said. 'It's not just that you're with Jimmy – though that's obviously a part of it. No, I think Paddy hates you because he knows he can never have you. And he's used to getting what he wants, or who he wants, *when* he wants.'

All of which Lucy knew to be true. 'Hark at you, with all the philosophy,' she said. 'Anyway, I'm sorry to drone on at you. I just feel so frustrated at having to stand by and watch my mate – *our* mate – fuck her life up with that twat.'

'But you have to, you know,' Gurdy said, his expression suddenly serious.

Lucy took a couple of chips. Why the hell hadn't she ordered chips? Like their absence would make everything, anything, okay.

Gurdy pushed the plate further towards her, clearly stuffed full with his burger. 'I mean it. Keep away from Paddy, obviously. But keep away from Vicky as well. Let her go with it.'

'Go with what?'

'What he's telling her to go with. Cutting you out—'

'I should bloody say so! Well, we'll just have to see how well that works out. Mr fucking perfect family – yeah, right. Let's see how that goes when he doesn't have muggins here to palm his precious daughter off to, eh?'

'Exactly. But, seriously, you just be there when it all goes tits up. Because I can assure you it will.'

It was like talking to Jimmy all over again. 'Gurdy, come on, out with it. What do you know that I don't?'

He shook his head. 'Nothing. Well, no more than you, I don't reckon. Only that he's different since he came out of jail. Really different.'

'Oh, like he's a big hard man now he's been inside?' Lucy asked, sitting back and rolling her eyes. 'Typical Paddy! Big-time gangster now, is he, eh?'

'No,' Gurdy said quietly. He really did look pretty serious. 'I don't know how much Jimmy tells you, Lucy, and I know I still earn from Paddy – and, to be honest, I daren't get out of it now. He'd go fucking ballistic if I tried, but he's like really fucking scary these days, mate. Mixing all sorts of drugs, always on the ale … honest, he's like a wild fucking animal most of the time, I swear.'

'I know, but that's same old same old, isn't it? This is Paddy big I am Allen we're talking about, after all.'

'No, seriously, it's worse than that. None of the other lads in town – the *normal* ones – will have anything to do with him these days. It's like he's a time bomb, waiting to go off.'

Lucy put down her knife and fork and plucked another serviette from the holder. She felt suddenly markedly more ill at ease. 'Gurdy, Jimmy tells me all kinds of stuff. Most of the time I'm not interested in what that prick does, as you know, but if you know what's good for you, you really should knock it off working for him.'

Gurdy sighed. 'I wish.'

'Look,' Lucy went on, 'I know you're saving for your future, and I'm glad you've kept me out of it, but honestly, Gurdy, the cops aren't far behind him – you do know that, don't you? And I'd hate you to get done with him when it all goes down. Christ, mate – you in prison. It doesn't bear thinking about.' He opened his mouth and gave her a lop-sided grin. 'And no jokes about bloody boyfriends, okay?'

Because it really was no joke. She had no idea how deeply he was into the shit Paddy Allen was – in an ideal world, only very little. And, God, wasn't life so unfair? He shouldn't even be doing anything for Paddy – shouldn't be doing anything illegal, full stop. And look at Vikram – doing so well for himself. The golden boy. Getting on. And all the while, poor Gurdy had led such a shitty life – forced to work in the family business, forced to be the good son … not to mention getting beaten by his dad if he refused to conform. She could so see how the money he made from Paddy mattered to him. It was going to be his ticket to a better legal life. But was it? Might it be his 'Go to Jail' card instead? Jimmy'd not said so, but he didn't know everything, did he? They might be sitting here, discussing what a shit to Vicky Paddy Allen was, when the greater victim might be Gurdy himself, swept along with Mo and Paddy when the police floodgates opened – straight into prison. And she really couldn't imagine how Gurdy would cope in prison.

'Surely you've saved up enough now to sort your life out and get away from him?' she said. 'Surely? I mean, how much can you need?'

'A thousand pounds,' Gurdy came back, in a heartbeat. 'That's all. My cousin has a curry shop in Leeds and he said I can buy into his place once I've enough. And once I have another grand, I can, and I will.' He grinned. 'I'll be gone like a bat out of hell, mate – just like Meat Loaf. I just need another grand or thereabouts, and I'm gone. I promise.' He reached across and grabbed her hand. 'I promise. First curry on me.'

If he got out before DI Daley and his team closed in. In comparison her and Vicky's spat mattered little. If she'd had a thousand pounds she would have given it to him there and then.

Chapter 20

Jimmy Daley was having a rare Saturday afternoon drinking session with his mates, and was making the most of it. It wasn't often he had the chance, as he was more often than not working, but with his apprenticeship soon going to be nearing its end, he was keen to do however many hours needed doing – the firm he worked for, Flowstar, were an up-and-coming plumbers, and there could be a good job with his name on at the end of it.

But today wasn't just about time with the lads – it was also an afternoon of celebration. Bradford City had scored a hat-trick in their first match of the season, and, as the previous season they'd only just escaped relegation by a whisper, the whole town were naturally elated.

And Lucy, bless her, hadn't minded at all. 'Go on,' she'd said. 'Go and celebrate, love, and have a drink for me too. I'm happy enough stopping in with Mum and Dad tonight, *really*. And you deserve it, love.'

She was a top bird, no question.

Even so, after the first two or three (or was it four?) pints, he'd begun to waver. However brave a face she put on things, Lucy was in a sad place, he knew that. Specially since Vicky – fucking shame on her – had completely cut her out, and she wasn't even getting the chance to mind the baby.

He wished she'd get it. Understand that he really didn't *care* about the baby stuff. That when the time came, they'd find a way round it together. And it wasn't like the doctor had even said 'never, ever'. Just 'unlikely', which wasn't the same thing at all, as his mam had kept saying. So he'd rung her again – it was an emotional kind of day, after all. And she'd called him a wet and told him to piss off and have a drink for her, and, since he could hear her dad in the background, laughing, he decided to do as he was told and stop worrying. Just celebrate and get pissed with his mates.

He was just emerging from the little corridor where the payphone was when he heard his friend Kenny calling. 'C'mon, lightweight!' he shouted through the din at the Belle Vue. 'Jimmy! Down that pint, mate – we're making a move.'

'Fuck off!' came the response from another mate of his, Jackie. 'I paid twenty fucking pence to get in here, if you don't mind. At least wait till I get my fucking money's worth!'

Which he was, and pretty much had been since they'd first tumbled into the place, particularly now, when the nearest barmaid – topless, just like they all were – was busy emptying and cleaning ashtrays on the adjacent tables.

It was another ritual in Bradford, post-match. You watched the footy, had a bit of agro with any daring opposing fans down Manningham Lane, and then you started off your Saturday afternoon session at the Belle Vue, where topless barmaids served your beer and a topless DJ played the records.

Not that Jimmy had any qualms about leaving. Better that than still be in when 'The Ointment' lads came in. Win or lose, they were the sort of die-hard footie fans (or more accurately, football hooligans) who didn't think they'd had a good day until they'd spilled blood in some form. Jimmy's dad would go mental if he got caught up in any of that shit. Once a copper's son, always a copper's son.

'Where we off next?' Jimmy had to yell over the swell of cheers and whistles. The strippers – another part of the attraction of the place – had just started climbing up on the filthy stage.

'Haigy's,' Kenny told him as they made their way to the exit doors – another pub, on Lumb Lane, which would be filled with the claret and amber of Bradford City fans, though the landlady who ran it wouldn't stand for any shit, so it was a safe bet that there wouldn't be any trouble. Which suited Jimmy just fine.

But by the time they'd done in there – there was only so much of the landlady-friendly sobriety a young lad could stomach – the night was still young and the party, which had grown with every pub they'd stopped in, moved inexorably towards town and the Boy and Barrel – this not least because they always put free pie and peas on on match days. Good for soaking up the pints of post-match beer.

The only bugbear was that the Boy and Barrel was one of Paddy Allen's usual haunts, and even with the beer on board (in fact, perhaps because of it) a run-in with him was the last thing he was looking for. In fact, the further away he stayed from Allen right now, the better.

'Sorry, mate,' he said to Kenny as they approached the noisy pub. 'I think I'll pass on going in there. You know how things are.'

'Paddy Allen?' Kenny said. 'You've no need to worry on that score. Didn't Jackie tell you back in Haigy's? He's banged up again, you silly twat.'

'Banged up?' Jimmy looked at him, shocked. Then shook his head. His dad hadn't said anything, and he definitely would have. 'Nah, mate,' he said. 'Not anymore. He got out just over a month ago.'

Kenny scratched his head. 'No, I'm sure he is. Ask Jackie. Was him who told me. Banged up again. I'm sure of it. Yesterday. Even this morning perhaps, come to think of it. Honest, mate – go and ask him. Sure I'm right. Get you a pint?'

It didn't take long to pin down the informant in question, and even as he did so, Jimmy wondered what the hell was going on. He'd been with his dad just before the football. Surely he'd have told him?

'Aye, he is,' Jackie confirmed. 'Or so your little Paki mate said, anyway. Whatshisname. Ghandeep, or summat?'

'Gurdip Banerjee?'

'That's the one. Saw him at half-time. In the pie queue.'

'And what did he say?'

'That it was an undercover cop that nicked him. Dunno what kind. You'll know more about that than me, obviously. In the Old Crown, not long after opening, trying to sell some dope or something. To the wrong bloke ...' He laughed. 'Can you fucking imagine? Wish I'd been there. Anyway, he busted him and had him carted off to the cells. He'll be there till Monday now, I imagine. You know, for court. So nothing to worry about. Sorry, mate. Assumed you knew. Top result, eh?'

Kenny arrived with drinks then, but, as the other two were absorbed back into the group and talk returned to the football, Jimmy stood apart, in a quandary. On the face of it, yes, it *was* a top result. Nice to see the sod behind bars again. But, on the other hand, he knew something the others definitely didn't know. And couldn't. And he was more certain than ever that his dad didn't know about this. Or at least hadn't when it happened. He might by now, of course. But should he assume that? No, he shouldn't. He popped his pint on top of the jukebox and slipped away to use the phone box up the street.

It smelt rank, and he popped the door open with one foot. 'You are kidding me,' his dad said. 'Christ, I hope you've got this wrong, son! Are you 100 per cent sure about the facts? Have you checked with anyone else?'

Jimmy hadn't. And he said so. Because there was absolutely no need. 'Dad, I'm telling you, it's fact. It's come from Gurdy, and he'd know.'

'Gurdy?'

'Gurdip. You know, Luce's friend, Gurdy. Does stuff for Allen.' They almost never called him Paddy; that would imply a measure of respect. 'Arrested this morning for dealing apparently and currently held down at Bridewell.'

'Shit,' his dad said. '*Shit.* Okay, Bye.'

Then he'd rung off – proper banged the phone down – presumably to hot-foot it back to work. To update his own team, whose efforts had now been so compromised. Or most likely, anyway. How had *that* happened?

'I thought your dad would have been pleased,' Lucy said, looking confused.

Jimmy had gone straight back to hers after speaking with his father. He'd only nipped back into the pub briefly to say goodnight, knowing he'd probably be missed. But he needn't have bothered, he'd decided, as he took a quick sip before abandoning his pint. Everyone, by now, was too pissed to even see straight, let alone notice he'd disappeared.

'You don't understand, Luce,' he said, pacing her living room now, still too wired to sit down. He was glad her mam and dad had gone to bed. 'My dad was proper angry. Proper furious,' he went on. 'You don't realise. That undercover cop – whoever he is – might just have fucked everything up for them.'

'Everything as in what?' she said, patting the space on the sofa beside her. 'Jimmy, tell me. I need to know what's going on!'

He sat down. Took her hand. Could he trust her? Of course he could. In almost all things. In everything that mattered to the two of them, at any rate. But there was still Vicky to be figured into all this. Vicky, who'd already shown herself to be a far cry from the loyal friend she'd always purported to be. She'd gone running to him, hadn't she? About Lucy. Had betrayed her confidence. Caused all that trouble. He found it hard to forgive her for that.

And Lucy understood that. She clearly knew only too well why he felt so reticent about discussing *anything* to do with that bastard Allen with her.

'Babe, look, I know how much you love Vicky – and I wouldn't want to change that – but that prick, well, he needs locking up and the key throwing away.'

'Course I know that. And I can't wait for it to happen, believe me. And now he's been dealing drugs again, he'll get put away again, won't he? He's on some sort of probation deal, after all, isn't he? Isn't that how it works? That he's got to keep his nose clean for twelve months or they'll sling him back inside again? I'm sure Vic told me that's how it usually works.' She raised her brows at his continued silence. 'Well, isn't it?'

'Yes, in theory,' he said. 'But not in this case. Not if my dad's doing what I imagine he is.'

'Which is what, exactly?'

'Making sure they let him go. Well, if the whole thing isn't already fucked up, which it might be. Fingers crossed I'm wrong. Fingers crossed he's already back down the pub.'

Lucy looked shocked. '*What*? That can't be right, Jimmy. Why on earth would your dad do that? He bloody hates Paddy!'

'Oh, you have no idea how much.' Decided, he took her other hand. 'Okay, so here's how it goes. And you must tell this to no one. And I mean *no one*. Seriously, Luce. You mustn't.' Then he proceeded to explain to her the extent of the task force who were involved in the operation. All working, as they had been, over many laborious months, to pull the plug on Rasta Mo's little drugs empire. Which had turned out to be bigger than anyone had imagined, and worth a considerable amount – an eye-watering amount – of money. And, of course, it meant Paddy would be tugged for it too, him being one of the main dealers.

'But that's not even the half of it,' Jimmy explained, keeping his voice low. Lucy's parents slept like babies – on other kinds of Saturday nights, it was one of their greatest virtues – but you never knew. 'There's also the prestige car business. Which is a huge operation. They steal them here and in Leeds and take them south to be sold. And Allen's always been a huge part of that too.'

He thought of the bastard's Capri and how much he looked forward to seeing him deprived of it. This time permanently, hopefully, because it would rot before he was out. 'Oh, I *see* ...' Lucy was saying. 'So this is some lone wolf who thought he was doing his good deed for the day but might mess it all up for them. That it?'

She was bright, was his Lucy, as well as beautiful. 'Exactly,' he told her. 'They're not quite ready to make the arrests yet. If they pre-empt things, i.e. don't have all the loose ends tied up, every scrap of evidence in place, the whole lot of them could walk away.'

'Or get off on some more minor charge?'

Again, Jimmy nodded. His father had told him that most of the evidence had been gathered, and the surveillance, over many months, had paid rich dividends. But this stupid undercover cop – who obviously had nothing to do with the task force and no idea who he'd been collaring – could have now put the whole thing in jeopardy.

'So they'll release him, just like that?' Lucy asked.

'That's the hope,' Jimmy answered. 'And perhaps they already have.'

Lucy pondered for a few moments. 'But won't Paddy wonder why?'

Jimmy shook his head. At least on that score he was reasonably confident. 'Will he fuck!' he said. 'Allen? The lad's that fucking arrogant that he'll walk out of the nick laughing at *them*, probably.'

'You think?' she said. She didn't sound convinced.

But Jimmy was. 'I *know*. He'll just assume it was lack of evidence. That's what they'll spin him, and he'll believe them, no question. You know what he's like. He'll just think he's got away with it. *Again*.'

Chapter 21

Paddy still couldn't quite believe his luck. Not even properly dark yet and here he was sauntering blithely into Arthur's Bar, like the events of the day hadn't even happened. Except the other unreal thing – which was truly amazing – was that he'd even talked a fucking copper into dropping him off on Manningham Lane. After everything. Unbe-fucking-lievable.

He needed a drink. He needed a big snort of coke even more. They'd let him go, but they hadn't sent him on his way with his gear. That would have been a miracle too far.

More importantly, feathers would have been ruffled. He'd been pulled and that was bound to have got about. Bloody everywhere by now, probably, specially with everyone being in town for the fucking football. And there'd be serious concern from those in the thick of things about the implications. So his first job was to track down Rasta Mo. Because just as he couldn't quite understand why the police had let him go, he knew Mo would need to be reassured. Be properly convinced that it was only his own personal gear he'd been caught with, even though it hadn't been. That Mo's gear was all hidden away, safe.

It was busy in the bar – there were few days when it wasn't. But whereas most of the local pubs were full of regular lads out on the town, Arthur's Bar had a more select clientele. Prostitutes and their pimps, drug dealers and assorted junkies – these were the regulars in Arthur's. Yes, you'd get the odd group of young lads wanting to impress each other by buying their first spliffs, but they were fodder as much as anything – specially the hooray-Henry types, who were sport. Mo enjoyed selling spliffs to them containing nothing more sinister than a few herbs for top whack, then would laugh as they pratted about, thinking they were stoned.

Paddy didn't imagine Mo would be laughing this evening, and was relieved when he located him where common sense had already told him he would be – tucked away in one of his 'offices'. In fact, a secluded corner of the main lounge/public bar, where he was sitting smoking, and sipping a glass of the dark rum he favoured, the rings on his hand winking a hello.

He was alone. Paddy wasn't sure if that was a good thing or a bad thing. 'Mo, mate,' he said, by way of greeting, keeping his limbs loose, his demeanour light. 'Don't worry, it's okay. All sorted. Nothing to worry about.'

'Oh, is that so?' Mo asked, putting both glass and cig down and blowing out a thin stream of smoke. He got up and then he grinned. But then, Mo always grinned. It meant nothing. He grinned when he was yanking your arm up your back, or stubbing out a cigarette on your knee.

Paddy spread his arms. 'I'm here, aren't I? Course it's okay.'

Mo's teeth were so white that they almost seemed to illuminate the dark space he'd been sitting in. He raised a hand, languidly, but with intention and precision, clamping it firmly around the stubble on Paddy's chin. 'So, tell me,' he said, 'there's *nothing* to worry about then, boy, no?'

Paddy clocked the emphasis he'd placed on the word 'boy'. Not to mention that his jaw was now gripped in what felt like a vice. The kind they often used down the garage. He had seen this side of Mo more than once and it wasn't pretty. He also spotted the familiar coked-up glint in his boss's eyes. He obviously already knew about Paddy getting the tug.

'It was just a little fuck-up that's all, Mo,' he said, as lightly as he could, given the physical constraints. He didn't try to pull away though. That was not what you did. But at least they were relatively hidden, away from prying eyes. This wasn't the sort of thing that was a good look for him, after all. He was supposed to be Mo's right-hand man – well, at least one of them. Not one of his joeys. 'If you've heard the full story, you'll already know,' he went on, trotting out even though he knew it wasn't true. 'That fuck-up of a copper really messed everything up. He never read me my rights, for one thing – and it was him that approached *me* for the blow. He's had a right doing for it, and it'll have done us a favour, won't it?'

'Will it?' Mo asked, the hand still firmly in place.

'Course it will,' Paddy said, trying to appear confident while the grip of Mo's fingers told him he should feel anything but. But if he stuck to his line, everything would be cool. 'Because now they'll have to back off from me for a bit, won't they? I've told them, too. I'll have them done for fucking harassment if there's any more of it. Told them good. I swear down, Mo. No worries.'

Mo released Paddy's chin and gave him a friendly slap on the arm before sitting back down on the wooden chair he'd just vacated.

'This had better be all it is,' Mo said. He pointed his finger at Paddy. 'And if any bizzies come sniffing my way, boy, I know where to come looking, you get me?'

Paddy nodded, relieved that his grilling was apparently over. He felt shaky, almost, and realised he'd eaten nothing since early that morning. And only then some shit cereal before he'd taken Vicky to work. He shouldn't have let her persuade him to stay over there, bottom line. Should have gone the fuck home – the baby'd kept him awake half the night anyway – then he wouldn't have dropped Vicky, and probably wouldn't have told Gurdy he'd meet him in the Crown to pass on the bent ten pound notes that needed delivering to a house up Holme Wood. He'd have more likely gone straight to the lock-up and met Gurdy there, and none of this weird shit would have happened.

Cause and effect. Funny how it sometimes worked out. Funny and baffling. 'I promise you, Mo,' he said. 'There's more chance of them cunts catching fucking Lord Lucan than they've got of nabbing me.'

He hesitated a moment, as Mo picked up his drink again. Dare he even suggest it? Why not, he decided. Ride his luck for a bit. Where was the harm? And a show of balls could only help his current situation, couldn't it? 'Now then,' he said, affecting a cockiness he didn't feel. 'I know I've got a bit of coke and the pills and that up at the lock-up' – and, boy, did he need some – 'but have you got any more gear you want me to shift? I thought I might as well get a good bit of work done while them lot down the nick are still licking their wounds.'

Mo nodded. 'Some Charlie and some brown coming in about ten minutes, if you want to have a go at that,' he said. He flicked his head slightly, his dreadlocks swaying either side of his head, like a pair of curtains. Or one of those bead blinds people hung off their kitchen doors. 'You can meet Pete round the back if you're up for it,' he finished.

Paddy nodded, both shocked and relieved. 'I'm definitely up for it.'

'Then on your way, and get it out of here.'

Paddy smiled as he shook Mo's big hand. It was over. And fucking heroin! He was *definitely* back in the good books, then. He'd never been involved in the movement of heroin before, but now it looked like Mo was trusting him to go up a peg in the pecking order. God, from worrying he'd get a pasting to promotion in a matter of minutes. What the fuck did *that* mean? He wasn't sure. You never knew where you really were with Mo. But right now, he chose to take it at face value, and make the most of it. It meant he was back in the fold, and was sure of a big earn if he played his cards right. What a peculiar day this was turning out to be. From a spell down at Bridewell to being entrusted with a consignment of the brown stuff. Unbelievable.

An hour later, having cut the cocaine and bagged what he needed, Paddy was walking down Manningham Lane towards town, feeling high. He'd buried the precious heroin, and had sampled sufficient of the coke stock to be able to chase most of the anxiety away. The malt whiskey was doing its job too, courtesy of Irish Pete, and while the question about what had happened and *how* it had happened was ever-present, Paddy once again felt strong enough to deal with it.

But how the fuck *had* it happened? That was the main thing that concerned him. How come a random cop would just walk up and try and score off him? It was almost as if he'd been watching him, trailing him, waiting to be at the right place at the right time for his moment. How else would he have known where he was going to be?

Chance. That was possible. But it didn't stack up. It had been nagging at him from the moment the sergeant had told him he was free to go, just as he was preparing himself for being slung in the cells, and expecting all kinds of shit to rain down on him come Monday.

And it was nagging at him because the arrest had been conducted to the letter. He did have his rights read and he'd been caught bang *to* rights. Every box ticked, right down to the gleeful expression the plod couldn't wipe from his greasy, self-satisfied face. Yet they'd let him go. Let him off with a fucking caution! It had all happened so quickly that he couldn't quite remember exactly what he had on him, but no way was it little enough that they'd let him off with a fucking caution. Not even with the bollocks the sergeant had told him about 'initiatives' and amnesties and all the rest of that shit.

No, now he could think straight – now the coke was sharpening his mind as well as his reflexes – he couldn't help but think that it had all been a little too simple. Who the fuck got arrested, bang to rights, cuffed and dragged off to the nick, only to be released a few hours later with a full apology?

Not the likes of Paddy Allen, he decided. The Paddy Allens of this world didn't get so lucky. And certainly not when they'd already made the acquaintance of Armley nick. Something was amiss, and the more Paddy thought about it, the more he was sure it was part of some bigger plan. To spook him, or maybe frame him – but then why let him off again? Or, and the thought sent a chill down his spine, perhaps they'd let him off, let him out, because they were *using* him, to get their hands on Mo.

He entered the Boy and Barrel – down to its last dregs and, conversely, plenty of likely business – and ordered a pint and a whisky. Then he brooded on events, speaking to no one. And no one approached him either. But then why fucking arrest him in the first place? What was all that about? He kept running it round and round his brain but it didn't make sense. Why fit him up just to let him go?

But the biggest question – the one that was really beginning to make him angry – was who'd helped them? What had led that copper to be in that place at exactly that time? Because someone *had* to have helped him. Jimmy Daley?

And who was the hotline to Jimmy fucking Daley? That bitch, Lucy Briggs. But he thought that unlikely. Vicky wouldn't dare cross him on that score. So who else? His little Paki lapdog, Gurdip Banerjee? He drained his whisky, feeling the heat trace a path down his gullet. Gurdip, whom he'd fixed up to meet at the Crown. Gurdip, who'd changed since he'd come out of prison.

And who'd been around the pair of them, no doubt, in his absence. Thick as thieves with fucking Daley, no doubt. Gurdip, who'd changed. What the fuck was going on with him? Creeping. Obsequious. Irritating. *Weird*. What the fuck might be going on there?

He drained his pint in another swallow, and, the coke sales temporarily forgotten, banged it back down on the bar and stalked out.

Chapter 22

Gurdy was in a jovial mood. No, he wasn't the biggest football fan in the world – in fact, he wasn't a football fan at all, truth be known – but there was something about the atmosphere on a match day in Bradford that made you forget your cares, feel magical, feel reckless.

He was feeling reckless now.

It was getting on for ten and he'd returned to the Old Crown – scene of Paddy's being pulled by the plain clothes copper. Not that Gurdy had witnessed it. By this time he'd been off in his Mini to Holme Wood, feeling scared – this was dealing with a whole other breed of people – but at the same time euphoric to be entrusted with moving Mo's cash around, and being deemed ready to be moved up in the pecking order.

It made no difference. Gurdy was still busy plotting his escape. He'd even made the trip to Leeds to visit the curry shop for himself. And though his cousin wasn't a favourite (he was a few years older than him and had an 'all work and no party' ethic reminiscent of his mother and father) Gurdy's excitement at the prospect of going into business hadn't abated. A partner. An equal. No more being at anyone's beck and call. And everyone said how Leeds was a place where a gay man could live his life unmolested.

Gurdy wasn't sure that properly applied when the gay man in question was a naïve Hindu lad with a pair of overbearing parents, but the physical distance would make all the difference in the world. In Leeds he could be free to be himself.

He felt free tonight. He didn't want to think disloyal thoughts, but knowing Paddy was banged up in Bridewell relaxed him. Yes, there might be all sorts of trouble down the line – definitely would, in fact – but from what he'd heard, and what he knew, Mo would remain out of the picture, and if Paddy had been pulled with just a bit of gear on him, then he might not even get a custodial sentence.

But he'd rant and he'd rage and think the world was out to get him, because that was the way Paddy was, mostly, these days – which was why Gurdy would never so much as snort a single pinch of the coke that was always so available. Dangerous drug, coke. They called it the party drug, didn't they? He'd have called it the fight drug himself.

But right now, he was in the mood to party; not least because one of the big draws of returning to the Old Crown was human – in the shape of a local DJ he'd met a couple of weeks back, and who'd provided him with his first ever opportunity to find out what being gay was about, in the men's bogs in a place called Mr B's.

He was called DJ Steve, which was hardly imaginative, but behind the name was an imagination that had made

Gurdy's eyes pop – not to mention a passing pang at the thought of going to Leeds. Still, he'd make hay while the sun shone, as one of his teachers used to say.

Steve was just setting up when Gurdy slipped through the doors, and as their eyes met, Gurdy knew that, whatever else was true, he was going to be partying tonight. Well, in theory. He'd just left the bar, clutching a whisky and coke, when his eyes met a pair he was altogether less pleased to meet – Paddy, large as life, was walking towards him.

What the fuck was Paddy doing here? He'd been nicked, hadn't he? In possession. No question about it. His brother had confirmed it. So how the fuck did he get out again so quickly, when there'd be no magistrate for him to go before till Monday?

Feeling an uncomfortable lurch in his stomach, Gurdy managed a smile, all thoughts of DJ Steve spirited away. And as Paddy got closer, Gurdy could see that he was smashed out of his skull. Great, trust him to be in the wrong place at completely the wrong time – Paddy would no doubt expect him to stand there and listen to one of his interminable ravings about how Jimmy Daley and his dad were stitching him up. Again.

Paddy banged a fist down on the bar. 'Is anyone serving here or what?' he barked, even though the barmaid, an older lady who was known for taking no shit off anyone, was so obviously already coming to do just that.

'Let me,' Gurdy said, reaching into his jeans pocket for money. 'What d'you want, mate? A whisky?'

'A slap round the chops, you keep up that caveman act,' the barmaid said.

'Promises, promises,' Paddy answered, winking, his demeanour changing completely. And to Gurdy's irritation, the woman winked back at him. Women really were their own worst enemies when it came to men, Gurdy decided. Surely the correct response would have been to put Paddy in his place. *Give* him the slap around the chops she'd both promised and he deserved. Yet, time and again, Gurdy had noticed it didn't usually work like that. The woman was standing there simpering at him now. He pulled a fiver out and placed it on the bar while Paddy sent her off to get him a double. Hey ho. They got what *they* deserved.

'So,' he said, since Paddy was too busy watching her backside to speak to him as she shoved a glass under the optic. 'They let you out, did they?'

'No,' Paddy said, turning to face him. 'They locked me up and threw away the fucking key. What's it look like?'

'Alright, mate,' Gurdy said, surprised by the vitriol in Paddy's voice. 'Keep your hair on. So what happened? I heard you were going to be stuck there till Monday. For possession, like. Though I assume you weren't carrying much of Mo's stuff—'

'Will you shut the fuck *up?*' Paddy hissed, his gaze shifting, darting here and there. 'No, I fucking wasn't,' he said, once the barmaid had set his drink down, picked the fiver up, opened the till and provided the change. 'But I was carrying. You knew I was carrying, Gurdip. But they let me go anyway. Strange that, don't you think?'

Gurdy did think it was strange, specially if Jimmy's dad had anything to do with it. Stranger still that he was no longer 'me little Paki mate'. Just Gurdip. Not Gurdy even, but Gurdip.

He nodded nervously, wondering why Paddy was being so strange with him. It wasn't like it was *his* fault, after all. 'Why go to the bother of pulling you in just to let you go again?' he agreed.

'My thoughts exactly,' Paddy said. 'And also strange, don't you think, that he should be there, in this very pub, where I hadn't even planned on being?'

'What d'you mean?' Gurdy said to him. 'You'd planned to meet me in here, hadn't you?' God, the morning seemed a lifetime ago now.

'Not initially,' Paddy told him. 'I wanted to meet you up the lock-up, remember?'

Gurdy wasn't sure he did remember. In his memory they'd always agreed to meet here. Because it made more sense. Going to the lock-up would have meant an unnecessary journey for both of them, wouldn't it?

Gurdy was just about to ask again what that had to do with anything, when Paddy said, 'Forget it. More to the point, why the *fuck* did they let me go?'

'How should I know?' Gurdy said. Paddy's glare was beginning to get to him. He wished he'd go and find someone else to drone on at. 'I don't work for the police, do I? Maybe they decided you didn't have enough on you.'

'Fuck-up, so they say,' Paddy said, taking a big gulp of his drink and watching Gurdy over the glass rim. He lowered it. 'They fucked up down the nick. The cretin didn't read my rights to me. Paperwork error. Illegal arrest. Clowns, the fucking lot of them,' he finished.

He hadn't taken his eyes from Gurdy as he'd said this. He still didn't.

'So your lucky day then,' said Gurdy, as Paddy finally let his gaze drop and drained his whisky. He banged his glass down on the bar just as he had his fist minutes earlier. Gurdy wished he'd just go away. 'Let me buy you another one,' he said. Perhaps if he did, Paddy *would* go. All he seemed to want to do, despite being released, was drown his sorrows. His brother would have called that reverse logic.

But then he did something weird. He clapped Gurdy on the back. 'My treat,' he said expansively. 'I've had a right touch from Mo today,' he added, his mouth now close to Gurdy's ear. 'Bigger than *anything* we've had in the past. This is the big one, pal, I'm telling you. The brown stuff. Pure heroin.' He touched his nose. 'After this you'll be able to fucking retire, mate – we'll both be able to retire. And you know the best news? Mo wants *you* in.'

'Me? He really said that to you?' Gurdy was stunned.

'If you want in, that is,' Paddy said, his eyes suddenly narrowing. Gurdy didn't want in. Not at all. Not a bit of it. Coke was one thing, but heroin was quite another. All he wanted to do was get away. And with this news, even more so.

'Cat got your tongue?' Paddy said. 'What with your global curry shop ambitions, I thought you'd be pleased.

You could open twenty fucking branches – everywhere from Leeds to fucking Bridlington.'

'I *am* pleased,' Gurdy said, anxious, wondering what the fuck Paddy knew about his plans. 'It's just a shock, that's all. You know …'

Paddy hoicked up the sleeve of his leather jacket to check his watch. Then put his finger to his nose again. 'Yeah,' he said. 'I do know. *Comprende?* I fucking *do* know.'

Then he turned around and walked away, right out of the pub, the offer of a drink forgotten. Gurdy would have called after him – *Comprende? Who do you think you are – Don Corleone?* – except none of their exchange felt remotely funny. Or explicable. What the fuck was really going on with Paddy? Who *did* know?

He finished his beer and turned his attention back to DJ Steve.

He didn't want to know; he just wanted to be left alone.

Chapter 23

Gurdy knew something wasn't right the very second Paddy put his foot to the floor. Why the hell had he agreed to get in his car? Why the hell hadn't he just said he'd follow him to wherever they were going on his own?

It had been a strange Tuesday morning all told. It had started normally enough – he'd gone to work in the garage, just as Paddy had asked him to the previous evening – but no Paddy himself – he'd simply not showed – even though there was a car they were supposed to be working on and he knew there were things Gurdy couldn't deal with on his own. He wasn't a fucking mechanic after all, was he?

And still no sign of Paddy, as the morning wore on, even though he'd said he'd be there around nine, after dropping Vicky off at work. So Gurdy had cracked on – daydreaming about DJ Steve, formulating his grand plans in Leeds – the latter ever more urgent now that brown had been brought into the equation. That was one line he was never going to cross. No way was he getting involved in dealing heroin.

But there was only so much he could do to the car. Paddy knew that. So when, by half eleven, Paddy still hadn't showed, Gurdy began to get anxious.

Either he'd had to do something unexpected for Mo and couldn't call, or – worse – the fucking cops had pulled him in again. Which wouldn't have surprised Gurdy, even though he fervently wished it otherwise – Paddy had been dealing coke so fucking blatantly on Sunday and Monday that it was almost like he was *asking* to be arrested again. Like they'd have to do it as a public bloody service.

Then the call from him, finally, just after twelve. 'Meet me at the lock-up at one.' No 'Hello', no 'How are you?' No explanation for his absence. Just the order barked at him. To which Gurdy'd obviously said okay. Then locked the garage, got in his Mini and drove there.

He grabbed the door handle, for stability. And now this. Paddy weird. Paddy antsy. Paddy scowling. And straight out of one car and into another. Into Paddy's Capri, at his insistence, which smelt of some sickly air freshener. One of several swinging from the rear-view mirror. Fruity.

Gurdy felt trapped now. Sweaty. And the smell made him nauseous. And, as the Capri began screaming down the road in what looked like the wrong direction, very frightened as well.

In truth he had always been frightened of Paddy. It had never been one of those relationships where he felt he could be himself. They were thin on the ground anyway – Vic and Luce, his brother Vikram. But he'd always accepted that – after all, he was an odd-ball, everyone knew that. And he'd never had what it took to build a circle of friends. And, besides, he'd always thought that was the way it worked with business. Yes, he was nervous of Paddy and his volatile behaviour, but the same went for Paddy, with Mo. He'd not witnessed it often but the couple of times he'd seen Paddy around the scary Rasta, he saw his own anxiety and fear mirrored in Paddy's eyes. That was obviously how it worked. That was why it was called a pecking order – with the lowliest in the chain, him, getting pecked the most.

Now, though, he was a million per cent *more* frightened of Paddy. This new version – knocked into shape during those nine months in prison – was one he no longer felt he knew. He'd been difficult to deal with from the minute he'd been released, as if he had to roll around town like some sort of gangster to prove a point that he was harder than everyone else. No longer just the local baker's wayward son, but a drug-fuelled not-to-be-messed-with ex-convict.

Convict. A hard word. Gurdy really hated 'hard'. Hated the whole notion of what men thought they had to be. Hated all those horrible masculine trappings – even more since he'd accepted the person *he* was. He was counting the days now till he could get out and reinvent himself too.

Away from here. Away from *this*. He thought of Steve. Just a shag, but a watershed moment. Get away so he could finally become himself.

He really had absolutely no idea where they were going. Obviously not to anywhere he'd been to before. So where? They seemed to be headed out of town. On some dodgy secret job for Mo perhaps? Hadn't Paddy already mentioned the word 'mission'? He hoped not. Lucy's concerns kept coming back to him and he feared for his liberty. Couldn't get the tone of her voice out of his head – her implication that some sort of 'net' was closing in.

They screamed towards another junction, and Paddy glanced left and right, looking for crossing traffic, and, as he did so, Gurdy noticed just how manic he really looked. His eyes seemed glazed and unfocussed, like he was looking but not seeing, and Gurdy wondered how much – and what – he might have taken. Always the bloody drugs, these days. Paddy seemed always high on something, and no longer just in the nights, but in the days. Tenfold, since he'd come out of prison. When Gurdy felt braver, he'd say something. Someone had to say *something*. Didn't he realise what he was doing to himself?

He brushed clammy hands along the legs of his jeans. 'Pads, mate, what's going on? Where are we off to?'

Paddy swung the car onto the main road, a grin plastered on his face now, and, instead of answering, simply clicked on the radio. It blared a dance song, mid-track – 'I'm gonna run away from you' – which was so entirely at odds with the mood in the car that, had he not been so dry-mouthed with fear, Gurdy might have laughed.

And the fear was only growing as they got further out of town. Paddy Allen was a lunatic of the highest fucking order, and this little trip they were taking was all wrong. All so *wrong*.

And as the car sped past bits of town that Gurdy knew to be dodgy, he felt his insides begin to churn. Why wasn't Paddy speaking? Why wasn't he telling him where they were going? 'Paddy!' he said again, adding a little volume to his voice now that it was having to compete with the radio. 'Stop messing around, man. Where are we off to, and why are you driving so fucking *fast*? There'll be coppers all over up here.'

Paddy glanced at him, that same crazed look in his eyes. 'No coppers where we're going, my little Paki mate,' he said. 'In fact I doubt we'll be disturbed by anyone at all.'

Gurdy's insides churned some more. What the fuck did *that* mean? 'Please stop, Paddy,' he tried. 'I really need a piss, and I feel sick.'

'You fucking pussy,' Paddy taunted, laughing so much that he was actually rocking in the driver seat, making the car buck and lurch. 'You think I'm fucking stupid, eh? Eh?'

Then, out of nowhere, he landed a punch on Gurdy's ear.

A hard one. 'Fuck, that *hurt*!' Gurdy gasped, astonished.

Paddy glared. 'It was supposed to! You think I'm as fucking stupid as that fucking Jimmy? Eh? Or his ugly fucking bird, eh?'

Gurdy's terror now ramped up to a whole new level. 'Bloody hell, Pad – what the fuck are you *on* about, mate?'

'I'm fucking *on* to you, "mate",' he hissed. 'Got it? I fucking know what you've been up to. I know *everything*.'

Gurdy couldn't help it. He suddenly lost control of his bladder and could only look down in horror as a hot urine stain began to bloom across the crotch of his jeans. Fuck, and the smell. It made his eyes smart.

Though Paddy didn't seem to notice. He was banging his fists on the steering wheel as he drove – down some country lane, hedgerows zipping by in a green blur. Fuck! What the hell was all this about?

'I swear, Pad, I don't know what you're on about,' he pleaded. 'I'd never do or say anything against you. You *know* that. I'm *loyal*, man. I swear on my mother's life.'

Another stinging punch connected with the side of his head. He saw stars – tiny diamonds that danced around in front of him, and all he could think was how hard it must be to drive a car and punch him all at the same time. Perhaps they'd crash now, as well, and he welcomed it.

'Shut the fuck up, you Paki cunt! It's all down to you! You and that fucking Daley have been plotting against me all along. Shagging my bird, too? Eh? Eh? It's *all* making fucking sense now. That it? You forget, "mate", that I'm NOT A FUCKING IDIOT! I've seen stuff. I've got fucking eyes in my head!'

Cringing now, braced for the next punch, and pressing his body against the car door, Gurdy was spared the necessity of trying to respond to Paddy's nonsense. And spared another punch, too, as Paddy needed both hands on the wheel to turn the car into a broken concrete forecourt beyond which stood a big old metal building, largely screened from the road by high fences and trees.

He thought he knew where he might be now. At one of Mo's fabled hideaways. But there was no time to ponder the whys and the wherefores of the situation as Paddy leapt from the driver's seat, scooted round the bonnet and yanked open the passenger door to drag Gurdy out by his hair.

And then came the next humiliation. It was pointless trying to fight it. The body did what it did – you couldn't control it. And he'd now lost control over his sphincter as well. And it was pointless trying to struggle, to try and get away, because Paddy, who was a good five inches taller than he was, could beat him to a pulp with one hand behind his back. So there was nothing for it but to allow himself to be dragged along, stumbling and sobbing, into a filthy, deserted building in the middle of nowhere.

Only now, Paddy saw how his body had betrayed him. Smelled the smell. Saw the shit running from the bottom of his jeans. 'You fucking, dirty, smelly *cunt*.' He booted Gurdy in the back of the knees. They obediently buckled.

'Just wait,' Paddy raged. 'Just you wait till I tell everyone what a shitty-arsed cunt you are, you fucking *pussy*!'

Gurdy realised he was in the hands of what was commonly referred to as a raving maniac.

Perhaps he always had been.

Vicky was annoyed. It was almost half six already and it was only a bloody Tuesday, for Christ's sake. One of the few nights in the week when she could be sure of getting home on time. She hated being beholden to her mother at the best of times, and this would make her worse.

She was mostly annoyed with Leanne, though. It was all very well her having her bloody aunty in for a cheeky end-of-the-day perm, knowing the boss was away, but to expect Vicky to have to stay late to help her bloody wasn't.

'I can't be doing this all the time, Lee,' she snapped out of earshot of the hapless aunty. 'My little Chantelle hates being left all day with my mam as it is. And I can almost hear the steam hissing from her ears from here. I'm going to have to set off.'

Leanne seemed to find that funny. But not in a good way. 'For Christ's sake, Vic, keep your hair on. She's only a baby!' Vicky wasn't sure if she meant Chantelle or her mum. Either would apply, after all. 'Look, I said I'd slip you some extra tip money, and I will, because I'm grateful. But you know, you really don't need to worry about your little one like this – she won't even know who she's with at her age.'

Vicky was about to ask Leanne when it was she'd taken her diploma in being a mother, but Lee looked past her and tipped her head. 'Looks like you've got a lift home anyway. Paddy's here for you.'

Paddy? Why would Paddy be outside? She wasn't supposed to be seeing him till later. If she saw him at all that was. He'd been all peculiar this morning when he'd dropped her. She hoped there wasn't something bad going on with Mo. Though as everything to do with Mo had the word 'bad' stamped across it, she knew that might well be a vain hope.

'I wonder what's up with him?' Vicky mused as she peered out of the front window. He looked seriously agitated, stepping from foot to foot on the pavement, and taking deep, continual drags on a cigarette. 'God, I hope he hasn't already been to call for me and my mum's wound him up.'

'Hmm,' said Leanne. 'By the look of him, you'd best get off, I reckon. Here,' she said, handing Vicky her jacket off the coat stand. 'I'll finish up and lock-up. Go on, get going. He looks really narky, doesn't he? And you just come straight back in if he looks like kicking off!'

Vicky pulled her jacket on, grabbed her bag and hurried out onto the pavement, slightly alarmed by her friend's anxious words. What did Leanne think might happen? Did Paddy look dangerous to her or something?

Evidently. And if she was still looking out of the window, she'd have even more cause to think so, Vicky thought, as Paddy grabbed her roughly by the arm and almost shoved her into the passenger seat of the Capri. There was a Morrisons carrier bag flat on the seat, which she made to move before sitting down. 'Leave it,' he commanded. She didn't argue.

'Fucking hell, Paddy!' she said instead, as he climbed in beside her. 'Calm *down*! What the fuck's wrong with you anyway?'

Paddy gripped the steering wheel, as if it might be planning to fly off and roll away – she wouldn't have blamed it – and stared straight ahead as he gunned the engine, his jaw twitching. He was high on something. The sod. High on what, though? He seemed so edgy. 'Paddy, have you been shoving that shit up your nose again?' she asked, twisting in her seat, angry. 'Only I asked you to stop all that now you're a dad, and *you* said—'

'Fucking shut your stupid mouth!' Paddy snapped as he pulled away from the kerb, apparently not giving a toss about the oncoming traffic. He narrowly missed scraping a van, the driver of which tooted his horn angrily, to which Paddy leaned almost half his torso out the window, in order to shout a furious 'Fuck off!' at him.

Stunned now, Vicky gripped her seat belt and cringed. 'Paddy, you're scaring me,' she said in a smaller voice, anxious not to inflame him further. 'Will you please just stop it and tell me what the hell's going on? Is it Mam, something she's said?' She waited for him to answer, but he didn't. 'Or something else? Something to do with Mo? Babes, I can't help you if you won't tell me. Come on, calm yourself down. Tell me what's wound you up.'

Out on a quieter road, he finally seemed to register her question. Though she noticed his knuckles were still white against the wheel.

'Did you know?' Paddy suddenly asked, turning his head to glare at her. 'Did you know I'd got locked up on Saturday morning? Locked up and then released?'

Vicky was really confused now. 'Locked up? Locked up for what?' She shook her head. 'On *Saturday*?'

Again the silence.

'On Saturday?' she said again. 'Why didn't you tell me?'

He was looking at her so intently that she feared they were going to crash. 'For fuck's sake, Paddy, keep your eyes on the road!' She also realised that they weren't heading to her house, they were heading away from it. Ditto his.

Where were they going then? And Saturday? Locked up? And he'd said nothing!

She felt suddenly irritable as well as anxious. What kind of game was he playing? 'Oh, Paddy, for God's sake, what is going on? What did you *do*?'

Paddy snorted. 'You bloody did know, didn't you? You already bloody knew!'

'Knew *what*? For God's sake, what are you *on* about?'

He grinned suddenly. Manically. 'You're fucking in on it too, aren't you? My own bird in cahoots with those slimy bastards! How the fuck do you know that I did *anything*? Eh? *Eh*? Gurdy phone you up and give you the gen, did he?'

'Because you *must* have done something!' she retorted. What was all this nonsense about Gurdy? 'Or did they just arrest you because they didn't like your brand of jeans?'

He made a noise in his throat. One of what she thought was frustration, but which reminded her she'd do better to shut up when he was in this state. This state – on the bloody drugs – that he was so often in these days. Only worse. Where the hell was he taking her?

Some distance by the look of it, and she sat tight, clutching her seat belt, while he weaved in and out of the traffic at the end of Manningham Lane and they continued on to God knew where out in the sticks. She felt like crying, but some obstinate part of her refused to. She wasn't going to act like the stupid girl he obviously thought she was. Oh, but *Gurdy* – what was all that nonsense about him? She started putting things together, remembering past conversations, remembering his paranoia about who'd said what to whom when he was inside. It made her feel even more fearful. 'What do you mean about Gurdy?' she finally ventured after five silent, high-speed minutes. 'I've not spoken to Gurdy since back last week. What's he done? Is it him that's got you mad? Is that it? He's your friend, Pad,' she pointed out. 'He wouldn't hurt you.'

Paddy laughed then. A cold, manic laugh that sent shivers down Vicky's spine. 'Hurt me?' Paddy scoffed. He sounded so, so strange. 'That Paki cunt couldn't hurt himself!'

He stopped laughing. Then slowed down a little before continuing. 'Can I trust you, Vic?' he said suddenly, his voice now low and conspiratorial. 'I mean, can I *really*? I need to know, babes. This is important.'

'Course you can trust me,' Vicky said, venturing a hand to his thigh and squeezing. He glanced down at it. Nodded. Found a smile for her. 'You are my world, Paddy, you know that,' she said, sensing an urgent need to talk him down a bit. 'What is it, babe? Whatever it is, *tell* me.'

In answer, he flipped down the stalk for the indicator, and turned the car into a yard beyond which stood a huge tin building. Corrugated roof. Very old. Like a shed. In what looked like a field. Surrounded by a fence, a bunch of bushes, a garland of monster-sized weeds. Isolated. That was the word that came to mind.

Paddy stopped the car, yanked on the handbrake and pulled the key from the ignition. Then he twisted in his seat and took her hands.

His huge pupils were like an advance guard, paving the way for what he was about to tell her. His hands were sweating. 'It's Gurdy, babe. He's a treacherous cunt, and I've found him out.'

Vicky shook her head. '*No*, Paddy. He *wouldn't*.'

'Shhh,' he said, stroking a thumb across the back of her hand. 'Listen, I have the facts now. I don't know when it all started but him and that Jimmy have been working together with the cops to bring me down, I swear it.'

'But that's—'

Now his hands gripped hers more tightly. 'That's the reason I've brought you here,' he said quietly, speaking slowly, as if to an infant. 'So you can bear witness. So you can listen to him admit it.'

'*What?*' she said, feeling her gorge rise. Was Gurdy *in* there? Or – God – in the *boot*? For a moment she thought that must be it.

She swallowed. 'Paddy, please don't tell me that you have Gurdy in there.' He had to be wrong. Gurdy was a loyal, loyal friend. He would never, ever grass on Paddy, no matter what. Christ, yes, Jimmy might – probably would. But Gurdy? Never.

She said so. 'You'll see,' Paddy said, reaching behind him to open his car door. 'Come on. Come with me, babe, you'll see.'

What choice did she have? So she followed him on shaky legs to the big corrugated and padlocked door, and stood silently while he sorted through his fob for the correct key. He had a key to a place like this? Chilling.

Finally he did it, released the padlock, and pushed the door open, where Vicky's nostrils were assaulted by a foul faecal smell.

And her eyes to the sight of her poor defenceless friend, gagged and bleeding, tied to a chair, in the middle of the empty shed.

Chapter 24

The lock-up still smelt of good, honest business. Of engine oil and petrol. Of hard graft and rubber. As it would. It was still haunted by the remnants of the past, when it had been the place where Mo had first plied his trade. Proper trade it had been, too – he'd sold car parts and tyres, almost all of it legit. Many moons ago, this had been, back when Paddy was just a boy and at a time before Mo realised that there was a great deal more money to be made on the wrong side of the law.

It was growing dark. There was no longer any electricity or running water, and the only light was what was filtering through the long-ago smashed-out windows, leaking in, along with the ivy and taller weeds. But that was fine. There was still plenty of daylight available. Plenty enough for him to complete his secret mission.

Secret mission. A bit rich, that, but he liked it, even so. Even as he was aware of his own grandiosity, he liked that his brain was so fucking razor-sharp. He shut the doors again, vaguely conscious of Vicky wrenching herself from his grasp, crossing the cavernous empty space and kicking up dust. He hoped she had the intelligence to understand why this was necessary.

Clearly not. 'For fuck's sake, Pad!' she yelled at him, her voice shrill and aggressive. 'What the fuck are you *on*! For Christ's sake, *untie* him!'

Paddy studied Gurdy with scientific interest as he approached him. Still in pain, obviously. Still groaning. Still bleeding. Still staring at him, wide-eyed, from behind the drool and blood-soaked gag.

'Had any flashbacks yet, you black cunt?' he asked him brightly. The words boomed and echoed in the shell of the building. 'Eh?' he said, rather liking the way his voice filled the space. Like he was in a Bond movie, almost.

Vicky had sunk down beside Gurdy, and was trying to lift his head up. 'He can't answer you!' she screamed at him. 'Untie him right now, Paddy! God, I can't believe what you've done. He's my fucking *friend*!'

Paddy felt something shift in his stomach. Not like Gurdy – filthy cunt that he was – just a shifting of possibilities. How dare she stick up for this sneaking fucking grass? Even *now*. Even after he'd explained everything. 'Are you right in the head?' he barked at her. 'I've just *told* you, Vic. He's been on a right fucking grassing spree! Thinks I'm as thick as him and Jimmy, he does,' he added. And would have added more, but she was screaming at him again.

'No!' she yelled, clambering up off her knees and heading towards him. 'He wouldn't *do* that. Christ, Paddy, you're not thinking straight. Please take that thing off.

Please take that thing off.' She was trying to get round him now. 'Take it off so he can explain.'

Paddy caught movement just behind her. The lying fucker was actually trying to nod! It made him want to hit him all over again. He clenched his fists. '*Explain*?' he roared. Why the fuck didn't Vicky get it?

He reached into his jeans, immediately clear what was needed. He pulled out his coke stash and set up three lines on the nearest window ledge.

'For fuck's sake!' Vicky squeaked. He ignored her. He snorted them fast and then carefully wiped his nose. Then turned around to see Vicky frantically tugging at the rope he'd used to tie up Gurdy.

Not that she'd succeed. Because he'd tied it like a pro. So he could leave her to it while he did another couple of lines. But it was the principle. Always the principle. Such arrogance. Such fucking *disloyalty*. Who was her fucking boyfriend here? Who mattered most?

'You stupid cow,' he growled as he stomped across the floor. Bits of glass crunched like cornflakes beneath his boots. He grabbed her by the shoulder, then grasped an arm and tried to hurl her out of reach, but as she'd grabbed the chair back, it toppled and crashed onto its side as she slumped in a heap a yard away.

Since Gurdip's head was on the floor now, he kicked it.

Vicky sobbed. A sort of keening noise. 'Keep out of this, Vic, I mean it. Stop trying to interfere. I only brought you here to hear his confession. Because when I get nicked, and I will, you can depend on that – see what you've done to me? – I want *everyone* to know that it was this fucker who saw to it.'

Vicky was whimpering on the floor now. Like she *still* didn't get it. 'Please, Paddy,' she said, 'I'm begging you. Just take that thing off his mouth. Please. Look. He can hardly breathe.'

She'd started crawling. Like an insect. Across the dusty, rubbish-strewn floor. Soon her face was only inches away from Gurdy's.

Was he breathing? Paddy stood and watched Gurdy's chest rise and fall. In and out. In and out. Yes, he was.

'Don't worry about that, babes,' he told Vicky, righting the chair one-handed. He had the strength of ten men. Much good *that* would do him. The second thought booted the first into touch. Much fucking good *that* would do him.

'It's coming off, babe,' he told her. 'It has to come off. Remember? Because I *need* you to *hear* his *confession*.'

He scanned the room, the corners of which were already growing gloomy. Where had he put down the crowbar? Sighting it under a window he strolled across to retrieve it. Then returned to his trembling victim.

He yanked the gag down. 'You ready to tell the truth yet?' he asked, smacking Gurdy around the face for good measure.

Vicky squealed again, but he ignored her. Instead he looked into Gurdy's eyes, which were bloodshot and wet. Why the hell hadn't he seen what he was seeing now before? This prick was so obviously working as some kind of double agent. Just wait till he told Mo about him.

Gurdy licked his lips and spoke, and Vicky squeaked again behind him. This time Paddy silenced her by raising the crowbar. Not that he'd ever hurt her. Not really. But she needed to shut the fuck up and *listen*. 'Please, Paddy,' Gurdy whispered. 'Please don't hit me anymore. I swear, I never told a soul, not a soul.' He raised his head slightly. Blood dripped onto his shirt. Why always a shirt? Did he think he was going to a fucking wedding? 'I don't know why you think I would. Honest, mate,' Gurdy said with difficulty, 'I was earning good money off you. Why would I betray you?'

Paddy felt crosser. That was another fucking point. 'Yeah, you were, you treacherous cunt!' he yelled into Gurdy's face. 'But your fucking face, mate. It said it all. Your fucking face! Now …' He swung the crowbar hard against Gurdy's legs, causing him to howl out in pain. 'You fucking admit, in front of her. In front of your fucking *girl-friend*.' He pointed at Vicky. 'Admit what you done, and all this will be over.'

'I can't!' Gurdy gasped, once he was capable of speaking. 'I never, Pad. I never! I don't know what you're saying!' Then dissolved into screaming as Paddy swung the metal bar again, this time coming down on his back and shoulders. 'Stop fucking crying, you fucking nancy!' Paddy told him, the screams getting on his nerves now. 'Save your lungs for telling me the fucking truth!'

'He is!' Vicky screeched now. She was on her feet again and hitting him. 'I'm not his fucking girlfriend, you moron! He's fucking gay! Jesus, you thick bastard! He's gay!'

Moron. Thick bastard. That riled him. And as he obviously couldn't hit her he swung the bar at Gurdy's face, causing blood and snot to spray onto his T-shirt. Which made him hate the fucker even more.

As if he could. Fucking gay! So in Daley's pants instead then? That bastard had always looked like a faggot to him, so it figured. He swung the bar again and the chair crashed down, putting Gurdy on the floor again. He was now trying his best to curl up into a foetal position while Vicky once again tried to fiddle with his bonds.

Paddy nudged him with his foot. 'What's that?' he asked. Then made a big show of holding his hand behind one of ears to amplify the sound. Not that either of them were actually looking. 'Did you say something, Gurdip?' he asked, bending down. 'Was that an admission you were spitting out?' He knelt on the floor amid the blood, piss and shit. 'Come on, you little cunt,' he said, right in Gurdy's foul-smelling face. 'A bit louder so we can all hear it.'

'Paddy,' Gurdy gurgled, his eyelids beginning to flicker shut. 'I never told. Nothing. To no one. About anything. The only person I ever told anything about anything was Vik.' He coughed and spluttered. 'Who I trust with my life.'

His eyes closed, and Paddy stood up. Then he met Vicky's eyes. Unusually, he found he couldn't read them. What the fuck? What the *fuck*? But he couldn't hurt Vicky. So, abandoning the crowbar, he pulled his foot back then smashed it into the middle of Gurdy's face, where it connected with a satisfying crack.

His own bastard bird. His own girlfriend!

She could clearly read his eyes. The hurt in them. The shock. 'Vic! You told Vic!' He screamed, kicking Gurdy's face a second time. 'You wanted to shag my fucking missus as well, you cunt?'

He raised his foot for a third time, but felt strong hands grab his arm.

Her! His own Vic! Another fucking traitor! He tried to throw Vicky off but she was like a lunatic – and a strong one. And she also had the crowbar in her hand. She surely wouldn't. Would she?

'Fuck, Vic. Fucking *you?*'

She raised the bar. 'Paddy, stop it NOW!'

'Fuck, Vic,' he tried again. 'Him and *you?*' He eyed the crowbar. Perhaps she would. Could he block it?

'Vik as in Vikram!' she screamed at him. 'He meant fucking *Vikram*, you stupid, evil bastard! His brother! His *brother!*' Tears were streaming down her face, two wet tracks through her make-up. 'And now you've fucking *killed* him!' she yelled.

She swung the bar then, and, his arms flailing too late, it connected.

He went down slowly, the floor rising up to say hello. Then a brush, a playful thump, almost. Then nothing.

Chapter 25

Vicky's hands wouldn't stop shaking. She held them up and was mesmerised. She knew this. Knew *about* this. She was in shock.

The memory came from nowhere, bright as freshly spilled blood. School. Being in the hall. A talk from two policemen about road safety. She remembered the screen being erected and a film being shown. The motes of dust dancing in the beam from the projector.

The images. One or more? She couldn't quite remember. Just the boy. The little boy who'd been run over by a drunk-driver. She'd never heard the expression 'drunk-driver' before then. She remembered the horror, though. The little boy being covered in blood. The way his leg was almost hanging off. Could it have really been? Would they *really* have shown that to children? She wasn't sure where reality ended and her imagination had picked up the story, but what she did recall was the way he shook, and his haunted, staring eyes. The way he couldn't speak. Couldn't focus. Couldn't respond to his crying mother.

That's the effect of shock, one of the policemen had said, in response to someone's question. *That's the body's way of protecting itself.*

* * *

She lowered her hands from her face and rolled onto her side. She had no idea how long she'd been lying there, howling. Could have been minutes. Could have been hours. Time had no meaning. But it was dark. Fully dark. A darkness that was protecting her, she knew – as was the numbness in her heart – from the full horror of what she had witnessed. Of what Paddy had *done*.

Paddy. She felt a scream rise in her gut and try to escape her. She clamped a hand against her mouth, then the other hand, pressing frantically, tasting dirt on them, and something else, something she didn't dare even guess at – clamping both against her face as if unable to contain what was inside of her, then pulling her knees up to her chest and shivering, waiting for the shock to re-engulf her.

More time passed. But this time she was aware of its passing. She was in a kind of fugue but she was still aware of it moving inexorably forward. Coming to claim her from the 'pause' button she had pressed. But then a noise. A low moan, and she initially thought 'Gurdy!' but when she risked opening her eyes, forcing herself to accept what she couldn't, the hump on the floor was still there, outlined by the moonlight, still moulded round the upturned metal chair. She stared. And as still as the building itself.

It hit her again then. Paddy. It was *Paddy* who was moaning. Paddy who – oh, *God* – she had walloped round the head.

She scrabbled up onto her hands and knees, feeling shards of something pressing into them. Then, effortfully, as if she'd been kicked, to her feet. He moaned again, and though she couldn't see him, she was aware of him moving. Then a slice of darkness crossed one of the windows. He was lurching towards her.

Instinctively (it had to be, because by rights she should surely run from him) she held out her arms and let him stumble into them. 'Shit, Paddy. Shit!' she whispered. Did the dead hear? But still she whispered. 'Shit, Paddy, what have you done?'

'Fuck,' he said. 'Fuck,' then his head fell against hers, warm and heavy. And bringing with it with the beaten-metal smell of blood.

As she held him, and shushed him, she tried to think straight. Shake off the nausea that had begun to grip her. 'Come on,' she said, trying to balance the dead weight of him. Was he *crying*? 'We need to get outside. Get the doors open. Get some *air*.'

He was barely responsive, but she managed to shuffle the pair of them back to the big metal doors, haul one of them open and let the light – such as it was – spill in. She staggered out with him then, holding him up before plopping him down again on what looked like an oil drum, whereupon he immediately put his head in his hands and moaned some more.

Then she turned around to where she could see back into the nightmare they'd just exited. To what was left of her friend. And saw a shaft of light – a guiding star? What the *fuck*? – shining down on the blood and gore where his face ought to be; a sick halo illuminating exactly what Paddy had done. She span around, ran blindly to the side of the building and vomited her guts up into the weedy grass.

Once she'd found the wherewithal to stand up straight again, her stomach voided, details began to catch Vicky's unwilling attention. She was still wearing the pinafore she'd been in when he'd come to get her. Pink. Very old. Been through the washer a zillion times. Only now, as she tried to cough the sick from her throat, did she see how it was pebble-dashed with blood. She retched again, feeling dizzy, her body convulsing of its own accord, just as it had in childbirth. Giving birth to Chantelle. She kept her head down till the feeling passed. Fuck. *Chantelle*. What the hell was she going to do now?

Then his voice. Another whisper. 'Vic, babe.' He sounded broken.

She turned around. 'Paddy, Christ! What the fuck have you *done*?'

He was crying. Sitting on the oil drum exactly where she'd left him.

She walked across to him, wiping her mouth on her skirt. Pulling it up from beneath the pinafore – the murderously stained pinafore – and dabbing at her mouth with the hem.

He held his arms out and, as she got to him, he flung both of them around her, properly sobbing now, his face buried against her stomach.

Like a child might. Like a daughter might with a mum. Though not her mum.

She stood and let him, looking up into a perfectly starry sky. Not the moon, then. Just the starlight. A multitude of constellations. The Plough. The Great Bear. The Brave Hunter, Orion. She could barely identify any of them but it suddenly struck her that she must learn them, so she could show them to her daughter. Thinking of Chantelle made something clutch at her, and she thought she might be sick again. But she breathed, deep and long, pushing the wave down.

She stroked Paddy's head rhythmically, almost instinctively, and he responded by lifting his face to her. 'I don't know what ...' he began. 'I just can't ...' Then he faltered. 'That wasn't me,' he said finally. 'I took something bad, babe ...' His voice was all panicky. 'Babe, I *took* something.'

Her hand, sweeping over his curls, felt the bump where she'd hit him. She could have killed him, she thought distractedly. Just like he'd killed Gurdy.

He lifted his own hand and placed it over hers. It was blood-blackened. Crusted. A claw come to claim her. 'Babe,' he whispered. '*Babe*, you have to *help* me.'

She left him outside. He kept on crying, and she couldn't concentrate on anything with him crying. Being such a mess. Being such a junkie. A remorseful snivelling *junkie*. Besides, she didn't want him in there, she decided.

Was she still in shock? She had no idea, only that a stillness had come over her. The 'capable head' her boss said she had on her shoulders. At the interview. That was why he'd given her the job.

She tried not to look at Gurdy. Instead she scanned the far reaches of the building, her eye eventually resting on something heaped in the corner. She walked across to it. It was a dust sheet. A big one.

She had no idea what to do. Only that she had to do something. So she grabbed it and shook it out and took it back to where Gurdy lay.

The blood. That was what you did. You tried to clear up all the blood. But there was just so much. He was lying on a lake of it, for one thing. And all about him, spatters and globs of the stuff – so much so that she didn't know where to start. She started anyway, screwing up a corner of the dust sheet and applying it to the floor, but the more she scrubbed the worse it looked, even in the darkness.

Water. She needed water. But there wasn't any water. It was useless. But she kept scrubbing even so. Making circles around the circle of blood that demarcated where he'd taken his last breath. She started to wail as the reality hit and was startled when she felt Paddy place his hand on her arm.

'Stop, babe.' Paddy's voice. A hand stilling her arm. 'Stop, babe,' he said, softly. 'There's no point.'

He was no longer snivelling. Both his touch and voice were firm. And, in that instant she felt a wave of relief. He could take charge now, couldn't he? Make it all go away. And he did. First the dust sheet, which he tugged from her hands, gently. Then pulling her back to her feet. It was as if a switch had been flicked and the Paddy that had been broken had been replaced by the old, calm and calculating one. The one who could deal with this mess. Take control. 'You go outside,' he said. 'I know what to do.'

Vicky did as instructed, but stood and watched from the doorway. Watched as Paddy ripped part of the dust sheet to make a rag. Watched as he bent down next to Gurdy and picked up the crowbar. Wiped the worst of the blood from it, then wrapped it inside the rag, before pushing the package inside the front of his bomber jacket.

Then he stood for a bit, his eyes scanning the interior, his gaze finally coming to rest on the body by his feet, and lingering there for a long, thoughtful moment. Or was it? Vicky wished she could read his mind.

Then he came back outside and, taking her arm, urged her towards his car. 'Come on,' he whispered. 'Let's get out of here.'

Just like he was a character in a movie. 'But what about Gurdy?' she said. 'Won't they—'

'Shhh,' he said. 'Shhhh!' He patted his front, where the crowbar was. 'This is all we need. We can leave him here, babes,' he said, as he opened the passenger door for her. 'When he's found, the cops will think it was a drug-related killing. Or a racist attack. Or something like that. And without a weapon, they can't pin any of it on us.'

On us. Not on me. He'd said on *us*. She stripped off her pinafore, and bundled it up into a ball, inside out, then placed it in the footwell before getting into the car. Pinafore. *Pin it*. It was a ball of damning evidence. *Were* they both responsible? Was that what he was saying? But he was right: she had been there and had done nothing to stop it. Her Paddy had murdered her friend before her eyes and she had allowed it. Just stood there and let him.

No, that wasn't right. She'd tried. She'd tried her best. Or had she? She could have run away, couldn't she? Run away and screamed for help. Or just screamed the place down. But she had done that, hadn't she? She'd screamed and she'd yelled *at* him and then – yes, she *had* done it – she'd stopped him by hitting him with the crowbar. But too late. She had not acted quickly enough. She'd been too scared and too blind to see what he'd been doing. He was mad from the coke – and fuck knew what else, these days – and perhaps he had planned to kill Gurdy all along.

Was that true? She stole a glance at him. His face looked like granite. Bluish, where his stubble had started sprouting on his chin. Grey, black and blue. Like a rock. Still and calm now. Just staring ahead, driving the car, being Paddy. All trace of the monster she'd witnessed long gone, now the grip of the drugs had gone away.

But was he a monster? Was her boyfriend a killer? Was the father *of her child* a cold-blooded killer? He turned to look at her, as if feeling the strength of her scrutiny, and she realised she loved him just as much as she feared him.

'Wassup! Whaaaathe fu … Whassgoing on … Whasssa – Vicky!' Vicky's mam blinked her way out of her slumber. 'What the *fuck* time d'you call this, young lady!'

They had moved like assassins, by mutual agreement. Paddy up the stairs so he could get himself sorted – strip his clothes off, run a bath, get into it, clean up – while Vicky, of necessity, given the far more difficult task, went to check on Chantelle and face her mother.

She opened the door into the front room very quietly, and was rewarded with a minute or so of grace. Chantelle was spark out on the floor, on her crocheted blanket, beneath the arch of her baby gym, as if she'd fallen asleep mid-play. As was Vicky's mam, snoring lightly, on the sofa, close beside her, one arm flung out as if reaching for her granddaughter's head.

Tears sprang in Vicky's eyes. For all the memories she didn't have. For the thought that way back, during a time she couldn't remember, the baby in this tableau might have been her. For the knowledge that, despite everything, her mam did love her granddaughter. For the enormity of what she might now lose.

'It's almost ten to eleven!' her mam spluttered now. 'Where the hell have you *been*? I've been thinking all bloody sorts. Nearly phoned the police!'

'Mam, shhh,' Vicky pleaded. 'You'll wake up the baby!'

'I'll give you wake up the sodding baby, my girl! Who the *hell* d'you think you are, stopping out, leaving muggins here to babysit? I've been worried sick, I have, wondering what's happened to you – worried sick! Thinking you've had a car crash, or been raped, thinking God knows what else! Where the hell have you been? And why the hell didn't you *phone* me?'

In a corner of Vicky's mind a revelation registered. That this was true. That despite all appearances to the contrary, her mother worried about her. Her mother might even love her.

But this was no time to dwell on motherly love. Motherly belief was so obviously more important. 'I'm *so* sorry, Mum,' she trotted out, as per the story they'd agreed. 'Paddy picked me up from work, and on the way home he had to go out of town to deliver a car part. So we made the detour, and he had a puncture. Hit a nail in the road. And—'

'And it's taken him this sodding long to fix it? You think I was born yesterday?'

'Mam, listen! I'm trying to *tell* you. His spare was flat too. So he had to walk miles to find a phone box – we were in the middle of, like, nowhere – but he couldn't, so he went on, and—'

'And what were *you* doing?'

'I was waiting in the *car* for him. Mam, will you just let me finish? And he couldn't find a phone box but he eventually found a petrol station, and got some of that stuff you can inject into flat tyres so you can fix the puncture temporarily, but it took ages to do and then we had to drive back *really* slowly, and' – she raised her arms and held her hands out, palms up – '*that's* why we're so late. I'm sorry, Mam. I would have called but once we were back on our way home it seemed quicker to just come home than drive round and round ...'

'Round and bleeding round,' her mother huffed, reaching down to pick up Chantelle, who was now stirring. She sniffed her bottom. 'Well, you can bloody change her and put her to bleeding bed! Where's lover boy anyway?'

Vicky indicated with a nod as she took the baby. Her precious, precious baby. 'Having a bath,' she said. 'He got covered in filth sorting the tyre out.'

'Oh, so just use all my hot water, why don't you?' she yelled upstairs, as she shoved her feet into her slippers and toddled off into the kitchen.

Paddy was lying on Vicky's bed, staring at the ceiling. She'd thought he might have fallen asleep, she'd been so long changing the baby, giving her a bottle and settling her down again – down in her basket in the front room, for the time being at least. She could bring her up and put her down in her cot later.

Her warm, living baby. She thought of Gurdy; she couldn't stop herself. Of his body lying cold and dead and wet in a lake of blood, and had to fight to stop the images from filling her mind's eye.

Paddy turned over on his side to look at her. He was naked, apart from a pair of boxers. 'I thought it best to stay put,' he whispered, beckoning her towards him. 'Didn't want to set your mam off even more.'

Vicky unbuttoned her blouse, took her bra off and stepped out of her work skirt. Then took her tights off and went across to join him. He'd watched her throughout and a wild thought entered her head – would he be expecting to have sex? But no. She could see as soon as she lay down beside him – his eyes were full of tears, the skin around them all puffy. He'd been lying here crying again.

She placed a palm on his cheek. 'What the fuck have I done, babe?' he whispered.

'It's the drugs, Paddy. You know that,' she said, because it was. 'It's the drugs that have done this. Not you.'

'Tell that to the judge,' he said wretchedly. 'Tell that to fucking *Gurdy*.'

'But it *is*,' she persisted. 'That bloody *animal*, that bloody Mo! You should never have got mixed up in *any* of it, ever. It's not like you had nothing else you could do,' she went on, beginning to warm to her theme. 'Is it? You'd have *never* have done this were it not for the drugs. Oh, babe, and going to *prison*. Being away from us for so long ...'

'Which I'm going to be again,' he said. 'Oh, fuck! What have I *done*?' he swallowed another sob. 'Babe, you are going to stand by me, aren't you?'

She shifted position so she could look at him face to face. Feel the heat of his breath on her cheeks. 'You don't even have to ask that,' she said, knowing it to be true now. No matter what – and she knew her grief for Gurdy would all too soon hit her. But no matter what, she understood. She knew who and what were to blame here. And, whatever happened, she would stand by him. They'd be fine. He had said so. No evidence. They'd be fine. Poor Gurdy would be buried, and then the world would move on. It would all go away, and they'd keep their dreadful secret. But if it didn't. If she did have to fight for him, she would. Whatever happened, she would stand by her man. 'Pad,

I *love* you,' she told him. 'You're Chantelle's father and I love you.'

He drew both his arms around her and held her tight. Almost too tight.

'Fuck, I love you,' he said into her ear. 'Fuck, how I love you! I'll stop, Vic. I promise. I'll do anything. *Anything*. I don't think I could go on living if I didn't have you. I don't know what the hell I've ever done to deserve you. But, fuck, I love you – I *need* you, babe. You're my *life*.'

He loosened his grip on her a bit then, so he could smother her with kisses. Tiny little kisses, all over her face. Little individual declarations of undying love that tore into her because he'd never done such a thing, ever. That ripped into her and almost burst her heart.

Because this should have been the happiest moment of her life.

Chapter 26

Vicky woke up to find her mother looming over her. Shaking her and hissing her name.

'What, Mam?' she whispered angrily, wondering what the hell she was doing there. Chantelle was right there, in her cot, sleeping soundly. But wouldn't be for long. What the hell was her mum doing, barging in there?

'Get up!' her mam barked at her. 'You too,' she said to Paddy, while he groaned and rubbed his eyes. 'Come on! The pair of you, hurry up!'

'Why?' Vicky said, her brain firing darts of fear and shock. She somehow found the words she knew she needed to say and got them out. 'What the fuck is going on?'

'Frigging cops are here, that's what,' her mam said, jabbing a finger into Vicky's shoulder. 'Probably for this fucker, here, lying there like the picture of bloody innocence. Get *up*, Vicky! The neighbours'll be having a field day if the knocking gets any louder and I'm not opening the door to them till you two are up.'

Vicky tried to think. Find more words. The police? Downstairs? *Now?* She pulled the covers off, keeping her face away so she wouldn't have to meet her mother's eyes. 'Go let them in,' she said. 'We're coming. Tell them we're coming down. Okay? It'll be a mistake. That's all it'll be, Mam. Keep your hair on. Just a mistake.'

'Yeah, and I came down in the last shower of rain. Mistake, my eye,' she said, before stomping off back down the stairs.

Paddy was still coming to. Christ, how could he not get what was happening? 'Shit,' she said. 'Shit! Paddy, the police are here! Get your bloody head together! Get your jeans on!' she said, yanking the covers off him too.

He snapped to attention. 'I can't!' he said. 'They've got blood on them, haven't they? Oh, fuck …'

'Then find some trackies. The grey ones. *There*.' She pointed. 'And keep calm,' she said. '*Calm*, okay? Don't wind them up.' Then she wondered if, actually, he should do exactly that. That's what he would do, if he was innocent. Kick off. That was *exactly* what he would do.

To top it all, Chantelle woke up now and started grizzling. Vicky grabbed a T-shirt and her own trackies, and yanked both of them on. Then picked up the baby and jiggled her on her hip while Paddy, wide awake now, stuffed his legs into his trackies. 'What about a top?' he asked.

Christ, he was like a child. 'Forget the top! Just make yourself decent!'

'Half fucking six!' he said. 'Half fucking six? How'd they *know*?'

'We don't know they *do* know,' she said. 'It could be anything. *Think*, babe. Get your head straight. We don't know why they've come here. We're surprised. Half asleep. Just woken up, okay? This is a *shock*.'

She surprised herself by how quickly she was thinking. Blotting the fear out. *Just tell the story.* As per the whispered discussions that had continued into the small hours. *Just tell the story and everything will be okay.*

'How could they have found him?' Paddy asked plaintively.

Why couldn't he just get his fucking head straight?

'How should I know? Stop thinking! Christ, Paddy, come *on.*'

It was Jimmy's dad who was waiting for them in the front room. Was that a good thing or a bad thing? Could it perhaps be that they hadn't found Gurdy? She grabbed at the thought that perhaps this was unrelated. Something to do with Paddy's arrest at the weekend. There was another copper too. Youngish. In uniform. One she didn't know.

She held Chantelle against her like a shield.

'What's he s'posed to have done *this* time?' she asked them, as cockily as she could muster. 'You do realise we have a baby to look after, don't you? Waking us up at this bloody time!'

Jimmy's dad met her stony gaze, looking sad. No other word for it. 'Look, Vicky, we're here in connection with a murder inquiry. The body of Gurdip Banerjee was found a couple of hours ago and we'd like you both to come in for questioning.'

Vicky heard her mum gasp behind her. '*What?*' she said, feigning shock, feeling sick.

'Why us?' Paddy asked. 'What's it got to do with us? Why are you arresting us?'

'We're not arresting you, not at this point, but you do need to come in and answer some questions. Down at the station,' he continued, in a toneless voice. 'So I suggest you go and put something warm on ...' He glanced at Vicky's mam then and frowned. 'And, Vicky, if you need to, to make some arrangements to have your daughter looked after.'

The growing fear was also genuine, even if the words were a confection. 'What, *Gurdy?*' she gasped, her throat catching. 'You mean Gurdy is *dead?* What's happened?' She looked desperately at Paddy, then back at Jimmy's father. 'What's happened?' she said again. 'And why do you want to speak to us about it? I don't understand. We've been here all night!'

She'd been aware of her mam sitting down on the armchair by the window. Now she stood up again, slowly, on heavy-seeming legs.

'They have,' she said. 'Been with me. Here—.' She reached her arms out to take the baby. 'Give her here. I'm her *grandmother*,' she added, scowling at both policemen, her voice indignant. 'I'm fine to have her till you're done.'

Vicky could have hugged her mother – did she mean to stand by them? – but she simply handed over the baby, her mind whirring with the effort of trying to know how to act. 'Okay,' she said. 'Of course. If we can help in any way, of *course* we will. I'll go and dress. But Gurdy ... who'd have done that? Oh my God, I can't *believe* it. C'mon, babe,' she said to Paddy. 'We have to *help* them!'

Paddy, beside her, was clenching his fists. 'They don't want our help, babe,' he said, looking at Jimmy's dad, not her. 'They've already made up their fucking minds that we've something to do with it. But this time, they'll see they fucked up.'

Jimmy's dad ignored Paddy. Acted like he wasn't even there. Or, if he was, that he had nothing of any value to say. Just that sad look, to her. 'One at a time, love,' he told her, gesturing towards the hall. 'Not together. You first.' He nodded towards the other officer. 'My colleague will accompany you, okay? He'll wait outside till you're dressed.' He turned and looked at Paddy then. 'And then this young *gentleman* can go and get something on as well.'

Vicky turned towards the door, the way he'd said 'gentleman' sending a chill through her. And she realised that he didn't look sad anymore.

There were two cars parked outside. One marked, one not. Both occupied by a uniformed driver. Vicky went first, just as the sun was coming up, bringing with it the promise of a bright late summer's day. She walked up the path and through the gate, the uniformed officer beckoning her to the marked car – which would no doubt set the curtains twitching, just as her mother had predicted.

She didn't turn around. She felt a welling of something too big to keep a lid on, knowing that Paddy was behind her – probably giving it lots of attitude – and that her mam would be on the doorstep, with Chantelle, confused and sleepy, on her hip. Vicky was grateful for what Leanne had said, even though she'd pooh-poohed it at the time – that her daughter would have no memory of this.

She climbed into the back seat of the car with the policeman, who said only, 'Up you shove, love', nothing more. And marvelled at the enormity of what had happened – *was* happening. The fact that two officers and four cars had arrived just after dawn. Like in *The Bill*, or some similarly clichéd cop show. Like they were taking this non-arrest (for Jimmy's dad had assured her they weren't arresting them) all too seriously for comfort. Making sure that, as of now – as of when she'd gone back upstairs to put some clothes on – she wouldn't be able to speak to Paddy on her own.

So when would she be able to speak to him next? It hit her hard, like a punch, that she had absolutely no idea. Which threw her into a panic, trying to remember what they'd agreed on. The flat tyre, the hike to find help, the can of tyre-weld, the long fandango of Paddy fixing the puncture on the roadside. The fact that she must try to be vague on all counts. No, she couldn't remember where the puncture happened. No, she didn't remember where he'd got the stuff from. It was dark. It was remote. All the details were just a blur now. Why the hell would she make a note of every little frigging thing anyway? She wasn't expecting to have to answer twenty questions!

But when she was 'processed' – another word she thought she'd probably gotten off the telly – and shown into an interview room, it was *all* gone. Only to be replaced by the logistics of what *had* actually happened. Him pulling up half a mile or so away, to chuck her work pinny in some random skip full of rubble, then, nearer Clayton, making a detour and pulling up again, on Bradford Road, jumping a small wall that led to the patch of woodland that everyone just knew as the 'fillas' – and hiding the crowbar, or so he'd said, under some rocks.

She tried to keep her mind still. To breathe. To bring the fiction to the fore. To keep calm and look calm – just shocked and bereaved. God, did Lucy even know yet? She might well do. If the police had found him, the news would have travelled fast. Thinking of Lucy, of what she didn't know, of what Vicky must never, ever tell her, just made the whole thing more wretched. How could they be blood sisters when she carried such a terrible, terrible secret? And if Lucy ever did know, would she ever call Vicky her sister ever again? It was no good. She'd have given anything to turn the clock back, bring Gurdy back again. But when it had come to it, she'd failed to protect him.

And were they leaving her in here expressly to torture her? Did they have a CCTV camera mounted in a hidden place high on the walls? Were they watching her now, reading her body language? Oh, God, she hoped not. Because try as she might – *Keep calm, babe. They have no evidence. They can't touch us* – her whole body seemed intent on conducting a mutiny. Her stomach kept convulsing, even though it was empty, hollowed out, grumbling with annoyance, and her legs couldn't stop shaking. Her bloody legs wouldn't stop *shaking*! She'd never experienced anything like it in her life.

And then, suddenly, into the room came two officers she didn't recognise. Not Jimmy's dad. (Was he busy interrogating Paddy at this moment? Probably. He'd love that. He'd love that he'd finally got him in his sights. Even if only temporarily.) But a man in a grey suit and a woman in a navy one. Jacket and skirt, stiff, looking like something out of the forces.

'Vicky,' the woman said, sitting down opposite on one of the two wooden chairs. And in such a way that made Vicky just want to let it go, every bit of it. Tell the truth. Get it over. Just tell her what had happened. Make Paddy's case. Tell her about the drugs. Tell her how it wasn't him – it was the drugs. But she couldn't; Paddy needed her and she would not let him down. She was strong enough. She put her mask back in place.

They 'took her statement' as they put it for the best part of three hours. Taking her, minute by minute, through the events of the previous day. And all the while, the male policeman wrote her words down. She knew, even as he was writing, in his curly, schoolboy hand, that he didn't believe a word she was saying. The female officer was gentle, acting like she *did* believe it, all of it, and giving Vicky time to think – 'Take your time, love, just think back, get it straight' – and when a constable came in, some two hours into the nightmare, made a point of saying, before handing over photographs from an envelope, that Vicky might want to take a breath before looking at them.

And there Gurdy was, in daylight. Or perhaps an arc light. So bright. Every detail she'd tried so hard to forget now picked out in glorious technicolour. Had she anything in her gut, she would have brought it up then and there. Instead she could only retch, because her shock and grief were genuine, and the male officer had opened the door of the room and asked for someone to bring some tissues and more water.

That was when it hit her. Would they have shown her had they not thought her guilty? Paddy must be wrong, she thought, panicking. They must have something. *Must* have.

And then another knock. It was almost a relief. And a male voice. Was it Jimmy's dad now, behind the opened door?

The policeman who'd answered it sat down again. Nodded to the female officer. She looked at Vicky sadly.

And *then* they arrested her.

HMP New Hall, which Vicky found herself approaching five hours later, didn't look like a prison at all. It looked nothing like Armley, with its intimidating walls and turrets, more like a holiday camp, she thought as she peered out through the grille of the back window of the security van – there were lights coming on and, partly hidden by trees, she thought she could even see a tennis court. It looked like an outward-bound centre for school kids, she decided – a place to learn rock climbing, or canoeing, or volleyball – stuff like that. It looked innocent. Welcoming.

Like a port in a storm. A perfect storm which had swept her up and catapulted her into an ever more terrifying nightmare.

Once they'd arrested her, around lunchtime, she had been moved again. This time to a cell, which was down a corridor, down some stairs, and then across another corridor, like some subterranean lair.

There she'd been given a sandwich, which she couldn't eat, and a carton of orange juice, which she'd managed. And had been visited by another man in a suit, this time apparently a court-appointed lawyer, who'd been given the task to represent her, if she wished.

She thought of Lucy – was she at this moment sitting at the switchboard at the solicitors? Could this very man – who was short and wide and looked a bit like a bulldog – even work at the same firm? It was possible, even if not probable, and shame overcame her. She was in a cell, going before a magistrate, inhabiting a world she'd always known about – existed on the edges of, with Paddy, truth be told. But a world she'd never once thought of as being anything to do with her.

It had been bad enough being a prison visitor – she'd never really felt comfortable in that horrible place – but a prisoner. A prisoner *herself*? She couldn't quite believe it was going to happen.

But the solicitor had been clear. They had evidence to put her at the scene now, apparently. He didn't say what, but he was firm on that point. So unless she was prepared to change her story and testify against Paddy, she would be tried for Gurdy's murder as well.

'You do realise that, don't you?' he asked her, not unkindly. 'Unless you tell them it was Allen – Paddy – you will both be tried for murder. Vicky, you do see that, don't you?'

Vicky was frightened to open her mouth, not knowing quite what to say to him. Aware that what he'd told her was already coming true. *They'll try to trick you*, he'd explained to her, as they'd lain there in the small hours. *They'll try to trick you into saying something that will incriminate me, I promise. Trick you into telling them what I did, then promising you'll go free, but then they'll get you on a technicality anyway.*

She'd asked him what sort of technicality, just so she knew what to expect, but he'd laughed a humourless laugh. *Don't even think about it*, he'd told her. *Just trust me, they'll find something to do you for. They always do. So you'll never be free.*

She'd straightened her back and met the solicitor's eye. 'Of course I know that,' she told him briskly. 'But they can't convict us for something we never did, can they?'

'No,' he said. 'That's true. But think carefully about this, Vicky. Think about your child … Chantelle, isn't it?' He let it hang there, waiting for her to speak.

She spoke, as per the plan: she must just stick to the plan. 'I don't know how that so-called evidence got there

– whatever it is they've got – and, for all I know, the cops could have put it there. It has been *known*,' she added, trying to emulate Paddy's usual sarcastic tone. 'And that Officer Daley has had it in for Paddy for *ages* – everyone knows that. So I wouldn't put *anything* past him.'

'As you wish,' the solicitor said mildly. His name was Mr Grey, and, in the dim light, he looked it. Did he really want to help her, or *was* he out to trick her? She couldn't tell. She wished she shared Paddy's confidence that it was all going to be okay. How could he possibly know that? 'But I'll still do my best to get you bail,' Mr Grey said, as if she'd just ruined her chance of it. 'I have to tell you it's a long shot, but as you have a child … Well, let's see, eh?'

He didn't say 'Don't hold your breath' but he might as well have done.

And here she was, early evening, in prison. At New Hall. No bail. Not today. And what was Chantelle doing now, right this minute? Vicky ached for her. She'd never in her short life felt so far away.

The woman who checked her in seemed to sense Vicky's upset. What did she already know about her? Everything she needed to, probably, Vicky guessed. She was kindly, and patient, and gave her a welcome bit of privacy, showing her into a place where she could shower and change – into prison clothes, a baggy boiler suit – and at least have some space to collect her thoughts. She said she was called Miss Teague, which made Vicky feel like she was back in school again. That's how she'd play it, she decided. Treat it like a weird kind of school trip. Hopefully a short one. Perhaps that would help the pain and fear go away.

And the continuing holiday camp impression helped as well. New Hall looked bright and lively, as opposed to Armley's relentless dark and oppressive aura, and, once she was inside, the impression only increased. From the outside it looked more like a series of office blocks than a prison, with manicured gardens, trees planted everywhere, and even greenhouses, which were apparently 'fully operational'. Inside, there were dorms for the prisoners to sleep in – no *Porridge*-style cells here, with iron bars for walls – a large gymnasium, a sports hall, a well-equipped dining area (whatever that meant) and even TV rooms to relax in.

It was about as far from her idea of what a prison might look like as could be. Even the room-mates Miss Teague introduced her to seemed a world away from her imaginings – three girls, all of whom looked to be in their twenties, and who welcomed her in with what looked like genuine warmth. Even their names seemed straight from an Enid Blyton novel – Susan, Amanda and Marlene.

Vicky was glad none of them asked why she was there.

But for all that she'd been stockpiling reasons to keep her chin up, the edifice she'd created was as flimsy as a house of cards, and when the other girls went off to the TV room – it was now getting on for nine – she climbed into her bed, under the thin beige blanket, and curled up into a terrified ball, knowing that whatever happened now – either to her or to Paddy – her life as she knew it was over.

She fell asleep praying for Gurdy's beautiful soul.

Chapter 27

Gurdy was cremated at Scholemoor Crematorium, just minutes away from where he'd spent his entire life. *Leeds*, Lucy kept thinking. He never even made it as far as bloody *Leeds*. And now he never would.

It was a sunny afternoon, but it had rained heavily earlier in the day, which meant everything green (the crematorium was set in the centre of a large and leafy cemetery) had been pressed down by the weight of water clinging to it, and hung down as if in prayer, and dripped as if crying, along with most of the hundreds' strong crowd of mourners.

Lucy and Jimmy stayed on the periphery. She'd sent a card to Gurdy's parents, but she didn't want to intrude now. Vikram, trying to be strong for his near-hysterical mother (whom his father could only just about keep on her feet), looked as stiff, brittle and frozen as if caught in freeze-frame. She thought if she approached him to say anything about what Gurdy had meant to her, she might completely shatter his composure.

There was to be no sprinkling of Gurdy's ashes here, and Lucy was pleased. Knowing the circumstances of his death she found it such a grim thing to contemplate – in death as in life, to be thrown to the ground in such a way. She knew it was silly – there was no relationship between the violence of his death and the ritual of sprinkling the ashes of loved ones, not in any religion. But the Hindu way, as she remembered Gurdy himself telling her when an aunt had died a couple of years back, was to sprinkle a loved one's ashes over the flowing water of the Ganges, so his were going to be sent back to a relative in India. So he'd finally escaped. And a good bit further than Leeds.

But no Vicky here to say farewell to her friend. It was wrong. Just so wrong. Her in prison. It had all been so much to take in, and Lucy wasn't sure she had yet, even though every day for the past dozen or so since the grim news had broken, she'd walked round to Vicky's mam's house to offer to help with the baby, and had so far – to her delight, despite her sadness and anxiety – been able to look after Chantelle twice.

Because who knew how long this was all going to go on, with Vicky in prison on remand for Gurdy's murder?

'Christ, Mo's here!' Jimmy hissed at her. 'There's front for you.'

They were at the back – part of the bulge of people who couldn't quite fit into the crematorium. So many family members, extended family members, all trying to pack inside before the service began. Who *were* all these hordes of weeping people? What a shame Gurdy would never know how much he was loved.

'Mo?' she asked, shocked, following Jimmy's gaze to a far corner of the kind of ante-room area outside the crematorium itself. And he was right. You'd spot those trademark dreadlocks from a mile. He was here with another man Lucy thought she recognised. Older. 'And who's that?' she asked Jimmy.

'Irish Pete,' he told her grimly. 'They have some nerve, turning up here.'

'Perhaps they felt they must. Perhaps they wanted to pay their respects. Gurdy worked in Mo's garage, after all.'

'And who I don't doubt would have thrown him to the lions, had he needed to,' Jimmy said. 'Well, they still have it coming …'

'Jimmy, stop that. Not today. Today's supposed to be about Gurdy.'

In fact, though she knew Jimmy didn't quite see it the way she did, Lucy thought Mo's intentions were probably genuine. She knew, because Jimmy'd told her, that the reason Gurdy's body had been found so incredibly quickly was because they had inside information. She didn't know all the details, only that a couple of people had seen Paddy in some sort of meltdown, and it was generally agreed that he was paranoid about someone trying to frame him after the arrest, and when Mo couldn't find Gurdy where he'd expected to, at the garage, it didn't take much for the grapevine to start jangling. And the remote lock-up, where Paddy'd taken Gurdy, belonged to Mo.

Not that anyone could officially make the connection. It had been an anonymous tip-off, and everyone was content with that, for now. The axe would fall on Mo's operation sooner or later. But, in the meantime, Lucy chose to believe Mo *was* there paying respects. For all that Mo was the number one hard man in their part of Bradford, only a sick bastard like Paddy Allen could want to harm Gurdy.

'No honour among thieves?' she asked Jimmy. 'Is that it? Anyway, shush, now. The service is about to begin.'

'I'm going to have another go to see if she'll agree to see me,' she told Jimmy, once the cremation had taken place and they were hurrying back to get in Jimmy's car. They didn't want to linger, because they both had to get back to work, and, being at the back, they didn't have to. Lucy couldn't bear to see the smoke rising from the chimney anyway. 'I'm just not having it,' she said. 'She has *got* to tell the truth.'

'She'd be insane not to,' Jimmy agreed. 'But she obviously hasn't this far. You've got to face it, love. She clearly cares more about that psycho of a boyfriend of hers than she does about her own kid.'

He shook his head. Jimmy no longer had any time for Vicky. As far as he was concerned she had made her choice and had been in some way involved in Gurdy's murder. They had evidence to place her at the murder scene – rock-solid evidence, apparently – so everything she'd said to the police had been a lie. She had been there, whether Lucy could stomach the fact or not.

Lucy shook her head. 'Because he's spun her a load of nonsense, that's what I reckon. Because he's convinced her if she just keeps denying everything she'll be fine.'

'Which she won't because forensic evidence doesn't lie. And her lawyer would have already *told* her that. And she's clearly not taking his advice.'

Lucy wished she knew what the evidence Jimmy kept mentioning was. He said he didn't know, because it would have been against the law for his father to tell him. But she still bet he *did* know. She'd have put money on it. But being at the scene didn't mean she had anything to do with it. How'd he know Paddy hadn't beaten her as well? It was all a mess. Why the hell wasn't she telling the truth? How much more psycho (as Jimmy'd put it) did your boyfriend have to be before you ran for the bloody hills?

'But I know if I can just *see* her I can talk some sense into her. I know I can. Which is probably why she won't see me. Because she *knows* that.'

And all too well, because Vicky hadn't budged an inch. Lucy had tried three times to get a visiting order organised, without success, and her half dozen letters had all gone unanswered. Vicky had even refused to see her mum ('She reckons she'll be out soon, so there's no point me dragging there,' Mrs Robinson had told her in an unashamedly relieved tone) and there was no way she'd agree to have Chantelle go to see her – Lucy knew that before Vicky's mum had even told her.

But she had a plan. She'd been speaking to one of the solicitors in her office, and she'd written a long letter to Vicky in which she'd highly embellished the truth. She'd said that if Vicky continued to refuse to see both her and Chantelle, then it would be like she was an unfit mother

– not bothered about her kid – and that she could even lose her altogether. Chantelle might be taken into care because of it. That would be enough, *surely*, to make her change her mind.

Jimmy started the car. 'You know, you might need to brace yourself, Luce. You're so sure Vicky wouldn't have had anything to do with it, but you don't actually know that. She's changed. You already know that. Since Paddy's been back, she's changed. Dumped you like a hot brick, the minute he clicked his fingers, and—'

'*No,*' Lucy said.

'Seriously, love, you don't know what happened. You weren't there. Think about it. She does everything that bastard tells her to. Everything. I'm not saying she did it. I'm not saying she had a big part in it. But she was *there*. They were there *together*. Love, you've got to accept the possibility that she at least stood by and *let* him.'

'No,' Lucy said again. 'I refuse to believe it. She loved Gurdy as much as I did. No, either he's got something on her – made some threat – God, maybe even against the *baby* – I wouldn't bloody put it past him. Either that or he's convinced her that they can't possibly have any evidence, and she'll be safe. Either way, I'm going to find out.'

The plan worked so well and so quickly that Lucy almost felt guilty. But only up to a point because, actually, Vicky *could* lose Chantelle if she persisted in her lunacy. Not that she was planning on actually taking her along, despite what she'd said. That could wait till next time.

Though, God willing, there wouldn't be a next time. She felt sure that she only needed to talk some bloody sense into her friend and she'd snap out of whatever spell she'd been put under. Because there was one weapon that was more powerful than any other – that Paddy couldn't physically get to her. Yes, they could write – another thing she'd asked one of the solicitors at work – but only in the blandest of tones, because everything would be vetted by the prisons. God, she hoped he went down for *ever*.

The trip to New Hall was fiddly and very time-consuming. First a train, then another, then a walk, then a bus, and with her memories of what Vicky had told her about visiting Armley, she expected the whole business to be grim.

She was shocked, therefore, to find herself walking up a bright, leafy lane, to what, if you ignored the discreet perimeter fence, didn't look like a prison at all. In fact, the first brutal shock of the reality of her friend's incarceration was Vicky herself, who she saw from across the sunny visiting room, wearing something not dissimilar to the overalls Jimmy wore to do his plumbing, which hung off her. She had lost a lot of weight. More shocking still was to see quite how different she looked. With her hair unstyled and lank, and her face free of make-up, she looked ridiculously young. Just a girl.

The expression on Vicky's face, though, was chilling. There was shock – Lucy had forgotten that she'd lied about Chantelle – and then a steel that Lucy hadn't seen before.

All too soon though, the moment passed and they were in one another's arms, both crying, both overcome with emotion. 'I'm so sorry,' Lucy said, pulling tissues from her jacket pocket. 'Chantelle's fine, she really is. And I'm so sorry I had to lie to you. And I have photos. I borrowed a girl from work's Polaroid camera. They're not the best, but here you go.' She pulled these from her other jacket pocket and placed them on the table. Though Vicky didn't immediately pick them up. 'So it's not true?' she asked instead. 'The social aren't really sniffing around? Only some of the girls in here, the things they've told me ... God, I'd go *mad*, Luce. I'd lose it, I know I would.'

Lucy nudged the pictures towards her. 'No, I promise. And I hated to lie to you. But I had to, Vic, I had to. I had to come here and see you.' She lowered her voice, conscious of the prison officer standing just feet away. Did they listen in? Did they have to report stuff? She had no idea. 'I had to come,' she said, 'to try and make you see *sense*.'

Vicky was now looking at the pictures of Chantelle, however, and if she'd taken in what Lucy had just said, she made no sign of it. 'God, I can't bear it,' she said finally, lifting a picture to her mouth and kissing it. 'Is she missing me?'

'Course she's missing you, you div! But your mam's doing fine. She really is, Vic. And don't look so shocked. She's *coping*. Probably be the making of her, truth be told. And I'm helping all I can; I try to pop round every day, and I have her the odd night, to give her a bit of a break. So you don't have to worry, okay?' She leaned forward. 'But, Vic, look, you know why I'm really here. What the hell is going *on*?'

Vicky dropped her gaze, then put the pictures in a pile and raised her eyes to Lucy's again. 'I didn't do what they are saying, Luce. I would *never* hurt Gurdy.'

'Christ, I *know* that. Course I do. But – look at me, Vicky – you've got to tell them the *truth*.'

'I am telling the truth,' she said. 'I'd never hurt him, ever. I—' She pressed the heels of her hands to her eyes.

'But you were *there*, Vic,' Lucy persisted. 'They *know* you were. You've got to come clean about it now. There's just no point – look, I know what's going on. You're protecting Paddy, aren't you? You—'

'Will you shut the fuck *up*?' Vicky hissed, gesturing towards the nearby officer. 'Paddy was with *me*. That's what I told the police, and that's what I'm sticking to.'

'But it's not true!'

'That's what I told the police and that's what I'm sticking to,' Vicky said again, looking even more childlike with the tears that were coursing down her face. 'I have to. Because … because, you know, Lucy. Because I have to. He's Chantelle's father, and she needs him, and I *have* to see this through.'

Lucy lost her rag, she couldn't help it. 'And you're her *mother*! And let me tell you, she needs you a great deal more than that murdering bloody monster!'

'It's not *him*. It wasn't *him*, Lucy. You just don't realise. It was the *drugs*!'

So an admission at least, finally. She couldn't backtrack on that now. Lucy pressed home her advantage. 'Yeah, but it's not the drugs that go to trial, is it? It's not the drugs that go to prison. It's *you*. Because you will, you know. You're not going to get off this. Whatever he's told you, Vic, he's wrong. You are not going to get away with this. They have evidence. You know that. Why are you being so bloody naïve?'

'They don't. I *know* they don't. He's lying just to scare us.'

'What's all this "us", for God's sake? Vicky, are you completely deranged? Jimmy's dad isn't lying, mate. You're an accessory to murder, and unless you tell the truth you're going to make everything *so* much worse!' She snatched up the photos and shook them in her friend's face. '*Think*, Vicky, for fuck's sake. I don't know what he's said to you, but think of this one. She *needs* you. Is that what it's come to, that you believe his shit over everyone, now? Is *that* it? Despite having watched him *kill* someone? Vic, you're *insane*.'

Vicky snatched the photos, leapt to her feet and scraped her chair back.

Lucy was confused at first. Visiting time was no way over yet. Could she just leave then?

'Can I go back, please,' Vicky said to the officer, turning her back on Lucy. The officer nodded. Apparently so.

Lucy stood too. 'Please, mate,' she said, casting an apologetic glance towards the prison officer. 'Please, mate, don't chuck your life away. Not for him.' She stood and waited. Nothing. 'Look, you know I'll be there for you,' she went on. 'And Jimmy and I, you know we'll take care of Chantelle for you. Okay?' Again she waited. This was unbelievable. It really was like Vicky had been irrevocably brainwashed. Lucy tried again. '*Okay*, Vic?'

But her friend just walked away.

Chapter 28

Lucy didn't realise. She was so stuck on her hatred of Paddy that she couldn't see an inch beyond her nose. Which was why there was no point in arguing with her. Or trying to explain how things were. How things could be, and would be. How her Paddy, another victim in all this, was clean now, and he was never going back to drugs again. He'd made her a promise and he was already proving he could stick to it.

He'd written daily. Lengthy letters full of loving words and reassurances. Always measured – the fucking screws got to read everything, obviously – but always clear, even if she did have to read between the lines a bit, that she needed only to stick to the statement she'd made. That they couldn't touch either of them, because they weren't there.

And though she wished she could talk to him, and have a proper chat about it – about the real 'it' rather than the fiction – she'd accepted and believed that was the way it was going to be. That they'd be unable to convict them because they couldn't without evidence. Didn't matter about anyone seeing Paddy's car, or whatever other cock and bull they'd come up with – without physical evidence, they couldn't convict anyone. And there wasn't any evidence. So they were safe. Whatever Lucy said – and God knew what lines Jimmy had told her to spin her – Vicky knew what she was talking about. There was no way in the world anyone would find the crowbar – it was a million-to-one shot. A billion-to-one shot. All she had to do was hold her nerve.

Lucy had written too, of course. A huge long letter which came two days after she'd made her visit to New Hall. Saying the same thing; that she must think of Chantelle. But didn't she realise? That was exactly what she *was* doing. If she changed her story – she couldn't quite think of it as 'Tell them Paddy had killed Gurdy', as he hadn't *been* Paddy when he'd carried it out – then he might, probably would, go to prison for murder. Because, as Mr Grey had kept pointing out (hypothetically, obviously, since they hadn't been at the scene, had they?), she would then become a witness to the crime. And if Paddy was tried for murder, which there was no question he would be, then she'd almost certainly be tried as an accessory to murder (Mr Grey had explained that also, at length) which, though he kept saying they'd be lenient, since she'd be ensuring Paddy's conviction, meant that she'd be convicted and given a custodial sentence too. And where did *that* leave her baby daughter? Christ! An *orphan*.

She had had so much time to think. That was the thing no one realised. And she'd thought, and she'd thought and she'd worked everything out. Which was why it angered her so much that Lucy couldn't even *see* it. She wasn't being stupid – much less 'deranged', as Lucy'd called her. She was being *smart*. Trying to find the silver lining in the biggest cloud of her entire bloody life. Standing by Paddy wasn't the lunatic behaviour of a stupid 'brainwashed' girl-friend. Looked at every which way, it was the only thing she *could* do.

But now she was beginning to fray around the edges. She was in the showers, having just played a game of netball. She'd been in New Hall five weeks now and, exactly as she'd thought when she'd first swept through the gates in the security van, it really was a lot like being back in school. She was in a dorm now – twelve of them in there – like something out of a Mallory Towers book. And, just like in school, they were very into exercise. Feeling low? Get some exercise. Feeling angry? Get some exercise. Feeling like you want to slit your throat? Get some sodding exercise. And though she'd been reluctant at first, to say the least, they had turned out to be right: it was the main thing that was keeping her sane.

But this morning, even being hot and sweaty and gasping couldn't stop the edges fraying. She'd not heard from Paddy in three days. And however hard she tried to push them away, Lucy's words kept returning. That he'd drop her in it in a heartbeat if the boot were on the other foot. That he had no loyalty to Vicky whatsoever.

Sod her, she thought, as she turned her face up to the shower head. It wasn't like she had a choice, was it? And there would be a good reason. Perhaps he'd reached his quota – who knew? Perhaps the post had been delayed. There could be all sorts of reasons why she hadn't heard from him. And he was clean now – that was the main thing. Able to think straight at last. She felt a pang of sympathy. For all that she had so many horrors to deal with, he was going to have to live with what he'd done for the rest of his life. God, it must have hit him hard. She hoped he was okay.

'He might even be in lock-up,' Susan, one of the girls in the dorm, suggested when she returned from the showers and confirmed she was once again letterless. 'Got into some fight, or other, and be banged up – they don't get access to letters or materials when that happens.'

Susan knew about that sort of thing. Knew all sorts of things about a world that Vicky didn't. Her boyfriend was apparently an 'accomplished thief' – her words – who had been responsible for a spate of armed robberies on jewellery shops in Leeds and Middlesbrough. And she herself was inside for stolen cheque books and forgery, and would apparently be in New Hall for two years this time – it wasn't her first sentence. She'd been to prison previously for the same offence.

That must be it, Vicky reassured herself, when there was nothing from Paddy the next day. Just a scrawl from her mam, droning on about how Chantelle was teething and giving her all sorts of headaches, and, irritatingly, some rant about what was going on on one of her bloody soaps on TV. Paddy had a short temper at the best of times, and withdrawing from coke and weed (and God only knew what else) was hard, so he would have been in a foul mood before he started. And if someone had wound him up, well, he would have definitely been up for a scrap.

Thank God New Hall was nothing like that. But then it wouldn't be, would it? It was more like a kind of holding pen for women who couldn't quite get their lives together mostly. One girl, Tanya, had laughed when she'd explained, in all seriousness, that whenever her kids were getting too much to handle, she'd go on a shoplifting spree with the express intention of getting nicked so she could have a few weeks' peace and quiet.

'But what about your kids?' Vicky had asked her, astonished.

'Oh, me mam has them. Or they go to foster homes,' she'd explained. 'They're used to it. They quite like going to foster homes, actually. You should see all the clothes and toys and shit they come back with.'

It was another world, though not one she ever felt inclined to share with Paddy. He'd only write back and moan about her having it so easy while he was marking out time in the hell-hole of Armley.

'If you write back at all, that is,' she said to his picture as she lay down that night. Her mam – hold the front page – had sent it in a package. A double-sided picture, that she'd protected with loads of Sellotape. A photo of Chantelle on one side and Paddy on the other. She slipped it back under her pillow and tried to drift away. It was hard, sleeping, these days, even without Chantelle to wake her, because the horrors and heebie-jeebies always came during the night. She'd often wake up terrified and sobbing, after some mish-mash of what had happened had swirled in her brain, creating the recipe for the perfect nightmare.

Was this a nightmare? She had no idea what time it was. Only that the dorm was dark. Unusually dark. When she opened her eyes she could see no more than she'd been able to when they were shut. Which was weird on its own. There was always a little light to see by. It came in under the door, from the always lighted corridor. But it wasn't just the blackness. It was that weird sleep paralysis thing she sometimes got, when she had to fight her way out of a nightmare when she couldn't move to run away.

But this wasn't that. She realised she was being pinned to her bed. By rough hands. Strong hands. Hands that were gripping her shoulders and forearms. More than one person. What the fuck was going on? She opened her mouth to shout out, but it was immediately silenced by something. Something bulky, shoved between her lips, making her retch. She could barely even groan. Whatever she'd been gagged with was pushing on the back of her throat.

Then, suddenly, a spray. Some sort of liquid. Her face wet. She tried to swing it from side to side but it made no difference. The sharp smell of chemicals. What the hell was being done to her? The wetness, the coldness, all over her head and face and neck. What was it? Fuck, it smelled like hairspray! But why would anyone want to spray hairspray all over her? She squeezed her eyes shut as hard and as tight as she could. Who was this? What were they doing?

This was New Hall. Like a school! Where were the warders? Why weren't they protecting her?

She jerked and bucked. Where were Susan and Amanda and bloody Marlene? Where were all the others? Was this one of them? Two of them? Was this some kind of sick joke they were playing on her? More hairspray – it was that, she was sure of it, bloody hairspray being sprayed on her! She tried desperately to make a sound – any sound. Why hadn't someone come to help her? Then a new sound. A rasp, and it all become obvious. A white blinding light, and a whump, her scream silent, then searing pain, as her whole head exploded into flames.

Chapter 29

Vicky came round to the sound of something beeping.

It sounded like a smoke alarm – the one in the back room at work. The one that always went off when she or Leanne tried to use the crappy toaster.

Or the alarm by her bed. On and on and on, it went. Shit. She had overslept. She should wake up and get the fuck on with it. She'd be late otherwise, and Lee would give her so much shit.

But she couldn't seem to do it. She felt sick. Dizzy as well. As if she'd downed too many vodkas. And her head hurt. She frowned. Which made it hurt even more. Enough to make her cry out in pain.

'Hush, sweetheart.'

She nearly had a heart attack – who the hell was *that*? Not her mam. Her mam never called her sweetheart. She tried to open her eyes, so she could see who was talking to her. That hurt as well. But she couldn't seem to get them open, try as she might. And then the memory – and the horror, and the terror – all flooded in.

Scared witless now, Vicky tried to put her hands to her face, but one was jerked back immediately, as if restrained. And the other was immediately grabbed between strong hands. 'Shhh,' said the voice again. Female. One she recognised. Then, 'Nurse, nurse, can you come, please? She's awake.'

Imprisoned in darkness, Vicky felt her fear writhe inside her like some parasitic animal trying to escape. She felt suffocated as well as blind, aware, even as she tried to cry out, that her mouth wasn't working properly. She could only writhe herself, and moan, unable to form words.

'Shhh,' the kindly voice soothed. 'You're going to be okay, love. You're in hospital,' she added, to Vicky's as yet unasked question, 'being taken care of, okay? There's nothing to be scared of. Try to lay still. The nurse is on her way.'

Vicky recognised the voice. Or thought she did. Was it Miss Teague? The friendly prison officer? She rattled her restrained hand, and heard a metallic rattling close by.

'Shhh, love,' came the voice again. 'Don't get yourself in a panic. It's just a restraint. I'll see if I can get it taken off for you, okay?'

Vicky, remembering more and more now, heard a grotesque wail come from somewhere deep inside her. The smell of hairspray. The heat. The violence done to her. What *had* been done to her?

And how did she get here? She didn't even know what day it was, let alone what time of day. Had no memory of anything bar the violence that had been done to her. The monsters who had come in and attacked her in her own bed.

She gulped in air, painfully, through lips that were cracked and dry. Then felt a touch on her cheek and a dabbing of something cool. 'There you go,' came another female voice. 'Here, open your lips a little. That's the way. It's a straw. Have a suck, it's just water.'

She tried to suck, but it was as if there was some strange swollen growth where her lips had formally been and it was hard to keep them tight around the straw. She knew she was dribbling, because she could feel it dripping down her throat, but over a chin she couldn't feel, like she'd had an injection at the dentist. The fear writhed inside her again. What had been *done* to her?

'You've been attacked,' said Miss Teague later on. How much later? She'd been aware of waking up, being given something, then drifting off again. And had no concept of day and night. But here Miss Teague was, at her side again. She could smell her too-strong and musky middle-aged perfume eddying around her. And, now she'd been given more painkillers, could at least get her mouth around the things she wanted to ask.

It had been two nights ago. 'In your bed,' said Miss Teague, 'while you slept. They set fire to your hair, love,' she added, patting Vicky's arm as she said that. 'It was pretty bad.' *Pretty bad.* How did you work out what pretty bad meant? Did she have any hair left? Was she blind? Was she horribly disfigured?

'Your eyes are going to be fine,' Miss Teague reassured her. 'That much I can tell you. You've just got to keep the dressings on for a bit while the skin heals. I expect they'll change them later on, then you'll be able to see for yourself. And yes, you've got some nasty burns, I'm afraid. And your hair ...' She stopped talking.

'Has it *all* gone?' Vicky whispered, slurring through her unwieldy lips.

'For now,' Miss Teague told her. 'But it'll grow back, they think, in time. And, really, thank God it was just your hair. You could so easily have been blinded ...'

She seemed almost as upset about it as if she was Vicky's mam, and Vicky wondered if she had a daughter herself. Or, well, perhaps not her mam. Did her mam even *know*? Did anyone know? Lucy? Paddy? Christ, who'd *done* this to her?

She could feel her panic rising once again, and heard Miss Teague click-clacking off to ask the nurse to come and see to her. Heard the words 'more morphine'. But she didn't want morphine – she wanted to know who had done this. Who had she upset? Who had she annoyed? Why had it been done to her? She knew bad things happened in prisons. Had heard all kinds of lurid stories about bad things happening late at night, in dark corners and secret places. Knew too that the correct course of action if it was happening to someone else was to act like it wasn't. Her former room-mate Susan had told her that right at the start, hadn't she?

So did they stand by and listen? Could they have even been involved?

Miss Teague returned, and confirmed, having listened to Vicky's slurred entreaties, that, yes, she did know what had happened, and that the perpetrators had yet to be found and 'dealt with'. 'But you can be sure they will be,' Miss Teague said, more briskly. 'And, once you're feeling a little better, perhaps you can help us out with trying to piece together something from what we do know.'

'What *do* you know?' Vicky whispered.

'Not now, love. You need some painkillers. We can deal with that once you're feeling a bit more up to it,' Miss Teague said.

'I'm fine,' Vicky managed to say, though she couldn't have been feeling less fine. 'Tell me – what *do* you know? Please, Miss Teague. Tell me.'

There was a pause, then a sigh. 'Only that you had a piece of paper stuffed in your mouth.'

Vicky gasped, remembering it. Remembering that particular piece of violence. Being unable to speak. Of gagging on it. Suffocating. 'What did it say?'

Vicky could hear footsteps. The sound of one of the nurses approaching, in their sensibly quiet shoes. She was becoming attuned to it now. Then Miss Teague cleared her throat.

'Vicky, love, we need to talk to you about Patrick Allen.'

Chapter 30

Paddy. Lucy stared at the words swimming in front of her. If he'd been standing in front of her at that moment, she thought she might be able to kill him with her bare hands. But it was the guilt that clutched at her heart the most.

'Oh, God, babes,' she said to Jimmy. 'This is all *my* fault!'

Jimmy snatched the letter from Lucy's hands, with one of the sheets beginning to rip because it was so damp from her tears. She'd read and re-read it, and she'd been unable to stop crying, her tears plopping down and mingling with Vicky's, already dried onto the cheap lined prison paper. Like everyone, she knew the expression 'tear-stained letter', but had never seen one before. Well, now she had.

'It is not your fault!' Jimmy said, for the umpteenth time, irritably. 'For Christ's sake, you've got to stop this! It was that bastard burned her. Not you. Not *you*,' he said again, gripping her wrists.

It had happened three whole weeks back. It had been three whole *weeks* before she'd even known. And all that time, Vicky holed up in some recuperation place, in terrible pain. And the worst of it was that she must have felt so alone.

And there was no getting round that horrible, horrible truth. That, whatever Jimmy told her, she still felt so certain that she'd been key in the attack happening in the first place. If Paddy thought Vicky had grassed him up, then there *must* have been a reason. Because she'd never wavered. Not once had she caved in and talked. She had stuck doggedly by her man from the very first. Even though it was clear to everyone else on the planet that he was not a man at all. He was a monster.

And even with his paranoia – part of his basic personality, whatever nonsense about drugs Vicky had tried to convince her – the one thing he knew she'd been as solid on since the day they'd been arrested was that no way in the world was she going to grass him up. She'd said as much to Lucy, face to face, even as she'd pretty much admitted that he *had* killed Gurdy. That she was going to stand by him, for Chantelle's sake, for her own sake, forever, because she still believed that they were both going to get off. And he'd have known that. They'd been writing to each other regularly, both of them clearly off their heads. Not on drugs this time, but sheer stupidity.

But then *she'd* come along, hadn't she? And changed everything. Not with her visit. Because Vicky's position – protecting her bastard murdering boyfriend, for her entirely crazy reasons – had not changed an iota. No, it had been after that, when, frustrated that she'd been unable to talk any sense into Vicky, she had decided to take action.

Though not even action; all she'd wanted was to find out where Vicky really stood. If the evidence didn't stack up, could they *really* get away with it? Was it really true that, without a witness, and if the evidence was only circumstantial, they wouldn't be able to make a conviction stick? And if she *did* change her plea and agree to give up Paddy, what would her position be then? How would she be able to convince a court, assuming he told them she was an accomplice (which he would) that she was innocent? And if she didn't, would she go to prison for life as well?

It had seemed to Lucy to be the only way to proceed. In order to help her friend, it was no good trying to guess at things. She needed to *know* what her options were. And since she worked at a solicitors, it was the most natural thing in the world to ask one of the criminal lawyers. Who, she realised later, knew Paddy's hot-shot lawyer and who would of course spend time chatting to him on a day-to-day basis. They all did – sworn enemies in court they might be, but outside of it most of them were friends. And even she hadn't really seen the seriousness of the situation. Hadn't really considered how much Paddy's lawyer would encourage him to change his plea. He obviously knew he'd done it – everyone with half a brain knew he'd done it. So when she'd merrily chatted to the guy at work, it never occurred to her that the business of her even asking in the first place might be construed as the long-awaited broaching of Vicky's defences; a signal that, finally, she'd been persuaded to see sense and tell the truth. And, of course, why wouldn't he merrily chat away to Paddy's lawyer about it? It was an interesting case, wasn't it? A big one.

'It *is*,' she told Jimmy now. 'I know it is! It must be. That bloody lawyer will have told Paddy to expect the worst now, wouldn't he? Put two and two together, knowing I was asking about what would happen if she *did* give him up. What *else* would he think? He'd think she was *about* to. Oh, God, Jimmy, I've caused all this, I *know* I have.'

That it had been Paddy who'd arranged the attack wasn't in any doubt. No need for incriminating evidence in this case. He'd held his hands up to it immediately, because there was no point in doing otherwise. Convinced he was going down for life, he hadn't even done it as a warning. He'd arranged for Vicky to be attacked for pure revenge. He must have. Why else have some sick woman write 'Love Paddy' for him on the note that had been stuffed in Vicky's mouth?

Jimmy folded the three sheets of flimsy paper. 'Love, I've got to get to work. And so have you. But, look, stop this, okay? You don't know any of that. And even if it *is* true, it makes no difference. Think about it rationally. What do you want? What does Vicky's mam want? What does Chantelle want? Come on – what do we all want to happen most?'

'For Vicky to stop lying for him.'

'Exactly,' said Jimmy, before draining his coffee and picking up his car keys. 'For Vicky to return to bloody earth and see that cunt for what he is. And tell the *truth*.'

Jimmy rarely used the 'C' word. And only ever in relation to Paddy Allen. Lucy wondered if it would be reserved

313

for that exclusive use till the end of time. 'Yes, I know that,' she said, 'but—'

'No buts. Because this was *always* going to happen.' He waggled the letter in front of her before putting it down on the kitchen table. 'It was always going to happen, the very minute she opened her mouth. Always,' he said again. 'Doesn't matter what prompted it to happen. But the minute it did – it still *does*, God willing – he was going to lose his rag and get his revenge. Love, there's nothing you could have done about it, don't you see that?'

'God, it's unbelievable. How? I mean, that's what's really chilling. That he can even orchestrate something like that *while he's in another bloody prison*! And who'd do that for him? Who? What sort of woman would calmly set someone on fire? I can't believe anyone would do something so vile. Christ, and to someone like *Vicky*.'

Jimmy shook his head. Then put his arms around her, while she sniffed against his chest. 'Then you need your head testing, trust me,' he said softly. 'Babe, you don't know the half of it. And you don't want to. Specially not where that bastard is concerned.'

'But does your dad? I mean, *really*? Is it really that cut and dried? Isn't there still a chance he could get off? God, can you imagine? Him walking around free? The guy I spoke to at work says it's not that straightforward – that if they both keep denying they were even there, then it's almost impossible to do either of them for murder. They *need* Vicky's testimony, don't they?'

Jimmy shook his head. 'No, they don't. I mean, Christ,

if she doesn't speak up now, she must be seriously deranged. But they can place her at the scene anyway so they *will* be able to break her if she doesn't.'

'You keep saying that,' said Lucy. 'But can they? Can they *really?*'

'She was sick, babe,' Jimmy said. 'They have her *vomit* to use in evidence. And if you tell that to a living soul, I am in serious trouble. Or, rather my dad is, so don't, babe, not to *anyone. Ever.*'

Which gave Lucy a whole new dilemma. Vicky wouldn't see her. Didn't want Lucy or Chantelle – especially Chantelle – anywhere near her. Not when she looked like she did. Bald, she'd said. Fucked-up. A mess. Like a gargoyle. And *still*, if what she'd put in her letter was to be believed, convinced that her only choice was to stick to her story. Paddy had done what he'd done and she knew him for what he was now. But she'd thought long and hard – apparently – and decided she *still* couldn't risk changing her plea now, because if she admitted she'd been there, which she'd have to, to give up Paddy, they would also put her away for years and years, because there was little doubt that he'd want to take her along with him. So she had to hope – Vicky had treble underlined the word 'hope' – that, without sufficient evidence to convict her as an accessory for murder, they could only do her on some more minor charge.

Noooooo, Lucy thought, as, after Jimmy had left for work, she read the letter through again. Who the hell was advising Vicky? Who was her lawyer? How could she think in that way? But there was no getting away from it, Vicky was between a rock and a hard place. Damned if she did tell the truth – possibly with a long sentence in prospect (and in this Lucy's heart bled for both Vicky and Chantelle) – or damned if she didn't. Because Lucy knew that if she continued to lie for Paddy, she would be in mental anguish about Gurdy for the rest of her life.

So how the hell did she begin to find a way to help her?

Or did she have to accept her own truth? That she couldn't.

Chapter 31

She had deep second-degree burns – that's what the physio woman told her, anyway. Burns that weren't like when you accidentally touched your hair tongs. Deeper than that. Nastier. Still so incredibly painful. Yet a mere three weeks after she'd first been returned to the prison hospital wing to recuperate came the news that she was being discharged back to the general population.

'The scarring will fade, love,' the woman said, smiling the sympathetic but still undeniably breezy smile of someone who wasn't horribly disfigured. 'And we must be grateful for small mercies, mustn't we?' she added briskly. 'You're lucky there's no scarring to the scalp tissue. Which means your hair will grow back.'

'Will it, though?' Vicky asked her. Losing her hair had left her more traumatised than anything.

'Yes,' the physio woman told her. 'In its own time – which might be quite a time, so don't be too impatient. But it will, love. At least you can hang on to that.'

Vicky wasn't sure she had the strength to hang on to anything currently. What good was her hair to her anyway? Not when she couldn't even bear to look at her own reflection. Let alone show her face to the world. To her *daughter*.

It was such a painful trigger now. Every time she thought of Chantelle – which was often – she cried. Chantelle would recoil from her, she knew. She would be frightened to look at her. Vicky could see it so clearly. How she would run to her mam, to Lucy, to *anyone*. How she would recoil in disgust at the monster who was her mother and would run to anyone, in fear, to escape her.

The crying hurt, bleeding salt into already angry wounds. Tears that mingled with the liquid that seeped from her constantly. Plasma, the nurse had said. The body's response. Like her body was weeping at the devastation of her life too.

'Why can't I stay in here at least till I look a bit better?' she asked the physio. 'Everyone's going to be staring at me. I don't think I can bear it.'

The physio lady, one of two who'd been working with her since she'd returned from the hospital, dabbed at her cheeks tenderly. She was middle-aged. Mumsy. Unemotional in her tone, but not unkind. 'It's not up to me, love,' she said. 'I wish it was, I really do. But you're healing. The difference just this past week has been incredible. You're young and strong. You'll heal well, I promise.'

Vicky didn't feel young and strong. She felt old and weak. So much so that they'd put her on suicide watch. Could they see the will to keep going weeping out of her as well? But she was strong enough, just, to find the strength to keep on living. Whatever horrors lay ahead for her she had something to live for. She understood depression. She had been fearful of her mam's for so long. She knew depressed people often found themselves in such desperate places that they thought their nearest and dearest would be better off in a world without them in it. But she knew she wasn't one of them, and never would be. Chantelle was her flesh. A part of her.

Vicky also understood abandonment all too well. Knew how it felt to have a parent who had walked away from you. So there was no way in the *world*, even if she couldn't look after her for a while, that she was going to allow Chantelle to experience the agony of feeling that you weren't quite enough, weren't quite loved enough, to persuade that absent parent to stay.

She nodded sadly. Of course she would heal. On the outside, at least. And the physio lady looked like she knew what she was talking about. And while she healed she at least had the pain of the burns to distract her from the far greater pain in her heart. After all, what were a few jeers and stares and catcalls in comparison to the evil that had been unleashed on her in Paddy's name?

If she'd been frightened before, she was terrified now. It didn't matter how much they reassured her that the women in question had been dealt with and removed to another prison, the fact that they could do such a thing to her so easily meant she wasn't reassured in the least. That Paddy could get to her, from a distance of however many miles and all those brick walls, all those coils of barbed wire. They meant nothing. He could get to her *despite* them.

Could have his orders – and since when did he become so powerful that he could even make them? – carried out so easily. It was chilling.

Via visitors, they said. That crucial link to the real world. Paddy hadn't even bothered to deny it, apparently. It had come to his attention that she intended to serve him up – how? She fucking *hadn't*! – and, via his cell mate, who was mates with a lad who had a girlfriend in New Hall, he had managed to orchestrate the entire thing.

'But *why*?' Vicky had wanted to know, desperate to make some sort of sense of it. Of a fellow girl – *girls* – being prepared to do something so vile. 'Who would do that to a stranger? For what? What would persuade them to do something so cruel? They don't even know me!'

'Vicky, they don't need to,' Miss Teague had told her, in weary tones. And then reminded her, sadly, just how much she had to learn about prison life. She had been perceived to be a grass. The world was a cruel place. There were bad people in it. There were people, even females, who did such things for kicks.

And the upshot was a terror that had increased eightfold. The inability to sleep and, when she did sleep, the nightmares. And all her waking hours consumed by the ultimate nightmare – that Paddy, who she'd truly believed loved her, had disfigured her. Tried to re-model her in his own monstrous image, and succeeded. And in doing so, had killed her love for him dead.

'So now is the time,' Mr Grey had said, 'to talk.' He'd come to see her just a week after the attack, when she'd still been in Pinderfields Hospital, to prepare her for her upcoming preliminary hearing, and was anxious that she now tell the truth.

But Mr Grey, for all the letters after his name, didn't get it. There had been many hours for her to think about everything. And she could not have been clearer that she mustn't do that.

Mr Grey had become rather exasperated. 'How can you possibly *not* tell the truth now?' he'd asked her. 'After all *this*. How can you possibly maintain any loyalty to Allen?' And in a way that made Vicky realise he really did imagine that she might be that stupid. But why wouldn't he? She had been, for so long.

But of course, she *couldn't* explain what was so bloomin' bleedin' obvious, as her mam might have said. (Thinking about her mam, for all her failings, made Vicky cry as well.) She couldn't explain, because to admit what really happened would be to tell Mr Grey the truth, and if she told him the truth he had a duty to act on it. Yes, he could still defend her, because it was the court that had to prove stuff – she got that – but he could no longer stand up and say 'my client wasn't there'.

So she stuck to her guns. 'I wasn't there,' she told him. 'I wasn't *there*,' she kept telling him. Till eventually, he had no choice but to accept it.

And she knew she'd keep doing so till the end. The bitter end. Bitter, like her mam had been since her dad left. Because the alternative – to spew up all the poisonous gloop inside her, which would be such a relief, such a purging – would be to condemn herself, almost certainly, to many years behind bars. It was all so obvious. For some reason, Paddy thought she had betrayed him. And he must therefore know the upshot – presumably informed by his own lawyer – would be her testifying against him and, in all likelihood, a life sentence for murder.

Which was why she couldn't even flirt with the idea of confessing everything. Because she knew without doubt that he would take her down with him. He'd made it clear that her life was of no consequence to him, hadn't he? And, oh, how he'd enjoy all that power and revenge. He'd say she helped him. To arrange it. To lure Gurdy there. To *do* it. To hide all the evidence. To lie to the police.

And half of this she *had* done, had she not? She *was* an accessory to murder. There was no getting around that wretched fact. And she had since knocked several nails in the coffin of her own making, by lying, withholding evidence, continuing to protest both their innocence. It would be a small job for Paddy – how her heart thrummed with hate now – to apply the hammer to the nail that sealed the lid. And who would care? She was scum. He would take her down with him. And, were it not for Chantelle, perhaps they should.

But as things stood, there was hope. There was that slim thread of hope. And set against the certainty of long incarceration, it was the one thing she couldn't help but cling to, for her daughter.

* * *

322

Were it not for the guards, the police wandering about, the officials and the many preoccupied-looking barristers, Vicky thought she might be standing in a place of worship or a stately home. The golden scrolls sprouting from the walls, the words etched in Latin, the sweeping staircase, like something out of a Hollywood movie, down which some legendary actress might well glide. Such a beautiful place, to deal in such ugly business.

Her 'preliminary', the first step on the road to a frightening future, was the first time Vicky had been out in the wider world. Yes, she'd been offsite to Pinderfields Hospital, but of that she remembered nothing. She'd been unconscious when they'd taken her – they'd put her under, they told her, to spare her the pain – and though she'd been conscious when she'd been brought back to the hospital wing in New Hall, she'd been blinded by the bandages, and barely able to feel anything bar the hollowness in her heart.

Being out in the world now, albeit shackled to a prison warder, was a powerful reminder of the enormity of the future she was facing. To be locked up, perhaps for a decade or more. She'd tried not to, but in the long, sleepless nights since her return from New Hall, she kept doing it anyway; all the sums. How old she might be when she got out. How old Chantelle would be, too. How many more milestones in her infant daughter's life she might – *would* – never see. Lucy had written only the other day, as she did, full of news. This time, in particular, about a tooth. About how it had just appeared, as if from nowhere, and how they'd all laughed so much. And how Jimmy's dad had started calling her 'Toothy Gonzales', because of how she'd whiz around the place, mostly on her bottom, laughing like a lunatic, looking like a character out of *The Beano*. God, it hurt. It hurt so fucking much.

But she'd kept it to herself. Kept herself to herself, pretty much. She was back in the same dorm – albeit in a different bed – with the same group of girls and women, and though she did her best to ignore the stares, to accept the support, to join conversations, she couldn't quite get her head round the way things worked in prison. The fact that no one – not a single one of them – had come to her aid. No alarm raised – not till her screams did the job by themselves, anyway. No wrestling off her attackers. No running for help. And absolutely no telling tales.

She tried not to hold it against them. That was how it worked, and there was nothing you could do about it – not if you didn't want to become a target yourself. You kept your head down and your nose clean and you *never* told tales. If the world was a cruel place, a prison was an even crueller one. No place for principles. Every woman for herself.

Mr Grey was waiting when they went in, but seemed to have other things on his mind and, bar nodding an acknowledgement to her, barely spoke to her. This was a small thing – just a bit of necessary admin in a busy day. She knew what was required of her – turn up, confirm who she was and how she was going to plead, go back to New Hall. Then wait for the next bit, while the preparation for the trial got under way.

Well, so be it, she thought, as her number came up and she was ushered into the courtroom. She would just make the most of being able to look around her, breathe in the sweet, free air, and contemplate all the things she might now lose.

The judge's bench looked like an altar. It made it seem as if she'd entered some sort of holy place, as if she was already gone from the world. The empty court, vast and echoing, and a chill breeze on the air, as if the spirits of all those condemned before her. And everyone dressed in the same funereal shades of black and grey, as if to allow so much as a scarf's worth of colour into the room would be a mark of disrespect to the law.

In contrast, Vicky's worn and too-bright clothes (what had her mother been thinking?) seemed to shriek for attention, and she kept her head down for fear of meeting the expressions of distaste she was now so familiar with, but would never get used to. The ones that were whipped away so hurriedly and guiltily, to be replaced by worse ones – expressions of pity.

The judge, who'd swept in in robes, putting Vicky in mind of a retired Batman, had only one job to perform today. For both Vicky and Paddy, coming separately to court from their places of incarceration, he was there to hear them confirm their identities and how they intended to plead. A secret ritual – no members of the public allowed, thankfully – that set in motion the process that would see her here again, and the course of her life be decided.

She felt herself being nudged by the female prison officer who'd accompanied her to court. A stern, hefty woman who she didn't really know. 'This way,' she said, leading Vicky to the dock, where, in a few months' time she would submit to her fate. A bizarre thought came into her head as the gate was shut behind her. That this box in which she stood was in reality a basket, and that, by some miracle, the roof of the courthouse would open, and above it, a bright hot air balloon would be bobbing in the sky, a rainbow of colours.

Up she'd go then, up and up. And away. *Not guilty, not guilty, not guilty*, she'd sing down to them all. Then fly away with Chantelle over the rainbow.

She was given a card. 'Place your right hand on the Bible in front of you,' the court speaker said. 'And, when you're ready, read the words on the card.'

Vicky did as instructed. She had always been good at doing as instructed. Particularly where Paddy was concerned. Had that, in the end, been her undoing? It was almost noon, and she found herself wondering where he was now; had he stood in this exact spot already this morning? Or would he stand in her shoes later on today? She didn't know what she'd do if she saw him. Lunge for him? Scream at him?

'I swear by almighty God,' she said, shocked at the thinness of her voice. *You always were a mouthy bitch, Vic.* Her mam's voice. *Full of gob.* 'That the evidence I shall give,' she went on, pushing the words out more forcefully, 'shall be the truth, the whole truth, and nothing but the truth.'

Except that it wouldn't be. It couldn't be. She dare not risk it.

You're insane, Lucy had written to her. In letter after letter. You will *not* get away with this. You will make everything worse. Yes, you'll have to serve time (Lucy was suddenly so fucking well informed about everything) but if you don't serve him up then you might serve even more. You *will*. She'd kept saying that. *Will*, Vic, you *will*.

But what did Lucy know, really? She hadn't been there, had she? Didn't know how Vicky'd scrabbled around, trying to clean up the evidence. Didn't realise – because Lucy never once seemed to succumb to it – how readily Paddy could wind people around his little finger. Didn't know, because how could she, the things she had been witness to.

The things she had borne witness to. Myra Hindley. She kept thinking about Myra Hindley too. All the time. Myra Hindley, who got life. And *got* life. Years and years. Was she out, even now?

The judge startled her. 'Please state your full name for the court.'

'Victoria Alice Robinson,' she said. After *Alice in Wonderland*. One of the very last pretty memories she had of her dad. *My idea, that*, he'd said to her. *On account of your beautiful blonde hair*. Which hadn't stayed blonde. In protest at his abandoning her? She often wondered. Her mousey but precious hair, which wasn't even there anymore.

'And you live at 23 Tanton Crescent, Clayton. Is that correct?'

Home. 'Yes, it is,' she said, aching for it.

'Victoria Robinson,' he then said, his voice growing sterner, his eyebrows gathering above his pale eyes like thunderclouds. 'You are charged with being an accessory to the murder of Gurdip Banerjee. How do you plead?'

She thought of Gurdy then. How he'd pleaded – for his life, all shit and gore. Sideways on the floor with that fucking chair around him, cords biting into his ankles and wrists, face contorted in pain. And something else. Disbelief that this could actually be happening. That the man he called a friend could snuff his life out so easily. Utter shock. The question 'why?' burned onto his bleeding lips. Forever burned there. In freeze-frame, as his life ebbed away.

And she'd just stood there. Appalled, yes, in shock, yes, in terror, *yes. All* of those. But still she'd stood there. No matter that she couldn't have changed anything. She hadn't tried *hard* enough. She hadn't tried *soon* enough. No wonder that the sound of the bar finally connecting with Paddy's head had had such a hollow ring about it.

She would have to live with that knowledge for the rest of her life. And the knowledge that, right now, she was about to do the same. To stand by and let the process of law take control of her, in some vain hope of mitigating what she'd done – what *she'd* done.

She tensed, already anticipating the gasp from Mr Grey.

Then she cleared her throat. 'Guilty,' she said.

Chapter 32

Leeds Crown Court, March 1989

Lucy saw the bandana before anything else. And despite knowing Vicky had planned on wearing it – she had said so in her letter – the sight of it, a flash of black and white amid the greyness of the day, made her heart sing.

'Come *on*, Jimmy,' Lucy yelled as she ran across the cobbles leading to the entrance of the court. 'We can't be late. We've got to get in there before she does. Sitting right there, where she can see us. I promised her. Come *on*.'

Who knew Jimmy would turn out to be such a great dad? Well, everyone, Lucy supposed. She watched him shift Chantelle higher on his hip. She clung to him with all four limbs, like a baby koala, and, strong man that he was, he carried her weight effortlessly.

Chantelle was sixteen months old now. A ball of endless energy. No longer a baby, but a toddler, and a bright one. Though didn't everyone say that about their kids? Though not *their* kid, and she'd never once let herself forget that, even though they'd been charged with looking after her full-time ever since Vicky had stunned everyone by changing her plea. She wanted them to look after her so she'd have 'continuity of care', she'd written. Vicky saw counsellors regularly in prison, and their language had begun to pop up so often that it was almost as if it had become a part of hers now. Continuity of care, and because her own mam, with her bad back and her drinking, simply couldn't manage it. So for now, Chantelle was theirs. On loan for the duration, however long that was likely to turn out to be.

Which, despite knowing they really had now reached the final hurdle, Lucy also knew was still an unknown. She didn't dare to second guess it in case she jinxed it.

Because that bastard Allen – now safely back behind bars, given life – had done his very best to have her friend go down with him. Lucy had therefore attended as much of his trial as she'd been able to, both *for* Vicky, and so Paddy would make no mistake about how vehemently she wished to see him locked away again. Though it hadn't been easy. She'd never had such an education in shameless depravity – not least in the way, whenever he clocked her in the public gallery, his eyes would sweep up and down her in the same way they had always done. His dead, cold, reptilian eyes.

Gotta pity him. Who'd said that? Irish Pete? Vikram? But she didn't have to pity him and she wouldn't ever pity him. There was no mitigation, no extenuating circumstance, and no chemical justification, that could allow a chink of pity to infiltrate her heart.

But she'd been there, stuck it out. Used up half her holidays so she could keep Vicky informed, via the letters that were the only communication they'd had, because Vicky would not allow anyone to see her in prison. No one. And that included Chantelle.

So Lucy had this real fear, this afternoon, when it had come to the sentencing, that she might have done the wrong thing by having Jimmy take a half day off work, pick her up from her mam's and bring her down. Vicky'd told her not to. Do *not* bring her. She had triple underlined it. And gone on to explain, as she did all the time, that it was the only sensible option, for *both* their sakes. If she saw Chantelle, and was immediately returned to incarceration, she'd written that her heart might break into so many pieces that she'd never be able to put it back together again.

But Lucy had allowed herself the luxury of optimism. Ill-judged, perhaps, but she didn't think so. She had grilled Jimmy's dad, with whom they all lived now, pretty mercilessly, and, though he'd never tell her anything he shouldn't – he mustn't – it was the spaces between the words that mattered to her most. And if he didn't think she'd be going back to prison – and it seemed he, who knew the real Paddy Allen best, didn't – then that was good enough for her.

Jimmy caught up with her, and the three of them filed through the ornate glass and wooden doors into the enormous central chamber. It was an imposing place, dominated by a grand central staircase, up and down which various barristers and court officials scurried. And, as they milled around, Lucy was shocked to see so many familiar faces, too; not least various members of Gurdy's family, who'd been present throughout Paddy's trial, many of them, women and men alike, weeping openly. But today they looked different. They were here to see justice finally done, and their acknowledgement of Lucy – like they were all in the same unfortunate club – bolstered her confidence further. She hoped Vicky would register their presence here too, and feel the dignity and strength of their support.

Jimmy passed Chantelle to Lucy while he went over to the cork board that listed the day's proceedings, and she made her usual small protest. 'Back, JimJim! Back!' she squeaked indignantly. Never Dad. People often said so – all that 'Daddy's little angel' stuff, often – but they corrected them always. Their time wasn't yet. God willing, somehow, it would happen when it happened. Or if not, they would adopt. She stroked Chantelle's head. Maybe sooner rather than later.

'JimJim!' Chantelle squeaked again. Lucy shushed her. But then, hearing the echo in the vast space above them, she began upping the volume on every random noise she could think of, causing Lucy to wish she'd done the sensible thing and left her back at home with her mam. Instead she pulled out Chantelle's dummy from her ready-for-anything baby bag (soon to be Vicky's bag – her gift) and slipped it hastily between her lips.

'Here you go, baby,' she said, wondering if she'd even be taking her home tonight. She pushed the thought aside. That was the *plan*, wasn't it? 'Let's go find your mamma.'

* * *

It was warm in the court, so Lucy began unbuttoning Chantelle's coat immediately they sat down. It had only been a matter of weeks since they'd both been there to see Paddy sent down and Lucy could still visualise him, standing in the spot Vicky would soon inhabit – his last hurrah a pathetic attempt at a scowl which spectacularly failed to hide the fear and mortification on his face.

Lucy tried not to enjoy the memory too much. She was mostly just so glad Vicky hadn't had to take any part in it. True to her prediction, though Paddy had changed his plea to guilty once he'd been informed that Vicky had told the truth, he had tried to take Vicky along with him. Tried very hard indeed. Right up to the last, he had tried to stick the knife in and implicate her, telling lie upon lie upon lie. So, right up to the last, hung the wretched, scary spectre, that Vicky would have to face him in court.

And then, at the eleventh hour, a complete turnaround. 'Finally,' Jimmy's dad had said. 'Cordingley has knocked some ruddy sense into him. Not that it'll help him much at this stage.'

And it hadn't. Though Paddy had retracted what he'd said in all matters related to Vicky, the run-around he'd given everyone, plus his clear intention to have Vicky tried as an accomplice, meant the judge took a particularly dim view of him. Quite rightly. And had sentenced him accordingly.

* * *

Seeing Vicky properly after so long was a shock. It might have been anyway, of course, because her incarceration couldn't help but change her. But even putting aside the way she seemed so insubstantial between the two prison warders she was flanked by, her hands cuffed, and the raw, brutal power of the scars on her face (which weren't so much scars as a crude rearrangement of her friend's previously pretty features) Vicky looked to be a shell of the person she used to be. Gaunt and pale – in grim contrast to the livid pink striations around her mouth and cheeks – she looked a good couple of stone lighter, as if she was made of sticks instead of bones. She had an air about her, even so, and Lucy wished she could preserve it. It was one of strength. Of acceptance of whatever was coming next.

'God,' Lucy hissed at Jimmy, as she passed a wriggling Chantelle to him. 'I hope they're kind to her. Please God, let them be kind.'

Lucy followed Vicky's progress to the dock, where she was instructed to stand behind Perspex, keeping her eyes on her friend the whole time. She was almost willing Vicky to see them, and was eventually rewarded by her making eye contact, and then seeing a gasp – which she couldn't hear – as Vicky saw Chantelle.

Lucy exhaled in relief at her friend's answering smile. She'd done the right thing. Even if the worst happened and Vicky was taken down to serve a further sentence, she would at least have a chance to hug her daughter. Who might well, it was true, respond as Vicky had repeatedly said she would; with mistrust and fear at this ghoulish-looking virtual stranger, this scraggy, haunted girl, in her baggy prison clothes, with little hair to speak of, just the odd weedy sprouting, if the contours beneath the bandana were to be believed. It was true – Chantelle might even scream or cry or try to run away. But something told Lucy it wouldn't happen. Vicky was altogether too present in Chantelle's young life. Through the picture books she made for her, the letters she'd written and sent for her and, most of all, through the tapes she made of her reading her own stories, written just for Chantelle, out loud. Her voice was all. A mother's voice. A voice Chantelle would recognise. And, hey, you had to start somewhere, didn't you?

She turned to Chantelle and lifted her up in the direction of Vicky so that her friend could see her.

'Look, baby,' she said through tears she hadn't even realised she'd been shedding. 'Look, sweetie – Mamma! That's your mamma over there.'

There was no time for Chantelle to voice a reaction, however, as just at that moment an usher stood up and shouted 'Stand please!' as he introduced the judge.

Despite the damning evidence against her – the vomit at the scene, her being identified as being the passenger in Paddy's car driving away from the scene and other forensics – Vicky's defence lawyer had done a sterling job. And the act of violence Paddy had orchestrated from his cell in Armley Prison only strengthened her case. Her lawyer told of a manipulating, evil, cruel and possessive boyfriend, who had controlled her the whole of the time they'd been together, and of how horrified she had been to witness her best friend being murdered while she could only beg and plead for his life.

She had just that morning been found guilty of the charge she had pleaded guilty to. Of being an accessory to Gurdy's murder. However, justice had prevailed, and the extenuating circumstances were so overwhelming that the judge had already intimated he'd be lenient with her.

Even so, it was as if the whole court held their breath as he gave Vicky a custodial sentence. 'But because of time already served,' he added, while Vicky sobbed in the dock, 'you are free to leave this court straight away.'

Everyone in the court seemed to rise up as one, and the taut silence was replaced by the white noise of relief. It was only then, looking behind her, that Lucy fully appreciated just how many people had turned out to be present at Vicky's sentencing. Yes, Paddy's trial had been splashed all over the local papers almost daily, both as an example of the kind of thing drug abuse could lead to, and as an opportunity for those who made such things their business to mount a campaign against the crime barons of Bradford. (Rasta Mo had even turned up on the day of Paddy's verdict. 'To send a message,' Jimmy's dad had said sagely. 'That he's untouchable. And no doubt a warning to Allen too. Arrogant bastard,' he'd added. 'Little does he know ...')

But this turnout – this support – she'd not expected at all. Much less the throng of reporters and photographers who were waiting out the front, when she, Jimmy and Chantelle finally emerged.

Vicky, Lucy saw immediately, was already ahead of them, having been hurried out to the front by her solicitor. There were flashbulbs going off and she could see Vicky cringing – yes, there was obviously something to celebrate, but this was the last thing she needed.

'Here, take the baby,' Lucy said to Jimmy. 'I need to go and help her.' Then she headed off, trying to push her way through the throng of people, anxious to protect her friend from all the flashbulbs and questions.

She felt her arm grabbed. 'Hey, you're the friend, aren't you? I remember you from the Allen trial. It's you, isn't it?'

Lucy turned to find herself looking at an ageing reporter, pencil behind his ear, reporter's notebook in his hand, like he'd just beamed down from a 1970s cop show. She nodded. 'But I have to go. I have to get her away from all this.'

'Course,' the man said, lifting his other hand to reveal a huge previously unseen camera, which popped in her face.

'What on earth are you doing that for?' she asked him, blinking the brightness away.

'For the spread, love,' he said. 'This is going on the front page of the *Telegraph & Argos*. Bit of a story, this one is. Warms the cockles.'

'Yes, well, that's fine,' she said, 'but can you let me by, please? I need to get to my friend. You okay, mate?' she called then, catching Vicky's eye over the sea of people. She was on the steps still with her solicitor and, seeing Lucy, she raised a thumb.

'I'm on my way,' she mouthed, but once again her progress was arrested. 'Friend or sister?' the same reporter persisted. 'Someone's now saying you're sisters.'

'Sisters,' Lucy confirmed, feeling her face break into a smile, remembering something that had stuck with her since as long ago as she could remember. That a friend was both the best thing you could have and the best thing you could be.

She waved again at Vicky and cupped her hands around her lips. 'Blood sisters forever!' she yelled as loudly as she could.

Then turned to the startled reporter. 'And there's your headline.'

Epilogue

And the heavens shall declare his righteousness:
For God is judge himself.

Psalms 50:6

Lights Out

As I lay here in my eight by twelve
And I punch my fucking head
I scream at the useless cunt I am
Someone's going to end up dead

That slit of a window stifles me
And the stench is making me sick
Why was enough never enough?
Why was I such a prick?

Fuck off with your banging, the rest of you scum
I do not belong in this cell
My mates and my parents, they fucked up my life
And I cannot live by a bell

I'll tear off my shirt and I'll make it a rope
While I sort out the thoughts in my head
In seconds the noose will be where it belongs
And someone will end up dead.

On 20 April 1992 Paddy Allen was found hanging in his cell in Armley Prison, Leeds. He was pronounced dead at the scene. The poem was found in the pocket of the jeans he was wearing.

Acknowledgements

As always I'd like to thank our amazing team at HarperCollins, you do such a fantastic job and I'm so humbled that you believe in me. And dear Andrew, agent extra-ordinaire and then some, always fighting our corner and forever our champion. Last but by no means least, my super talented, super patient, partner in crime, the very beautiful Lynne Barrett-Lee, who is so much more than a co-author, and I'm proud to consider her my friend.